A thoroughly documented account of the 1967 guerrilla challenge in Bolivia, *The Defeat of Che Guevara* reconstructs events leading up to, during, and after the defeat of the insurgency. Against the background of the 1960s' attempt to extend Cuban influence throughout Latin America, the book provides an analysis of trends in Bolivian politics from 1952 to 1967. General Gary Prado Salmón evaluates the geographical setting of the insurgency, guerrilla preparations, and the Bolivian response. He identifies key strategic errors, including Che Guevara's failure to capture peasant support, and analyzes Che's own theories. Military historians will find no sensational revelations here; they will find previously unknown details that form a concise reconstruction of *The Defeat of Che Guevara*.

(continued on back flap)

THE DEFEAT OF
CHE GUEVARA

The Defeat of
CHE GUEVARA

Military Response to Guerrilla Challenge in Bolivia

GARY PRADO SALMÓN

Translated by John Deredita
Foreword by Lawrence H. Hall

New York
Westport, Connecticut
London

This is a translation of *La Guerrilla Inmolada: La Compaña del Che en Bolivia*,
copyright © 1987 by Gary Prado Salmón, Editorial Punto y Coma S.R.L.,
La Paz, Bolivia, publishers.

Library of Congress Cataloging-in-Publication Data

Prado Salmón, Gary.
  [Guerrilla inmolada. English]
  The defeat of Che Guevara : military response to guerrilla
challenge in Bolivia / Gary Prado Salmón ; translated by John
Deredita ; foreword by Lawrence H. Hall.
    p. cm.
  Translation of: La guerrilla inmolada.
  Includes bibliographical references.
  ISBN 0–275–93211–7 (alk. paper)
  1. Bolivia—History—1938–1982. 2. Guevara, Ernesto, 1926–1967.
3. Guerrillas—Bolivia—History—20th century. 4. Bolivia.
Ejército—Commando troops—History—20th century. 5. Bolivia—
History. Military. I. Title.
F3326.P7213   1990
984.05—dc20   89–29664

Library of Congress Catalog Card Number: 89–29664
ISBN: 0–275–93211–7

First published in 1990

Praeger Publishers, One Madison Avenue, New York, NY   10010
An imprint of Greenwood Publishing Group, Inc.

Printed in the United States of America

∞

The paper used in this book complies with the
Permanent Paper Standard issued by the National
Information Standards Organization (Z39.48–1984).

10 9 8 7 6 5 4 3 2 1

To the memory of the commissioned and noncommissioned officers, sergeants, trainees, privates, and civilian guides fallen in combat in 1967. Their example lives on in the barracks, where the Bolivia we desire is quietly being built: an authentically independent nation, conscious of its integrating role on the American continent.

CONTENTS

viii   Contents

ILLUSTRATIONS

All maps and tables follow the appendix, on page 257.

FOREWORD

The news of Ernesto "Che" Guevara's death in the remote mountains of southeastern Bolivia in early October 1967 was received with stunned disbelief throughout Latin America. Even after publication of the grisly final photograph of the famed guerrilla leader and theoretician in almost every newspaper in the western hemisphere, many refused to believe that he had been killed. Rumors of his death had sprung up two years earlier when he suddenly dropped out of sight in Cuba, and Fidel Castro's enigmatic explanation that Che had left to carry out "important missions" elsewhere triggered speculation that Guevara had met the same fate as others who clashed with the Cuban leader. Subsequent reports of his presence in Africa and other parts of the world and finally in Bolivia were followed by the Bolivian government's announcement on October 9, 1967, that Che had "died in combat" the previous day. The claim that the Bolivian Army, one of the least effective in South America, had defeated and killed Che Guevara was greeted with considerable skepticism by many.

When it later became known that Che had been wounded, captured, and then executed for attempting to establish a continental "foco," or base of operations for a guerrilla-led revolution, those who had aspired to follow in his footsteps were outraged and demoralized. The murder of a wounded prisoner was despicable, but even more disturbing in this case were the implications for those who had accepted without question Che's theories and directions for waging a successful guerrilla war.[1] Almost immediately, various books and articles appeared, most distorted and inaccurate, trying to explain what went wrong in Guevara's Bolivian campaign. Finally in 1987, twenty years after the event, a firsthand, authoritative account was published in Spanish by Bolivian Army General Gary Prado Salmón who, as a captain, had commanded the unit that captured and killed Che. Now we are fortunate to have this first-rate English translation by Professor

John F. Deredita of Prado's work. It will become a standard reference for those who study guerrilla warfare and, given the continuing importance of such struggles, will also provide a basic source of information for both guerrillas and those who seek to defeat them.

Fidel Castro's successful guerrilla campaign that led to the ouster of Cuban dictator Fulgencio Batista in January 1959 triggered a series of insurgencies throughout Latin America. The rebels were inspired by Castro and guided by Che's study, which presented, in clear, straightforward terms, the formula for victory in a guerrilla war. Published in many editions and languages, Guevara argued that, contrary to previously accepted doctrine, guerrillas could defeat modern armies, and he used the Cuban experience to "prove it." Even the communist leadership in Cuba, which had initially dismissed Castro as a meddlesome adventurer, eventually came to embrace Fidel's cause. Although the debate over when and why Castro became a Marxist-Leninist continues, the more important aspect of his revolution was as a model of successful guerrilla warfare. Che's study of the Cuban campaign and its lessons became a standard guide for guerrillas everywhere and earned him world renown.

Although his study of guerrilla warfare presented few really new ideas, other than perhaps his "foco" theory, Che's formula for success based on the Cuban campaign gave him an aura of invincibility. As a result, the news of his defeat and death by the Bolivian Army raised a series of questions and cast doubt on the validity of his thinking. The reality of his defeat by a second-rate army perplexed and discouraged many of his disciples and stirred considerable debate. Gary Prado's authoritative study effectively ends this debate by explaining exactly how and why Che was beaten. It also makes clear the point that guerrillas, regardless of who leads them, will not necessarily triumph, and reinforces a notion proposed by Chalmers Johnson that revolutions are case-specific. There are no universal laws of revolution and each can be fully understood only in its own context.[2]

Prado's detailed and generally objective analysis of the campaign is unmatched for its clarity and balance. His observations on the shortcomings of both the army and the guerrillas are honest and accurate and dramatically detail Che's failures against poorly prepared troops. The U.S.-trained Bolivian Rangers, including Prado's unit, did not get involved until the very end of the campaign, and Guevara was effectively defeated long before they arrived on the scene. Although we are told that Che would have chosen Peru rather than Bolivia to establish his continental foco, the very notion was probably flawed from the start.

The selection of such a remote, rugged, and lightly populated region made life difficult for the guerrillas from the outset, but their failure to gain the trust and support of the campesinos in the area was decisive. In fact, rather than helping Che and his followers, the locals routinely provided critical information about their movements to their pursuers. Gary

Prado's explanations of the reasons for this basic failure are especially informative. He makes it clear that the guerrillas were in the wrong place at the wrong time, and his discussion of disagreements between Che and the leader of the Bolivian Communist party, which he desperately needed for support, shows that that problem was also instrumental in his defeat. The author also explains how the composition of the guerrilla band caused serious internal dissension that helped destroy its effectiveness.

As a retired U.S. Army officer familiar with the Latin American military, I was particularly impressed with the author's frank discussions of the Bolivian Army's problems at all levels. Although one may disagree with some of Prado's introductory comments and historical interpretations of U.S. policies and actions in Latin America, it is difficult to fault his analysis of the Bolivian Army's reaction to the guerrilla threat—and the reasons for those reactions. His study benefits not only from his participation as commander of the unit that finally captured Guevara, but also from his familiarity with the region where the action took place. Having spent a great deal of time in the area while growing up gave him a firsthand knowledge of its terrain and peoples as well as its history. The guerrillas' lack of understanding of any of these elements ensured that they would be unable to gain the support of the population needed to operate effectively in the region of conflict.

Although then-Captain Prado's accounts of his conversations with Che after his capture cannot be substantiated, they ring true. The topics discussed and the general tenor of the conversations have an air of reality. The author also presents a logical, albeit unacceptable, explanation for the decision at the highest levels to kill Guevara and another guerrilla who had been captured with him. It is quite clear that, if it had been up to him, Prado would not have made that decision.

During the past five years I have been using Che Guevara's *Guerrilla Warfare* as a basic text in a course on Latin American Revolutions and Revolutionaries. The availability of this new study in eminently readable English will serve as the perfect companion volume. A vote of thanks also goes to Praeger publishers for their decision to bring this important work to a much broader reading public. I am pleased to have been part of the effort.

Lawrence H. Hall

NOTES

1. Ernesto Guevara, *Guerrilla Warfare*, trans. J. P. Morray (New York: Monthly Review Press, 1961).
2. Chalmers Johnson, *Revolutionary Change*, 2d ed. (Stanford, Calif.: Stanford University Press, 1982).

PREFACE

As soon as the operations against the guerrilla force commanded by Ernesto "Che" Guevara in Bolivia in 1967 were completed, many friends suggested that I should write about these events, which were to become an important part of the contemporary history of our country.

I always replied that I would do so in due time. I was not interested in joining the "mercenaries of the pen" who sought to profit by exploiting the guerrilla chief's image. I told my friends that I was preparing a serious, well-documented essay that would be, so to speak, "the other side of the coin," since the flood of publications, both well- and ill-intentioned, that had appeared after the incidents of Ñancahuazú and La Higuera had only sought to relate the events and encounters from the point of view of the guerrilla fighters, and more often than not to denigrate the role of the Bolivian army and of military men in general.

As is always the case, when political fervor clouds one's perspective, one commits errors and draws false conclusions that take on the appearance of truth.

Over these two past decades, I have been patiently accumulating materials and documents, preparing data and charts, reconstructing step by step what happened in those months of 1967 and before, in order to present a serious, objective, and solid work that would display the true nature of those events that put Bolivia and her armed forces in the forefront of the international news.

Now that passions have cooled and new winds are blowing over the continent, when efforts are being made to repair the damage done to Cuban-Bolivian relations on account of the support given by Cuba to the guerrilla operation, when other subjects occupy the attention of Latin Americans, I consider it opportune to bring this work to light so that a different basis for evaluating this chapter of our history may be available.

No sensational revelations are to be found here, but rather a series of small details, heretofore unknown, that will be useful in forming a clearer idea of everything that went on back then. It is by no means my intention to hide anything or to twist the facts. I am not looking for fame or recognition, since in a worthy military career, I have achieved a measure of respect and affection among my fellow soldiers and fellow citizens that does me honor. I have only one purpose: to contribute to a clarification of history that will enlighten present and future generations.

This book is also a homage to the Bolivian soldier, who, in the test, answered his country's call bravely and humbly, writing yet another page of our history in his own blood.

ACKNOWLEDGMENT

Many people have contributed to this work, from those who participated in the operations and provided me with documents, recollections, photographs, and anecdotes, to those who helped me morally and materially to accomplish it.

My thanks to General Simón Sejas Tordoya who, as Commander of the Army, gave me access to all existing documentation.

Special thanks to my wife Rosario for her work with the first draft; to Ana María and Delvy for copying and transcribing; to my daughter Cecilia for the layout of the first edition; to Eduardo Leva for its illustrations; to my son Gary for checking and coordinating its graphics and printing; to Eloy and Jaime for pagination and assembly.

This testimonial goes to all of them as proof of my affection and gratitude.

Part I

BACKGROUND

Chapter 1

THE INTERNATIONAL CLIMATE

Along with the traditional holiday celebrations, the beginning of the year 1959 brought Latin America news that gave rise to feelings of joy and solidarity. At dawn on January 1, Fulgencio Batista had fled Havana, defeated by the guerrilla insurgency that had begun with the landing of a group of young combatants from the *Granma* on December 2, 1956, and had grown to the point of totally defeating the dictator's well-armed and well-organized army. The guerrilla war waged in Cuba over nearly three years had revived an old Latin American experience. Its first expressions had been seen in the first quarter of the nineteenth century in Upper Peru (now Bolivia) and on the Venezuelan savannahs, the Colombian plains, and the pampas and canyons of northeastern Argentina, when groups of patriots, inspired by the idea of freedom, joined battle against the far superior forces of the Spanish army that occupied the Viceroyalties and Captaincies-General. This type of combat, aimed at weakening, demoralizing, and breaking down the organization of military forces in order to facilitate the triumph of a small group of men capable of steering a people toward liberation, led to the establishment throughout Spanish America of the republics that today make up the center and south of the hemisphere.

The uprising of Fidel Castro and his followers shared those characteristics. Its objective was the fall of Batista's government, which, although native to Cuba, was simply a reflection of foreign interests that were depriving Cuba of her national identity. The dictatorial Caribbean governments of the Trujillos, Somozas, and Batistas, strongly backed by North American interests, were turning their lands into political and ideological fiefdoms and at the same time exploiting their populations and dragging down morale.

For that reason, the insurgency of the young Cuban guerrillas received the backing of international and particularly Latin American public opinion, which is characterized by a deep love of liberty and by romanticism. Wide press coverage had accompanied the guerrillas' operations from the outset, turning the events into front-page news, especially during the last months of 1958, when their continual victories over the regular army and the unmistakable support of the Cuban people had made evident their chances for triumph.

When the new government was installed after the flight of Batista and his closest collaborators, the charismatic figure of Prime Minister Fidel Castro came into full view as he undertook the hard task of organizing his country and recovering her identity with the support of the principal commandants of the guerrilla forces.

The first international conflict for the new order arose when the North American government offered generous terms to the principal members of the fugitive dictatorship so that they could settle in the United States. Individuals with well-known track records who had exercised a violent, inhumane repression against the revolutionaries were welcomed with open arms, along with all those who out of fear of the new order began to leave Cuba and to set up in Florida their base of operations for organizing an eventual return to power. They were protected and supported by North American economic interests, which were beginning to feel adversely affected by the first measures undertaken by the new government. These same interests, eager to block any possibility of success for the revolutionary government, pressured the power centers of the United States to adopt measures designed to create difficulties for the Castroites.

Throughout 1959, the course of events in Cuba was carefully followed, in particular the mass exodus of an important sector of the middle class. Feeling threatened by the revolutionary forces, it left the country to settle in Miami and other Florida cities. The continual accusations and tensions produced between the Cuban and North American governments troubled the Latin American power groups that had shown sympathy for the revolution that was beginning on the Caribbean island. Conciliatory efforts to avoid greater problems were unsuccessful, and when in April of that year a small group of insurgents landed on the east coast of Panama with the intention of reenacting the Cuban epic and directly threatening the strategic position of the United States in the Canal Zone, alarm began to spread in the governments of the region. Although the Panamanian venture was quickly brought into check by the National Guard of that country, it prompted a state of alert in the North American military forces, and it drew attention for the first time to the expansion of what would be called Castroism, signifying the appearance of a guerrilla foco, or nucleus, with an intent of armed struggle.[1] The obvious material and moral backing by Cuba of the Panama venture created new difficulties and new verbal skirmishes, which began to alienate those who until that time had unconditionally supported Castro and his revolution. The appearance of guerrilla focos in Venezuela and Colombia in the months following, and the evident spread of the foco doctrine, particularly in Central America and the Caribbean, gave rise to consultations, agreements, and decisions that little by little began to isolate what political circles were beginning to regard as the destabilizing factor in Latin America.

When it was learned in the first months of 1960 that the Cuban government was acquiring large quantities of arms from European countries, the concern grew. The sabotage explosion in Havana harbor of the French ship *La Coubre* with a considerable cargo of arms and ammunition confirmed these findings and led to the first pronouncement condemning Cuba for its interference in the internal affairs of other nations, at a meeting of the Organization of American States (OAS) held in August.[2] In keeping with this measure and in view of the continual verbal attacks by Prime Minister Castro and the campaign of nationalizations and expropriations being undertaken in Cuba, the United States decided to suspend shipments of petroleum to Cuban refineries and to reduce the sugar quota assigned to that country for the United States market. A policy of economic blockade got under way, the effects of which began to be felt at the end of 1960. Tension between the two countries worsened and became untenable. As a way of exerting pressure, Cuba's northern neighbor kept on issuing visas for Cubans who wished to leave their country, on an average of fifteen hundred every month, creating internal problems and a poor international image for Cuba. As a way of halting this action, the Castro regime requested that the North American diplomatic mission in Havana be cut to eleven people. This was met on January 3, 1961, by the United States decision to break off diplomatic relations, simultaneously ordering that all North American residents leave the island, and entrusting United States interests to the Swiss diplomatic mission.

The new North American government headed by John F. Kennedy, who assumed office on January 20, 1961, found that its hands were effectively tied so far as policy toward Castro was concerned. Yielding to pressures, it completely abolished the Cuban sugar quota, and it could not prevent the landing of an invasion force of 1,500 trained men, armed and financed by the Central Intelligence Agency, at the Bay of Pigs in the province of Las Villas, after ineffective bombings of the major Cuban airports. For seventy-two hours heavy combat was sustained and the situation remained uncertain. President Kennedy's decision not to permit the intervention of North American military forces in support of the Cuban counterrevolutionaries condemned them to failure and facilitated the defeat and capture of the invaders by the revolutionary army, which thereby made a first public demonstration of its strength and armed readiness, attained in less than two years of the Castro government. The repercussions of this international incident were strong, and they amounted in the long run to a political and military victory for Fidel Castro.

In view of all these events, the climate of relations between Cuba and the United States—and the rest of the hemispheric nations—worsened and became a permanent source of accusations, rebukes, and a general breakdown of relations, of which the Soviet Union took advantage in order to raise its banners high on the Caribbean island and from that base to begin exercising political power on the continent. The public statement by the Cuban prime minister that he was a Marxist-Leninist, and his decision to convert his country into the first socialist nation of America, hardened positions. President Kennedy's attempt to regain influence over the Latin American community and its governments with an ambitious plan of economic cooperation to improve the living conditions of its inhabitants, under the name of the Alliance for Progress, began to achieve success when projects were undertaken on the continent that helped unite peoples through hard work and dedication.

But the continuing spread of Prime Minister Castro's unique ideas and his evident support for so-called liberation movements, which began to emerge in several countries, led the OAS, at the foreign ministers' conference held in Punta del Este, Uruguay for the purpose of taking measures against the Castro regime, to order the expulsion of Cuba from the hemispheric system. The resolution pointed out the danger that the existence of a communist government in Latin America posed for the continent and stressed its incompatibility with inter-American principles of peace. At the same time, it ordered the separation of the Cuban delegation from the Inter-American Defense Council, on the grounds that a communist regime with subversive motives could not form part of an organism created for the very purpose of defending the continent from that political doctrine. The OAS determination gave rise in turn to varying reactions within the Latin American nations, in several of which it was criticized amid public demonstrations, the circulation of protest literature, and other activities revealing attitudes contrary to the position assumed. These reactions demonstrated the growth of the Latin American political movement and the influence it was receiving from Cuba.

In view of these reactions and the overall state of affairs, the United States hardened its position and maintained, besides the economic boycott, close surveillance of the activities being carried out on Cuban territory, where the presence of Soviet military advisers was already permanent, and where the growing influx of arms and military equipment was transforming Cuba into a virtual fortress. This situation reached crisis proportions in October 1962, when President Kennedy, in addition to publicly denouncing Fidel Castro's exportation of his revolution to the rest of the continent, showed photographic evidence, obtained on reconnaissance flights by U–2 airplanes, of the installation of intermediate-range missiles that threatened other Caribbean nations and the southern United States. Kennedy requested OAS support for his government's determination to effect a naval blockade to prevent the arrival in Cuban ports of a dozen Soviet ships carrying key parts of offensive arms. The measure, which set the world on the edge of a nuclear confrontation, forced the Soviet Union to accept North American restrictions and to withdraw the missiles in question from Cuba without consulting Fidel Castro. This situation amounted to a political defeat for Cuba and for Soviet plans for expansion. It helped to isolate Fidel Castro definitively from any hope of reaching agreement with regional nations or with hemispheric international organizations. From the Cuban position there remained only the avenue of supporting through covert means the liberation movements that were coming alive in several countries—by sending economic aid, arms, and expert advisers. At the same time numerous contingents of young Latin Americans interested in university study were brought to Cuba to receive both ideological orientation and military training and to be transformed into future combatants on the fronts that would open up in the struggle that the Cuban government intended to lead against North American imperialism.[3]

The reaction was not long in coming. The total political and economic blockade of Cuba intensified from 1963 on, and although the focus of news attention began moving away from the American continent and toward Southeast Asia, this did not prevent the unleashing of an intense political struggle between the defenders of the Cuban Revolution and those who criticized it and attacked its submission to the dictates of a power outside of the continent.

Since the weakness of some governments jeopardized what was then called hemispheric security, United States pressure and military advice increased in order to provoke coups d'état that brought forth military governments with a clear anticommunist bias in the Dominican Republic, Honduras, Brazil, and Bolivia. At the same time more rigorous controls were being set up in order to monitor the activities of Fidel Castro's principal lieutenants, who had proclaimed the permanent necessity of broadening the scope of activity of the Cuban Revolution to include the rest of the continent.

The individual of most concern to the intelligence services of all nations was the minister of industry of the Cuban government, Ernesto "Che" Guevara: Argentine-born, a veteran of the Sierra Maestra, and known for his resolute support of liberation movements. The Council of Revolutionary Ministers had declared him a Cuban citizen in February 1959, for his valuable contribution to the guerrilla campaign. He had been in command of the La Cabaña fortress in Havana, sharing with Camilo Cienfuegos in the first months of the rebel government the tasks of military governor of the capital. He had had an important role in the definitive liquidation of the remains of Batista's army through the trials of many of its members and the execution of those judged guilty of capital offenses and other high crimes. When he was named president of the National Bank of Cuba in

November 1959, he drew comments and speculation with the appearance of his signature as simply "Che" on the new currency that he unexpectedly put into circulation. In 1960, he was named minister of industry, a function that he performed for four years without, however, abandoning international contacts, particularly with the socialist countries, who were directing the Castro regime's ideological orientation. Guevara's interviews with the major political leaders of the nations he visited, his performance at the OAS meeting in Punta del Este, the Brazilian president Jânio Quadros's conferral of a medal on him, and his other international activities kept him continually at the center of the news. This wounded the pride of some Cuban political leaders and gave rise to some disputes with them. They were concerned that this public figure often put the revolution at risk with his personalist attitudes but always found support from Fidel Castro.

In March 1965, after a lengthy trip through several Asian and African countries, Guevara returned to Havana, where he was officially welcomed by Prime Minister Castro and President Dorticós. That was the last official occasion where he was seen. Afterward, his behavior was shrouded in mystery and his absence from his ministerial post and all public events was noticed by those who had been close to him and those far away. Thus a series of explanations began to appear that made it very hard to determine clearly where he was. His absence from the ceremony organized on April 18, 1965, at the death of the old Cuban communist leader César Escalante, and from the May Day parade, made it even more difficult to track him down. Rumors began to circulate suggesting differences with Fidel Castro that could have led to Che's being shot, imprisoned, or exiled, or his having sought asylum in some friendly embassy awaiting the opportunity to leave Cuba. Nonetheless, continual mention was made of the possibility that his absence was due to some revolutionary enterprise authorized by the Cuban government itself. He was mentioned in connection with the revolutionary movement that arose in the Dominican Republic, and he was also depicted in the Andes, the backbone of the continent, organizing guerrilla movements aimed at widening the front against imperialism.

In this context, the continent was alarmed at the outbreak of guerrilla subversion in Peru, which was under constitutional government. Very quickly the encounters in the foothills of the Andes turned into violent confrontations that required the use of military force with the inevitable bombings, arrests, and accusations of atrocities on both sides. The support that the guerrilla fighters received from the historically marginal Indian population made the former more difficult to control.

The operations lasted a long eight months. They took a serious toll on the government, casting doubt on the legitimacy of representative democracy as a mechanism able to resist the advance of armed challenges to power. Doubts also arose within the armed forces of Peru as to the role they should play in these encounters, especially when they saw in crude relief the abysmal differences that existed between the inhabitants of the coast and the Indians of the sierra and realized that these differences could not be resolved by force of arms. This kind of thinking brought about in the relatively short period of two years the rise of power of a new military group, led by Gen. Juan Velasco Alvarado, which would attempt to modify existing power structures in order to eliminate the root causes of the subversion.

Even before the operations came to an end in Peru, the outbreak of guerrilla action in Paraguay also created alarm on the South American continent, although the foco was quickly put under control. Political and social conditions in Paraguay did not permit even the organization of a subversive movement. A vast military and police operation culminated in the capture of about a hundred communist guerrillas, and this put an end to the problem. Several dead and wounded were the result of this movement, which could not carry out its plan to create four centers of command in different regions of the country.

In that continental atmosphere of the outbreak of violence, ideological confrontations, and tensions, Havana served as the stage for the first Tricontinental Conference, which, with the motto of "confronting imperialist violence with revolutionary violence," became from the first a broad forum where methods and procedures were debated for establishing "the solidarity of the peoples of Asia, Africa, and Latin America in their struggle against American imperialism for the gaining and the consolidation of national independence on those three continents."

Without disguising its goals, the Conference, which brought together 500 delegates from various organizations in more than 100 nations, determined that all methods, including armed struggle, were valid for combating colonialism and neocolonialism. The attacks were focused particularly on the United States as the symbol of imperial power.

The effects of the Tricontinental discussions were felt immediately. Throughout 1966, the resolutions adopted were debated in political circles throughout South America, instructions were received, cadres were organized, and everything pointed to the establishment of guerrilla focos which, in line with the Havana agreements, would promote the confrontation intended to convert the entire continent to Castroite ideology within no more than five years' time. The feeling was that nothing could stop the liberation movements that were springing up in different regions.

This danger, in addition to domestic problems, put Argentina on the already lengthy list of countries with military governments. In June, Gen. Juan Carlos Onganía took power as a consequence of the military unrest caused by the political attitude of the militant left.

By the end of 1966, the entire continent looked back with concern over the seven years of Castro's government in Cuba and the effects of his regional policy. Things had undoubtedly changed, and one could not speak unequivocally of a preponderant United States hegemony. New winds were blowing over the continent from north to south and everyone was asking, "Where is Che?" His long disappearance of more than a year continued to be a source of worry and uneasiness for the intelligence services of the different countries, for politicians, and even for ordinary citizens who saw Commandant Guevara as a sympathetic, attractive character.

NOTES

1. The expedition had left Barabano, Cuba on April 18, landing on the 24th near the town of Nombre de Dios, Panama. The invasion force, numbering eighty-six men and one woman, included thirty Cubans. They all surrendered without firing a shot, yielding to the pleas of an OAS delegation that had been sent to the area. The Cuban prime minister denied any connection to the venture.

2. The OAS Assembly met in San José, Costa Rica at the request of Peru, in order to study the threat of communism in the hemisphere and to pass judgment on the Cuban and Dominican governments for their actions in defiance of hemispheric accords. Among other provisions, the San José Declaration condemned overseas intervention in the hemisphere and proposed the drafting and signing of a treaty opposing communism. The Cuban and Dominican delegates ended up leaving the meeting.

3. During the military operations conducted in Bolivia in 1967 against Che Guevara's guerrilla group, several Bolivian students were identified as members of it, as will be explained later.

Chapter 2

THE DOMESTIC SCENE

In Bolivia, the ruling Revolutionary Nationalist Movement (MNR, in its Spanish initials) faced internal divisions in 1959 as a result of the decision taken by its leader, Dr. Victor Paz Estenssoro, to run for a new term after having held the presidency between 1952 and 1956. This left Walter Guevara Arze, the third man in the party hierarchy, frustrated, and he himself sought the official candidacy. This decision, which in a few months was to cause the first split in the heretofore monolithic MNR and the birth of Guevara Arze's Authentic Revolutionary Party (PRA), would lead first to ideological skirmishes and then to armed encounters between the followers of the two political leaders. This created a difficult situation for President Hernán Siles Suazo, who was carrying out the constitutional term of office from 1956 to 1960 in a context of violent opposition by the Bolivian Socialist Phalanx (FSB) and other smaller groups, in addition to the problems generated by his own party. From 1959 on, frequent coup attempts and other subversive postures taken by the various groups began to provoke a growing and decisive participation by the armed forces in the solution of political problems.

In the Cochabamba Valley, from the end of 1959 through almost all of 1960, violent clashes occurred between *campesino* (peasant) sectors that followed Paz Estenssoro or Guevara Arze. Using the arms that had been distributed for the purpose of organizing the campesinos in the first years of the National Revolution (which had begun in 1952), these groups tried to impose their rule over the population settled in the fertile lands of what at that time constituted the Bolivian Breadbasket. The use of military troops succeeded in keeping the adversaries apart and neutralizing their actions, but the price paid was a weakening of political structures, an increase in the importance of military power, and in many cases the subordination of regional civil authorities to military commanders who effectively occupied the valley in order to restore peace.

As yet in 1960, domestic politics had not felt the effects of continental tensions, nor was it influenced by what was beginning to happen in the Caribbean. Once the general election had been held and the leader of the MNR had been newly installed as president, it was clear that given Paz Estenssoro's personality and his authority, he could lead national politics along the path defined by the National Revolution line. Paradoxically, domestic tensions reappeared, this time as a consequence of what was occurring in the rest of the continent. The United States decision to break relations with Cuba in January 1961 had its counterpart in Bolivia, as in all area nations, when in June of the same year the government requested that Cuba withdraw its diplomatic representative in Bolivia, Mauro García de Triana, for violating the principle of nonintervention in domestic affairs. He was accused of participating in a communist plot uncovered by security forces. This measure drew the immediate opposition of the powerful Bolivian Workers' Union (COB), headed by the vice-president of the republic, Juan Lechín Oquendo. The labor organization sought to lead a people's movement in support of the Cuban envoy and in repudiation of the government's decision, but it failed because the bulk of the population was indifferent to the issue. At that time, most Bolivians were not feeling the effects of propaganda, nor did they know in any detail what was happening outside of the national context. They considered it more important for the country to resolve its own problems before taking sides on behalf of this or that foreign ideological enterprise, since the program of revolutionary nationalism was still going full strength, and the visible progress that had been made in the political and economic spheres had created public satisfaction. Now that the first revolutionary stage—the breakdown of dominant structures—had been achieved, the people were eagerly awaiting takeoff into the economic and social development that was constantly being proclaimed in accord with the theory of development imposed on the continent from the beginning of the 1960s.

In advance of the meeting of OAS foreign ministers in Punta del Este, Uruguay, where it was anticipated that sanctions would be imposed on the Castro government, anticommunist organizations went about preparing a mass demonstration in order to pressure the government into voting against Cuba at the conference. A radio network that began transmitting from the early hours of the day prepared public opinion for the demonstration, alternating anticommunist slogans with detailed accounts of tortures, shootings, and other violations of human rights that, it was claimed, were occurring on the Caribbean island. The anti-Castro demonstration was held with a strong turnout of several thousand persons. Under the direction of Vice-President Lechín, the COB attempted to organize another mass movement on the next day, this time with orders to support Fidel Castro. This intent failed due to the indifference of labor groups and despite Lechín's attempt to convince them. Thus the first symptoms were felt in Bolivia of confrontation between traditional politics, which was heavily nationalist in content, and the emerging politics of Castroism, which until then had remained outside of national events.

Meanwhile, some subtler methods were being used to influence the country politically, notably the formation of cadres of student leaders who would be able to lead the masses in the future. To this end, since 1962 more than a hundred young Bolivians had been invited to pursue university studies in Havana, with scholarships from the Castro government, under the guise of contributing to the professionalization of needy students. The young students in fact did receive instruction within the Cuban university system, but at the same time they were politically indoctrinated and given military training so that they might later be used in the stage of forming and operating guerrilla focos throughout the continent. This intention was publicly censured in Bolivia in the early months of 1963. As might be expected, the denunciation provoked diverse reactions and feelings of defensiveness in the families of those who had traveled to Cuba to study. Officially, no statement was made, but the public retained the impression that a broad revolutionary movement was being initiated out of Havana which would have repercussions in the years to come.

An airplane accident served as a signal to the entire country, revealing to what extent a quiet war was being waged between the intelligence services of the United States and Cuba. On March 16, 1963, a Bolivian Airlines DC–6 on a scheduled flight between Arica, Chile and La Paz crashed, presumably because of technical failure, on the slopes of the Tacora Volcano in the Andes range, causing the death of all aboard. When it was learned that the Cuban diplomatic couriers Enrique Valdés and Juan Molen had been on the plane, intelligence personnel from the North American embassy in La Paz quickly appeared on the scene. Under the command of the military attaché, Lt. Col. Paul Wimert and with the support of helicopters sent from Lima, they arrived at the accident site before the rescue patrols and before the Cuban ambassador to Bolivia, Ramón Aja Castro. There was much speculation about the documents that had been carried by the diplomatic couriers, which seemingly were not found by the rescue patrols. It was thought that the North Americans had extracted them from the wreckage of the plane. Although no formal protest was lodged, the episode worsened relations among the countries of the hemisphere.

On the domestic political front, as a result of increasing military participation in the acts of the MNR government, Gen. René Barrientos Ortuño, commander of the Air Force, emerged as a political leader. Backed by the armed forces and campesino sectors, he undertook a vigorous campaign aimed at increasing his support and demonstrating that he was the most appropriate man to accompany Dr. Paz Estenssoro, who was preparing for reelection in 1964. Military pressure became more obvious when the military cell of the MNR, led by the commander-in-chief, Gen. Alfredo Ovando Candia, proclaimed General Barrientos a candidate for the vice-presidency, involving the military in the political game that was unfolding. This intervention became definitive in February when, although he had not been elected by the party convention, René Barrientos was named the running mate of Víctor Paz after an unsuccessful attempt on Barrientos's life that added to his popularity and unified the armed forces behind him. As part of his election campaign, Barrientos organized mass rallies of campesinos that culminated in Ucureña with the signing of the Military-Campesino Anticommunist Accord, joining the military cell of the MNR and the principal farm leaders. The Accord committed both parties to prevent the emergence of communist leaders in the agricultural sector and to defend the traditional values of the nation.

The appearance of an FSB guerrilla foco in the Alto Paraguá region of Santa Cruz Department, which in imitation of the Castro model intended to lead the resistance against the government, did not find the support its leadership expected and did not even elicit a significant military mobilization. A squadron of Ingavi Regiment was called up to reinforce the Fifth Division, which from its command post in Roboré was put in charge of the operations aimed at wiping out the threat, but because of the political loyalties of the FSB members, who were characterized as rightist, this attempt was not given any possibility of success—and the participants were allowed to disband out of weakness and fatigue and to take refuge next door in Brazil. Within the armed forces these events had little impact, in part because cordial relations were being maintained with those FSB members who were considered friends of the military. Although their antigovernment attitude also meant opposition to the elected vice-president, General Barrientos, there was no desire for confrontations that could mean the death of the guerrillas, and so the operations were limited to harassment and psychological pressure, until the guerrilla foco was disbanded.

Once the new government was installed on August 6, 1964, with Víctor Paz and René Barrientos as president and vice-president, respectively, one of its first acts was to comply with the OAS resolution to break off relations with the Castro regime. The announcement was received by the public with a sense of relief and expressions of support. The government justified its action in the following statement:

The government of Bolivia, in the ninth meeting of foreign ministers, held recently, expressed an attitude of unstinting defense of the principle of self-determination of peoples because this principle is inseparable from the birth of our republic, and defense of nonintervention in recognition of the painful experience we lived from the first years of our political independence to the beginnings of the National Revolution during the Villaroel government.[1]

This meeting was held in response to the complaint of Venezuela against the government of Cuba, for the purpose of considering the measures to be adopted against the acts of intervention and aggression by the government of Cuba which affect the territorial integrity and the sovereignty of Venezuela, as well as the effectiveness of its democratic institutions. Bolivia, in accord with the principles of nonintervention and self-determination, voted in favor of condemning the Cuban government. On the other hand, because it considered that the sanctions were not on a scale with the actions denounced, Bolivia voted against severing relations and interrupting commerce. That attitude was adopted purely on principle and was legal in nature, because Bolivia does not have a diplomatic nor a consular mission in Havana, and commercial relations are nonexistent. In the vote on suspending maritime traffic Bolivia abstained, calling attention to is unjust landlocked situation.

The foreign ministers' meeting, by a two-thirds majority, approved the sanctions against the Cuban government in conformity with Article 2, which states: "Decisions that require the application of measures mentioned in Article 8 will be mandatory for all states that are signatories to the present treaty and have ratified it."

Given the obligatory nature of the decision adopted at the foreign ministers' meeting, Bolivia, as a signatory of this treaty, which is the law of the land, considers itself bound to enforce it.

The government of Bolivia, in taking this step, hopes that all the differences that separate the nations of the continent will be resolved through the peaceful means indicated in international law.

Fidel Castro's diplomatic representative in La Paz, upon receipt from the Bolivian foreign minister of the notice of the breaking off of relations, reacted forcefully in public statements against the United States. In his eagerness to attack the Washington government, he made declarations that were interpreted as offensive to Bolivia. The measure had been approved on Thursday, August 13, by the Council of Ministers, which also determined that the date should be chosen with regard to political circumstances and to the most opportune moment, authorizing the foreign minister, with prior consultation with the president and with his approval, to make the announcement to the Cuban embassy. This occurred on August 22, 1964.

The November 4, 1964, uprising of the Bolivian military that deposed the constitutional president, Víctor Paz Estenssoro, and replaced him with a military junta had its domestic and foreign causes, which we will attempt to summarize.

On the domestic scene, the weakening of the MNR was evident after twelve years of government. Its major leaders—Siles Suazo, Lechín Oquendo, and Guevara Arze—had distanced themselves from the party leader over serious objections to the political leadership of the process of the National Revolution. This debilitated the party and created parallel organizations that, precisely because they had a common origin, became its severest opponents. By mid–1964, President Paz's power, gravely undermined, was backed mainly by the armed forces, which had drawn a virtual circle around him, controlling through military men the vice-presidency, the executive secretariat of the MNR, several department prefectures, and other bodies in which by necessity esprit de corps and subordination to the commands of the hierarchy prevailed. The orders of the high command slowly stifled the ability of the political apparatus to react. Beyond that, the continual intervention of the armed forces in the last few years to solve the various problems of internal security that had come up, had in some sense popularized or at least given notoriety to the major military authorities, who therefore gained increasing political visibility. This generated a type of leadership that was generally welcomed within the armed forces because it appealed to a latent desire for hegemony that had grown out of the frustrations borne since the 1952 revolution, when the army had been in effect defeated in the streets by the MNR and the *carabineros* (militarized police). Playing adroitly on those sentiments, Generals Ovando and Barrientos obtained the support of the officer corps for their purposes, along with another element: almost all of the major political leaders backed military action in order to get rid of Víctor Paz. This was a decisive factor that helped the military insurrection of November 4 to occur practically unopposed and to gain power within a few hours. The support of the political leaders gave the armed forces from the first a sense of satisfaction and even pride at having led a movement that carried with it a high degree of national consensus.

Foreign influences also played an important role. The menace that Castroism was beginning to pose in the hemisphere had already been defined in the upper echelons of North American politics. Faced with increased participation in the Southeast Asian war and with the Middle East at a boiling point, the State Department had left Latin America in the hands of the Pentagon, allowing it to direct and to carry out a policy aimed at containing the expansion of communism in the hemisphere. For this reason, through an increase in the activity of military missions and through support of the armed forces of regional nations, a strong military apparatus was consolidated. In many cases, such as in Brazil, the Dominican Republic, and Bolivia, the military seized direct power in order to ensure that a stop was put to nascent liberation movements.

Once the military government was installed in Bolivia, differences between Generals Ovando and Barrientos prevented its being given clear direction. A rapid weakening took place, which, although it was not evident to the citizenry, polarized the armed forces between those who intended to use the military presence in government progressively to push forward tasks that were important and necessary for the country, and those who saw the use of power as an instrument for the advancement of the armed forces and their followers without regard for the needs of the nation.

The popular movement, encouraged by leftist leaders, disagreed with some government measures. It sponsored acts in the outlying districts of La Paz and in the principal mining centers that provoked armed confrontations, violence, and destruction that caused concern in the armed forces and brought forth the announcement of a state of siege, the military occupation of mining centers, and even a call-up of reservists to active duty in order to increase total strength and to take a stand against the threats to the stability of the regime. After investigating the sources of these uprisings and detecting the participation of known leaders of the Communist party in the plans for and execution of the demonstrations in the mines and at Villa Victoria, the military government adopted a strongly anticommunist stance that was first seen in threats, then in repressive measures, and finally in the promulgation of the National Security Law. The latter was intended to serve as a coercive legal instrument to counteract the new methods of popular struggle that were evolving, to make up for deficiencies in the existing legislation. Basically aimed at halting the action of irregular armed groups that had strong foreign backing, this security law sought to subject participants in these actions to military justice.

The text of the law reads:

Gen. René Barrientos O.
Gen. Alfredo Ovando C.
Presidents of the Honorable Governing Military Junta

Considering:

That it is necessary to maintain, against the actions of foreign and domestic forces, the sovereignty and integrity of the national territory and the life of our citizens, the stability of our institutions, peace, and law and order, as the foundations of harmony and progress.

That the nation requires for its goals of development a permanent atmosphere of order and calm.

That for this purpose it is fitting to declare the Law of National Security.

From within the Governing Military Junta

Decree:

Article 1: In addition to those acts mentioned in Book I, Article 3 of the Penal Code, the following are crimes against the security of the State:

a) The formation of irregular armed groups or their incursion from outside our borders with the purpose of establishing geographical areas to be removed from government authority or trying to take over the government, seeking armed conflict with regular armed forces or the forces of public safety.

b) Intimidation, demoralization, or terror provoked in all or parts of the population by the explosion of bombs, acts of sharpshooters, and dangerous public acts. Sentence of three to four years in prison. If as a consequence of these acts lives are lost, those found guilty will be sentenced according to the provisions of the Penal Code. In the case of grave damages to property, sentence of four to eight years in prison.

c) Destruction of industrial facilities, communication lines, supply routes, transport, and the like, for the purposes of attacking the productive capacity or the economic endeavor of the nation: sentence of four to eight years in prison.

d) The clandestine possession, concealment, manufacture, distribution, or sale of arms, weapons, or explosives by subversive groups or individuals: sentence of three to six years in prison.

e) Maintaining contacts with foreign persons or associations with the intention of receiving instructions or training of any kind in order to commit the crimes outlined in the present Law Decree: sentence of six months to three years in prison.

f) Facilitating any means of committing or concealing acts of sabotage, terrorism, or the like, which offend state security; knowingly providing premises or headquarters to organizations, associations, or societies that encourage the perpetration of these crimes: sentence of six months to two years of confinement.

g) Inducing members of the armed forces or the organs of state security, through oral or written means or through any other means, to break discipline, to fail to carry out orders issued by their superiors, or to disobey government authorities.

h) Propaganda and agitation, whether oral or written, individual or collective which incites to violence for the purpose of taking over the national government, to the formation of irregular armed groups (guerrilla forces), to acts of terrorism and sabotage, to illegal occupation of goods belonging to the state, to illegal strikes, to disobedience of the laws and resolutions of the government, to the cutting of communication lines, to the paralyzing of public services, and to any act or event which interferes with the work of national development: sentence of six months to three years of confinement.

In the case that the previously described crime only constitutes a threat to a determined region, the authorities in charge of public safety can assign the perpetrators to residency in municipalities that are far away from their center of activities.

i) The revelation by public functionaries of confidential decisions or agreements related to internal or international security: sentence of six months to two years of confinement.

Article 2: When the crimes outlined in the previous article affect the Armed Forces of the Nation, their members, or property, those responsible shall be subject to the courts of military justice.

Article 3: If the crimes identified in this law are committed by military personnel or public functionaries, this will be considered an aggravating circumstance for the purposes of passing sentence. The Ministers of Government, Justice, and Immigration and National Defense will be in charge of the enforcement and fulfillment of the present Law Decree.

Given in the Government Palace of the city of La Paz, on the ninth day of September, 1965.

The legal provisions did not interrupt political activity, which began to develop with the military government as the center of interest. In order to relieve the pressure and to consolidate power, the government called elections for the middle of 1966, presenting as its candidate Gen. René Barrientos Ortuñño, who left General Ovando as president of the military junta in compliance with the terms of the constitution. The anticipation of future guerrilla operations drew commentary from the candidate, who said in one of his speeches, "If guerrilla forces are organized in the country, we will show them an adequate response."

When the elections were held with results favorable to General Barrientos, who undoubtedly had won wide political support based mainly on his standing with the campesinos and his tendency to visit every spot where a voter could be found, in a display of vitality that amazed the entire country despite protests from the opposing parties, he was installed on August 6 as constitutional president. This permitted the armed forces to withdraw discreetly from the governing function, leaving the president to administer the state with the support of the civil structure. In this period the traditional political parties lost all of their power and all of their issues, crushed under Barrientos's strong personality. The president exercised total control over political activities, ignoring party structures, even those which he had used. The entire country hung on his decisions and his whims, but there remained nevertheless a margin of relative freedom for the underground activity of the parties of the international left, which began to organize their cadres and to prepare their resistance to the Barrientos government. They characterized it as a military dictatorship, but they were alone in their opinion, since at least in appearance all of the apparatus provided for in the constitution was in operation and no major repression was being undertaken in those first months.

The good relations maintained by the government with regional nations and with the United States provided an opening for the consolidation of loans and aid that served to stabilize the domestic situation and to keep the armed forces out of political events. This made it possible to improve their professionalism at the same time that efforts were being made to supply the units with better resources.

This political mood of relative surface calm was to be violently shattered with the emergence of the guerrilla group of Ñancahuazú.

NOTE

1. The government of Maj. Gualberto Villaroel (1943–46) was a populist forerunner of the nationalist revolution of 1952.

Chapter 3

THE MILITARY
ENVIRONMENT

Until the end of the 1950s, the Bolivian armed forces, composed of the
national army and the air force (recently created as a separate entity),
were equipped with matériel acquired by the nation for the Chaco War
(1932–35). The soldier's basic hand weapon remained the Mauser 7.65–
caliber rifle, and support arms included heavy Colt and Vickers machine
guns, 81–mm. mortars, and some 75–mm. artillery pieces. A good part of
this equipment had been distributed to worker and peasant militias, which
to some extent replaced the military apparatus in the first years of the
National Revolution process begun in 1952. The air force possessed only
a few T–6 training planes and some C–47 transports.

The slow task of military recuperation, begun in 1954, began to show
results when the first military aid agreements with the United States were
signed. They became effective in 1958, when the first officers were sent to
the Panama Canal Zone to study the equipment the country was planning
to acquire. In 1959 the first shipment of American arms, intended to outfit
one infantry battalion, arrived in Bolivia. It was divided instead among
three companies in the units that at that time covered the principal missions
of internal security. One company of the Major Waldo Ballivián Presidential Escort Regiment,[1] one squadron of the Ingavi Group, and a company of soldiers from the Sergeant Max Paredes Noncommissioned Officers
School received this first portion of armaments, which consisted of M–1
Garand 30–caliber rifles, M–1 carbines of the same caliber, automatic rifles,
Browning light machine guns, 60–mm mortars, 3.5–inch rocket launchers,
and 57–mm recoilless rifles. These weapons, which had been used by the
United States in World War II and were being replaced in the U.S. Army
by other, more modern weapons, were sent to nearly all Latin American
nations to improve their armed forces' equipment and training, with a view
to establishing a common military doctrine against the threat that was

beginning to be felt from the Eastern bloc and was giving rise to the Cold War.

The receipt of this and other equipment that began to arrive in 1959 constituted an incentive to the Bolivian armed forces to complete the reorganization of existing units, the creation of new ones that were completely motorized, and the creation of specializations theretofore nonexistent in the army. In five years obsolete equipment was renewed, and an army was put together that was small but adequately equipped to face the problems that began to spring up in the hemisphere—basically those of internal security against the advent and the spread of guerrilla warfare.

Precisely at the beginning of the 1960s, the United States, aware of the risk that the establishment of Fidel Castro's government in Cuba entailed for hemispheric security, sponsored the First Conference of Commanders of the American Armies at the West Point military academy. At that time it was resolved to hold this kind of meeting annually in order to effect an adequate exchange of information, an analysis of points of strategy, and coordinated measures that would eventually permit joint action in the event of threats to the security of regional nations. In 1961, carrying out a plan previously drawn up, the commander of the Southern Force of the U.S. Army, based in the Canal Zone, made visits to several South American countries, among which Bolivia was included, to receive on-site information about the military aid program that was being developed and at the same time to become more closely familiarized with the activities that Latin American armies were engaging in. Emphasis was placed on what would become something like the military part of the Alliance for Progress launched by President Kennedy. It was called "Civic Action," and it consisted of the use of the manpower of soldiers, machines, and military vehicles, along with the technical abilities of military professionals, so that the armed forces would join in the effort of economic and social development that was sought in the region. It is important to note that this undertaking of Civic Action had a favorable outcome, particularly in the campesino sectors of Bolivia, because it replaced the image of the arrogant and abusive military man—who was to be feared—with that of a friend in uniform—who, through a shared effort, helped communities to solve some of their fundamental problems such as the need for drinking water, the building of schools and sanitary facilities, and the improvement of local highways. The psychological effects of this program had an important impact on all of the later acts of the armed forces when they burst on the political stage.

Military preparation, however, was not neglected. The experience gained by the North American army in 1960 and 1961 in Laos and Vietnam, along with careful study of the campaign waged by Fidel Castro to secure the liberation of Cuba, made evident the need for personnel trained in irregular warfare in order to face this new type of struggle, which was on the rise the world over and particularly in Latin America. The creation of the North American Special Forces, with their distinctive green berets, answered this need, and for this reason a first detachment of Special Forces made up of a captain, a lieutenant, and twelve specialist sergeants was sent to Bolivia in 1962 to carry out a training cycle with the national army. The topic was "Guerrilla Warfare and How to Combat It." As a first step, the army ordered that a course be given to all second-, third-, and fourth-year cadets in the Gualberto Villarroel Military College, which was also attended by an officer, lieutenant or second lieutenant, from each infantry, cavalry, or artillery regiment in the country. The course took place over three months, and a new language began to show up in military terminology. There was talk of raids, ambushes and counterambushes, long-range patrols, annihilation zones, hammer-and-anvil operations, survival—all of it new for the army, which began to develop in the subordinate cadres new tactics and techniques that would allow them to confront guerrilla forces. When this course was finished, the group of North American advisors traveled to Cochabamba, where another instruction period was organized, also with positive results, and then on to Challapata in Oruro Department, a traditional military garrison where the Lieutenant Méndez Arcos 24th Infantry Regiment was created. This was also an assault or Ranger unit that received specialized training adapted to the *altiplano* (high plateau) region, to provide readiness to meet problems of subversion that might occur in the nearby mining centers of Catavi and Siglo Veinte.

At that time—1963—subversive actions were not anticipated in the tropical regions of the country, especially because of their low demographic density and the limited political activity of their inhabitants. It was rather the mining centers that continually acted as a source of concern for the government, on account of the high level of politicization of labor organizations and the traditional combative stance of mineworkers.

The emergence of Gen. Alfredo Ovando C. upon being named commander-in-chief of the armed forces in mid–1963, after attending the Fourth Conference of Army Commanders held in Panama, was a sign of the direction being taken in military relations between Bolivia and the United States. The Fourth Conference of Army Commanders had met to discuss the theme of "Subversive activities threatening the solidarity of the western hemisphere and methods for combating them." From this perspective attention was paid to existing guerrilla movements in Guatemala (notably MR–13, a Sino-Trotskyist group led by Lt. Yon Sosa, a former army officer) to Colombian movements such as the Moscow-oriented FARC and the Castro-inspired ELN, and to the creation of the FALN in Venezuela—all of which were demanding increased attention from hemispheric military forces. What was significant about the naming of General Ovando as commander-in-chief was that it occurred two days after the visit to Bolivia of Gen. Theodore Boggart, commander of the Panama-based United States

Southern Force, who called on the president, Dr. Paz, and the leading military authorities of the moment.

When on November 4, 1964, the armed forces took over the government, ending twelve years of MNR hegemony, the military structure was buttressed by the unmistakable support it received from the Pentagon, which thereby began to close off the possibility of new points of subversion in the hemisphere. Minor attempts at guerrilla warfare in Argentina and Brazil, which were quickly controlled by the armed forces of those countries, strengthened the belief that by now adequate military preparation was being achieved for the purpose of standing up to the expansion of Castroite ideas. At the same time these ideas were being seriously questioned by the Soviet Union. Moscow looked askance at the Castroite strategy, which besides the high cost it bore, was removing a good number of regional communist movements from Soviet control. Clear ideological differences were beginning to surface among the different Latin American guerrilla leaders, some of whom blindly obeyed Moscow's doctrine of so-called peaceful coexistence, which encouraged Latin American communist parties to seek legal channels for their actions, and others of whom found the Castroite mandate for armed struggle more appealing. Besides these tendencies, there were pro-Chinese movements that rejected Soviet directives, and also of course the Trotskyites, energetically dedicated to sowing anarchy in the political struggle as a basic political objective. This dispersion of ideology and efforts weakened guerrilla attempts in the hemisphere and precluded adequate coordination among them for the purpose of confronting regular forces, which were thus in better shape for combating subversion. In some cases, such as in Venezuela and Colombia, there was such a gulf between the different guerrilla groups that they refused to support one another and even gave information to the armed forces to permit the destruction of their ideological rivals.

In Bolivia the armed forces, which were exercising power, adopted a clearly anticommunist policy, and in the Sixth Meeting of Army Commanders, held in 1965 with the theme of "Preventive Action Against Subversion," they received full information on what was happening in the hemisphere. This served as a basic preparation for maintaining a watchful attitude toward leftist political forces, who up to that time had seemed neither capable of nor interested in armed struggle against the military government. The government decreased tensions by holding general elections in 1966, which led to the inauguration of General Barrientos as constitutional president. Although the existence of a guerrilla movement in Peru made it necessary to take precautions at the border, and instructions were given to the armed forces to prepare their personnel against guerrilla threats, the attitude prevailed that the specific conditions of Bolivia made a problem of this type unlikely, in view of the clear support of the campesino class for the Barrientos government and in view of the military effort to get closer to popular sectors.

The visit of Gen. Robert Porter, commander of the United States Southern Force, reaffirmed this attitude, which was conveyed in the visitor's words: "The United States will increase its military aid to Bolivia, because it is clear that it is being used effectively; Bolivia is making good preparations to face the problem of guerrilla warfare should it arise."

In spite of this national and international outlook, one thing was clear by the end of 1966. Although some training courses had been given for subordinate personnel, and some coordination had been set up at the level of the Latin American armies, the problem of subversion was not considered fundamentally important at the higher levels of the armed forces— which is to say in the commands of the branches of service and their general staffs, and even in the military institutes. Subversion was treated in a very superficial theoretical framework, without a clear directive from the general staffs or the formation of specific plans aimed at combating the rise of guerrilla focos. In this way a first breach was opened between subordinate officers who were relatively equipped for unconventional warfare and a command structure that still clung to conventional warfare and was reluctant to change its traditional patterns or did not understand what the appearance of a guerrilla foco in the country could mean. The tactical exercises that were held at the end of 1966 with members of the Command and General Staff schools, the Weapons Application School, and the Cochabamba Noncommissioned Officers School, with the participation of all units of the Seventh Division and the attendance of the president of the republic and the high military command, were narrowly framed within the context of conventional war, as if the hemisphere were not being shaken by explosions of guerrilla violence stretching from Guatemala to the Andes.

NOTE

1. Individual units of the Bolivian armed forces typically bear the name of a historical personage or a geographic designation.

Part II

THE OPERATIONS ZONE

Chapter 4

GENERAL DESCRIPTION

The geographical area affected by the military operations of counterinsurgency in 1967 in the southeast of Bolivia forms a clearly defined rectangle.[1] Outside of it practically no impact of the guerrilla war was felt, and even within it, some sections felt only minimal impact.

BOUNDARIES

The northern boundary of this rectangle is formed by the portion of the Santa Cruz–Cochabamba paved highway that runs from Santa Cruz, the capital of the eastern department of the same name, to San Isidro, located at kilometer 223, already within the semitropical valleys. Its winding trail follows the mountainsides beginning at La Angostura (60 km), rising from 400 meters of altitude at Santa Cruz up to 2,300 m above sea level in the valleys.

The southern boundary is marked by the course of the Parapetí River, from its source in the Los Milagros Hills, in Chuquisaca Department, through Camiri, the most important population center in the area, to its intersection with the railroad line in San Antonio del Parapetí, an approximate length of 180 km.

The eastern boundary traces a line through the southeastern plains of Bolivia, beyond the last foothills of the Andes, along the Santa Cruz–Yacuiba railroad track, a length of 200 km from Santa Cruz station to San Antonio del Parapetí station.

The western boundary is marked by the Mizque River, the dividing line between Cochabamba and Santa Cruz departments, up to its confluence with the Grande River and continuing along the Grande to the mouth of the Azero River and up the Azero to the Los Milagros Hills, where it has its sources on the northern slope, while the southern slope gives rise to the Parapetí River.

The area of this rectangle includes approximately 40,000 km, comprising barely four percent of the territory of Bolivia.[2]

SECTORS OF THE REGION

To aid in understanding the geographical setting, and noting that military jurisdictional boundaries have certain geographical and topographical features and differ very clearly, we shall divide the operations zone into two sectors, using the course of the Grande River from east to west, from its confluence with the Azero River to the railroad line in Puerto Camacho (Abapó).

The northern sector was under the jurisdiction of the Eighth Division of the army, with its headquarters in the city of Santa Cruz; and the southern sector was under the Fourth Division, with its headquarters in Camiri.

TERRAIN

The terrain shows strong contrasts.

Northern sector: from the west, where the highest mountains are found—extensions of the Eastern Cordillera of the Andes, with heights approaching 3,000 m—the terrain descends eastward until it meets the humid plains in the Santa Cruz region, at an altitude of 500 m, forming abrupt longitudinal compartments running from north to south, cut by deep river beds. The valleys in this sector (Vallegrande, Postrervalle, San Isidro, Santa Ana) are relatively short but are intensively cultivated.

The plain east of the La Angostura–Florida line is uniform, descending gradually to meet the Grande River, outside of the boundaries of the rectangle, in the arc that this river forms around the city of Santa Cruz.

From west to east the prominent mountain ranges are those of Martín Gálvez, Marcos, Los Monos, San Marcos, Parabanó, and Abapó.

Southern sector: the extensions of the Andes Cordillera become four longitudinal compartments that become less tall the farther east they are located. The Inao range has peaks that average 2,000 m, the Yanahuanca range 1,800 m. The Incahuasi range reaches 1,500 m, and the Pirirenda-Lagunillas range, which stretches to the railroad line, averages 600 m.

All of these ranges, heavily eroded by the prevailing north-south winds, display deep gorges and steep slopes. Access is difficult, since they are cut off by rivers that flow through them.

HYDROGRAPHY

The Grande River is the most important body of water in the entire operations zone. After receiving the waters of the Mizque River in Cajones, its flow increases considerably, becoming an obstacle for men and vehicles during most of the year. Its current is strong because of the sloping terrain. The water draws a large amount of sediment and is unfit for consumption. It provides abundant fish. It runs incised from Cajones to Abapó, with steep banks that are difficult to reach except in places known to be fordable. It has an average width of 80 m, and it varies in depth from 1.2 to 5 m in the rainy season. Beginning at Abapó, it enters the plains, where it follows a meandering course, widens its bed, and slows its current.

In the northern sector, it is met by these main tributaries:

a) The La Pesca River, which rises in the Martín Gálvez range. Formed by the Piraimiri and Los Sitanos rivers, it has a significant flow of clear water. It presents no obstacle.

b) The Masicurí River, a middle-sized stream, runs between the Marcos and San Marcos ranges. It ends in the vicinity of Vado del Yeso. It presents no obstacle.

c) The Rosita River, formed by the Abapocito, Morocos, Suspiros, and Galarza rivers, flows between the San Marcos and Abapó ranges. It presents no obstacle.

In the southern sector the Grande River receives as tributaries:

a) The Azero River, which flows with clear water between the Los Milagros and Inao ranges, incised in deep gorges with steep banks. Its flow is not heavy, but its location and features make it a diagonal obstacle and an obligatory transit route because of the difficulty of movement in the heights that surround it.

b) The Ñancahuazú River, similar in features to the Azero, with a slightly lesser flow, runs between the Incahuasi and Pirirenda ranges and flows into the Grande River through deep gorges, which are practically inaccessible except through the streams of its minor tributaries. On its right bank it receives the La Overa and Tiraboy rivers, the Saladillo Canyon, and the Saladillo River; on its left bank, the Iripití River.

There are other, lesser streams in the operations zone, tributaries of the rivers that have been mentioned. They present no obstacle nor did they influence operations.

VEGETATION

In the northern sector, there is practically no vegetation at altitudes higher than 2,000 m. Only within canyons can sufficient cover be found.

Between 1,000 and 2,000 m there is plenty of vegetation, even on the peaks, covering the mountain ranges, particularly the San Marcos. It is a thick, thorny vegetation that slows movement, requiring paths to be opened for passage. Despite its abundance, the vegetation is poor in nutrients. There are no substantial wild fruits.

In the cultivated areas, generally on riverbanks or in small, protected valleys, corn, yucca, rice, squash, sugar cane, and peach, apple, and citrus fruit trees are grown. Potatoes and wheat are grown in the higher elevations.

In the southern sector, the vegetation is thicker and more lush. On account of its altitude and higher temperatures, there are trees 20–25 m high. Toward the east rises the Chaco plain, which is drier and has thorny vegetation. In 1967, there was no intensive cultivation here, only simple subsistence with products such as rice, corn, yucca, bananas, etc., and small-scale cattle and goat herding.

TRANSPORTATION ROUTES

Santa Cruz–Cochabamba, two-lane paved highway.

Santa Cruz–Abapó-Camiri, two-lane gravel road.

Camiri-Muyupampa-Monteagudo-Padilla-Sucre, two-lane gravel road.

Camiri-Charagua, single-lane gravel road.

Ipitá–El Espino, single-lane unpaved road.

Vallegrande-Mataral, two-lane gravel road.

Vallegrande-Pucará–Alto Seco, single-lane unpaved mountain road.

Vallegrande-Piraimiri–Loma Larga, two-lane unpaved road, to be extended to Masicurí.

Samaipata-Postrervalle-Quirusilla, two-lane unpaved road.

CLIMATE AND WEATHER CONDITIONS

The climate varies according to altitude. In elevations above 2,000 m the temperature averages 15° C, while at lower elevations it reaches an average of 26° C. During the summer (December to March), the temperatures rise to 40° C, with high humidity readings.

In winter (June to September), the *surazos*, massive cold fronts originating in Antarctica, cover the plains and the spurs of the mountains with winds, rains and drops in temperature to 8° C in the lower regions and 0° in the mountains.

The climate in the plains tends to change abruptly from hot to cold with the arrival of polar winds, with drops in temperature of as much as twenty degrees. These winds typically last four to five days. In contrast, the climate in the high elevations is cold and dry.

DISTANCES

From the location of the first guerrilla camp in the vicinity of the Ñan-cahuazú River, distances have been measured to the major urban centers of Bolivia *in a straight line*, for reference purposes only. It should be noted that the straight-line distance to Cochabamba is 375 km, but the real distance is 700 km on the route through Lagunillas, Ipitá, Abapó, and Santa Cruz.

To Santa Cruz	200 km
To Cochabamba	375 km
To La Paz	600 km
To Sucre	150 km
To Oruro	428 km
To Catavi-Siglo Veinte (mines)	375 km
To Camiri	75 km
To Vallegrande	90 km
To Samaipata	120 km

Similarly, the *straight-line* distances to the borders of neighboring countries are as follows:

To Argentina (Yacuiba, Bolivia)	330 km
To Brazil (Puerto Suárez, Bolivia)	625 km
To Paraguay (Hito Villazón, Bolivia)	210 km
To Peru (Desaguadero, Bolivia)	650 km
To Chile (Charaña, Bolivia)	650 km

NOTES

1. See Maps 1a, 1b, and 1c, which show the rectangular area described in this chapter, some principal campaign sites, and the South American geopolitical situation of the operations area, respectively.
2. See Map 1a.

Chapter 5

OTHER CHARACTERISTICS OF THE REGION

HISTORICAL BACKGROUND

The area affected by guerrilla operations in 1967 presents some interesting sociological and historical features that should be taken into account to better understand the outlook of its inhabitants, their way of being, and their environment.

A line runs from north to south marking the eastern limit reached by the Inca empire in its period of maximum expansion. The Inca advance was blocked not only by a hostile nature, to which the Quechua (the people of the Inca empire) were not accustomed, being inhabitants of mountains and valleys, but also by the aggressiveness of the plainsmen—the Chiriguanos—and other jungle peoples who opposed the occupying troops of the Inca ruler Huayna Capac.

As evidence of the line reached, there remain a series of Quechua-language place names that made news again in 1967: Samaipata, Pucará, Incahuasi, Muyupampa, Churo, and the like, as against Abapó, Ipitá, Ñancahuazú, Iripití—all Guaraní-language names.

The Spanish Conquest originated from two impulses. From Lima, an eastern advance was made covering more and more territory; from Asunción, the advance from the Paraguay River in search of the mountains and the riches they might hold.

The clashes among the Spaniards, their jurisdictional conflicts and internal wars, also left their mark in this region, in the towns founded by the men of Andrés Manso and by Ñuflo de Chávez. In the middle were the Indians, who resisted the Conquest until the Church subdued them little by little through the missions and the conversion of native communities.

During the War of Independence, one of the bloodiest battles was fought in the town of Florida between the Spanish forces and the rebels, led by Antonio Alvarez de Arenales and Ignacio Warnes. The victory of the Creole patriots decisively helped the city of Santa Cruz keep afloat the latent spirit of freedom, which risked being drowned in blood by the Goyeneche expedition out of Cochabamba.

Arenales and Warnes's troops, made up of Vallegrande and Santa Cruz residents and men from the cordillera, coordinated their operations along the Lagunillas route with Manuel Ascensio Padilla, who hounded the Spaniards in the high elevations from his base in La Laguna, Chuquisaca. The last royalist general, Javier Aguilera, withdrew to Vallegrande, where he was hunted down, captured, and executed in 1828, after the Republic had already been proclaimed.

With the coming of the Republic, the political division that was adopted respected to some extent the Spanish jurisdictions, and this region remained as a symbol of the fusion of three races—Hispanic, Quechua, and Guaraní—who developed unique traits and above all a feeling of pride and independence that endures today.

Remote from state power, the people of this area have grown used to relying on themselves, cultivating their customs and traditions, and developing their capabilities.

When the Chaco War (1932–35) focused Bolivia's attention on their territory, the men of the Southeast were the first to take up arms and the last to return to work. They had become sentinels of the national inheritance, guardians of the recently discovered oil wealth. The development of the "black gold" industry gave a new push to the region. Roads were opened, more men from other regions of the country arrived to join efforts with the residents of Cordillera Province, and through their influence new cities and towns grew up, assimilating the character of Vallegrande and Cordillera provinces.

These are the people whom Che wanted to draw into his guerrilla war.

THE MAIN SETTLEMENTS

Vallegrande. City founded in 1612. It became an important center of trade and commerce because of its location halfway between the plains and the highlands. Its capable and enterprising inhabitants took their activities as far as Lagunillas and went on to other cities, extending their family ties. From 1950 on, with the construction of the Cochabamba–Santa Cruz highway, 50 km away from the city, Vallegrande lost its prominence and entered into decline as the greater part of its population emigrated. It has always produced noteworthy individuals in all fields of knowledge.

Camiri. A new post–Chaco War city, a petroleum town from the beginning. Men and women from all Bolivian latitudes live there. Located on the bank of the Parapetí River, it was an important point in the supply system in the Chaco War, and after the war the army concerned itself with organizing and developing the city. The coexistence there of oilmen and the military has given birth to a thriving city in constant growth.

Abapó. Founded in 1771, it was an obligatory stopping point on the route between Santa Cruz and the towns of Cordillera Province, or for travelers on their way to the Argentine border, because of its location on the bank of the Grande River. The transit of travelers and vehicles was its principal business until the construction of the Santa Cruz–Yacuiba railroad, which ended the use of *chalanas*, the local version of the canoe.

Piraí. Former Church mission, higher in rank than Cabezas, Florida, and Abapó. It was also a *pascana* (stopping point, in the Quechua language) on the southern route. Currently, it is a small town serving the needs of the peasants of the area.

Gutiérrez. Built as a fort against the unruly, rebellious Chiriguanos. It was founded in 1836, during the government of Marshal Santa Cruz. After surviving continual Indian attacks, it attracted a stable population and became an important center of trade and commerce.

Ipitá. Located 10 km north of Gutiérrez, it is a small town from which a gap was opened by the state oil enterprise, known as YPFB (Bolivian State Oil Deposits). The gap reaches the vicinity of the Grande River.

Ipatí. A new town that grew up when the cart track to Sucre opened up. The track meets the Santa Cruz highway at Ipatí.

Laqunillas. Created shortly after Gutiérrez in the face of the Chiriguano threat, it is more protected than Gutiérrez, lying on the Incahuasi range. The capital of Cordillera Province, it is the meeting point between the eastern and western zones, although it is located far from the major roads. Its traditional link to Vallegrande by bridle paths is constantly renewed. The construction of the Vallegrande highway between Masicuí and Lagunillas, undertaken in 1976 by Pando 3rd Engineer Battalion of the army, has come to a halt, prolonging the isolation of the two provincial capitals.

Population Figures in 1967

Santa Cruz	137,406
Vallegrande	7,841
Samaipata	1,696
Lagunillas	932
Camiri	12,871
Ipitá	282
Florida	280
Anapó	965

Pucará	611
Postrervalle	588
La Higuera	296
Muyupampa	876
El Picacho	114
Alto Seco	420

Source: Bolivian National Institute of Statistics.

PSYCHO-SOCIAL CHARACTERISTICS

Discounting the population of the city of Santa Cruz, which was virtually unaffected by the guerrilla war, we can see that aside from Camiri and Vallegrande, which are small cities, the other settlements are just barely hamlets, groupings of residents who know one another and live together with a constant exchange of products and commodities. Strong family ties unite almost all of the residents of Vallegrande and Cordillera provinces, who have spread throughout the region. It is a common occurrence to find acquaintances, relatives, and friends in any of the settlements.[1] Those ties have lasted for centuries.

The population, mainly devoted to agriculture, has owned its land for several generations. The Agrarian Reform, decreed by the government of the National Revolution in 1953, did not affect this region, which lacked the *latifundios* (large, privately owned landed estates) of the altiplano and valleys and the conditions of exploitation and servitude of western Bolivia.

The countryman of Vallegrande and Cordillera speaks Spanish, has received elementary education in the area's schools, which often have been built and maintained with his support. He has routinely fulfilled his required military service and has returned to his land to resume work as his elders have before him. He is proud of his freedom and independence. He feels as Bolivian as anyone, and although he knows that his region is backward and lacking in many things, he overcomes its deficiencies with initiative and perseverance. He is brave and enterprising. He does not fear nature, but rather knows her secrets and uses them to his advantage. He likes to hunt and fish to supplement his food supply, and he works the land with love and dedication.

His male elders were almost all veterans of the Chaco War, and they proudly bore their official status as Glorious Sons of the Fatherland. They liked to recount their war exploits and the poverty they endured—as a lesson to the young. In every town there is a chapter of the War Veterans Organization, and they are in general highly respected by everyone.

The Catholic Church has exercised a strong influence on the residents of this area since colonial times. The antiquity of its churches and missions is a source of pride; several date from the seventeenth century. Although there are few priests, those who are there practice their ministry in vast areas, using all means of transportation to reach every town, every community, on its patron saint's day, which constitutes a veritable social event.

The descendants of the original Chiriguano tribes are settled in the vicinity of the southern towns of Cordillera Province. There are small reservations of Izoceños, Matacos, and other tribes in the Chaco plain, outside of the area of guerrilla operations.

In this setting, the guerrilla foco made its appearance in 1967.

NOTE

1. The author is descended on his father's side from a traditional Vallegrande family and spent his childhood in that province.

Part III

THE OPERATIONS

Chapter 6

PREPARATIONS

The decision to set up a training center for guerrillas in Bolivia that could later become a foco generating armed struggle all over the South American continent was made in the last phase of the Tricontinental Conference held in Havana in January 1966. This international meeting laid down important guidelines because it marked the definitive alignment of the Cuban government with the Soviet Union, expressed in Prime Minister Castro's heavy attacks on the People's Republic of China and on the Maoist line that some Latin American revolutionary movements were following. The themes of the Conference drew clear lines for the battle against imperialism,[1] and although armed struggle was not explicitly advocated, it was ultimately necessary to adopt behind the scenes the proposition made by surrogates such as Salvador Allende, representing the great absent figure of the meeting, Commandant Guevara.

The plan presented at Che's behest stated that a "national guerrilla war," as an expression of revolutionary leadership, or in other words, the isolated attempt of a group in one country to achieve or to influence change, had little possibility of success. To put things on a positive basis, it was essential to set up a regional coordination, at least on the political and logistical fronts, that would allow for the greatest concentration of effort to achieve specific objectives, especially in the case of border areas. Although the creator of the strategy agreed that the military aspect could be left to the initiative of local commandants, general supervision was still needed.

For this purpose, the plan proposed by Che stressed the need to establish in South America, preferably in a country that provided access to several others through common borders, an international base that would serve as a continental and even intercontinental training center from which revolutionary columns would set forth after being instructed. Their first goal would be to take complete control of the base country; then they would penetrate neighboring countries to reinforce existing focos or to create them where necessary.

This plan held that the region chosen as a base should be sufficiently isolated to facilitate the task at hand and should also include geographical conditions of climate and terrain similar or identical to those in the regions where the revolutionaries in training would have to operate. The base region would therefore constitute "a multiregional training center" or a "political-military school" that would do the work of an instruction center for future commands of the continent-wide revolution. Ultimately, after the struggle had begun in the different countries, it would become a central point of political and military coordination that would be the basis of a permanent, shared continental general staff that would lead all the "armies of national liberation" that were to ignite the revolutionary fire in all of Latin America.

When this plan was accepted, somewhat reluctantly, by Fidel Castro, as a way of pleasing his old comrade at arms and as a bold move that would spread the influence of the Cuban revolution to other areas, the basic logistical details were worked out. They consisted basically of the allotment of economic support for the deployment of forces, the acquisition of arms and equipment, and maintenance during the first months of operation. A base group of Cuban veterans were assigned to this mission, among them members of the Central Committee of the Cuban Communist party. They had experience not only in the Sierra Maestra, but also in other revolutionary operations in Latin America and in the thwarted campaign in the Congo. They would constitute the core of the international base to be set up in South America. In order to accomplish this, Che had some leeway to choose the country and coordinate the support systems with local organizations, recruit combatants, establish liaison, and do everything necessary to set the accepted plan in motion.

The choice of a country finally boiled down to Bolivia or Peru. The decision imposed by Cuba was to begin the struggle in Bolivia and later in Peru. Foremost in this decision were factors such as the failure of armed struggle in Peru, ending first in the death of Hugo Blanco and then of Luis de la Fuente, which gave rise to the belief that leaks or infiltrations had existed that threatened Che's presence in Peru. The Cubans preferred to have him in Bolivia, where they hoped to encounter better conditions. Although at first this decision irritated the Peruvian delegates who were coordinating their efforts with the advance Cuban echelons in Bolivia, it was finally accepted with the compromise that select Peruvian elements would participate in the training and the first operations with the Cubans, and then move on to their own country together with some Cubans.

The decision to choose Bolivia as a base, though justifiable because the country was geopolitically positioned in the center of the continent, with long, poorly controlled borders on five countries, and because it seemed to correspond strategically to the general plan outlined by Che, apparently did not take into account the domestic Bolivian situation which in mid–1966 could be summarized in the following points:

—Gen. René Barrientos had just been elected constitutional president of the republic with a coalition of political parties that guaranteed him a measure of support in the cities and a more or less normal functioning of the state apparatus.

—Since 1962, General Barrientos had carried out a domestic political campaign aimed at capturing the sympathy and support of the majority campesino sector of the nation, which had transformed him into an important political figure. At the same time he had garnered obvious sympathy and solidarity because of his easy access to the campesinos and his almost paternalistic way of dealing with them, cleverly exploiting social traits that were deeply rooted in the rural workers.

—The position of the Bolivian armed forces vis-à-vis most sectors of the nation was not uncomfortable. Military participation in the efforts being undertaken to achieve development had permitted the armed forces to grow close to the people, not only through programs like Civic Action, but even in direct participation with the community through the relations maintained between the authorities, most of whom were military, and the commanders of local garrisons. Perhaps the only sector that out of tradition kept some distance from the military was the miners, despite the fact that in some mining centers like Huanuni, Quechisla, and lesser centers, the military occupations of 1965 and 1966 had not generated friction, and on the contrary there was some measure of cordial relations with the workers.

—The majority of the soldiers in the Bolivian army come from the campesino class, who consider it their true obligation to fulfill the draft. They find better living conditions in the barracks than at home and in many cases receive training in technical fields that prepares them for future civilian life.

—A unique characteristic of Bolivians is their nationalism, which automatically brings them together when foreign interference is felt in domestic affairs. We are very protective of our individuality as a people and that is one of the main reasons why foreign doctrines only flourish in small groups of intellectuals or heavily politicized groups, while the great majority has always supported the main points of revolutionary nationalism, which in its different tendencies became deeply rooted in Bolivian political life.

—By the end of 1966, the economic situation of the country was relatively favorable. Oil production was increasing noticeably, agriculture was spreading rapidly in the lands of the valleys and the East, and a modest industrial expansion was underway that, together with infrastructure work being accomplished, absorbed a good share of the available manpower. All these factors together made for a stable outlook, hardly apt for the outbreak of subversion.

In any case, the decision to choose Bolivia as the base country for the continental plan was already made, simply in response to some general evaluations and the unreliable information supplied on the one hand by the Bolivian adherents of Castroism and on the other by the Bolivian students in Cuba.

This decision prompted the trip to Bolivia by the first contingent designated to make contact with the local Communist party cells and other sympathizers in order to begin preparing the urban support base, to facilitate the arrival of the other combatants, and most importantly to take the necessary security measures for receiving and transporting the leader of the operation, Ernesto Guevara. To this end, in mid-May 1966, when the green light was definitively given to the project, Ricardo was sent to La Paz together with a group of the Bolivian Communist Party (PCB) who at that time were attending a political-military course in Cuba.[2] Meanwhile, the rest of the matrix Cuban team met with Che at a country house near Havana to complete their training and to coordinate the task that lay ahead. They left in different groups. First Pombo and Tuma traveled by way of Prague-Frankfort-Zurich-Dakar-Rio–São Paulo, arriving in Santa Cruz on July 25, where they were received by Ricardo and escorted to La Paz. Taking the same route, Rolando, Urbano, and Braulio arrived in the capital on November 18. Together with Pacho and Rubio, Guevara left Madrid for São Paulo and arrived in La Paz on November 3, traveling immediately to the Southeast to set up the base camp at Ñancahuazú. Upon his arrival, Che was briefed by Ricardo and the other advanced cadres on the work undertaken thus far. They first had established contact with the hierarchy of the PCB to gain their support, and then had recruited volunteers for the combat force. These negotiations had suffered a series of interruptions and reverses which had prevented anything positive from being concluded. The meetings with the first secretary of the PCB, Mario Monje, got off to a bad start because each side had a different view of the way to take power. While the PCB leader favored a general uprising that would produce the needed explosion, Ricardo and the other Cubans, following the instructions they had brought with them from Cuba, insisted on the need to establish the guerrilla foco first. Here a first basic difference of opinion showed up that would later have serious effects on the conduct of the guerrilla war.

In fact, the Cuban group did not behave honestly with its Bolivian counterpart, disguising the continental character that they wished to give to the movement and failing to outline the role the PCB was to play. The whole operation was explained simply as a means of cooperating with the Bolivian insurrectional movement. This position concurred with what Monje and Fidel Castro had outlined on the occasion of their meeting held in Cuba in May 1966, where the Cuban prime minister had shown agreement with the idea that the Bolivian revolution should be led by Bolivians and had promised "not to interfere in domestic affairs in Bolivia." When Monje became aware that a subversive apparatus parallel to his party mechanism was being formed, he refused to become involved with it and asked to travel to Cuba once again for an interview with Fidel Castro that would clarify the situation. This request was delayed, and meanwhile the preparations of the Cuban group, aided by those Bolivians who followed their orders against the decisions of the PCB, continued in accelerated fashion so that the base camp could be set up. When Monje arrived in Havana in December, Castro set his mind to rest and asked him to meet with Che Guevara in a border zone of Bolivia that would be revealed to him in due time. Monje therefore returned to La Paz and received Guevara's emissary, with whom he planned his trip to Camiri for the interview. It was held on the last day of 1966, and we will discuss it later.

The second task of the advance group was to determine which zone could best serve the purposes of the master plan. Once the first contacts were made and the first evaluations completed, four areas were discussed as the most appropriate: Alto Beni, the La Paz Yungas (the steep semi-tropical valleys of La Paz Department), the tropical zone of Cochabamba, and southern Santa Cruz. Different committees traveled to do reconnaissance in September and October, and in those circumstances, an intrusion occurred that nearly held up the whole operation. Regis Debray had arrived in Bolivia.[3] He had been entrusted in Cuba with a geopolitical study, and for that purpose he was traveling through Caranavi, Los Yungas, and Cochabamba, meeting up with the Cubans' reconnaissance mission, and touching the sensitivity of Monje and the PCB Central Committee by making contact with the so called "divisionists" of the Óscar Zamora group, who did not accept Moscow's leadership. The Cubans avoided Debray and continued their reconnaissance until they decided that southern Santa Cruz was the best area. They dismissed Alto Beni and Los Yungas because in those regions, where many highland families were settling, sponsored by the government, an insurgent group would be at pains to remain undetected for any length of time. Among the factors that favored Santa Cruz were: the tropical nature of the region, its low demographic density, and its varied terrain, including the last foothills of the Andes chain. Another decisive factor was the existence of oil fields that were of fundamental importance to the national economy. It was, however, an error to assume that these oil fields could significantly affect the United States. The insurgents believed that Bolivian exports were of real value to that market, but in fact the deposits located in the chosen zone—Camiri and Tatarenda—were used almost entirely to produce fuel for domestic consumption, while Gulf Oil, which had concession in Caranda, in northern Santa Cruz, was just beginning commercial exploitation.

Pursuing its aim, the advance group sent Rodolfo with Coco to acquire a farm in El Pincal, near Lagunillas and Gutiérrez, where corn and other produce intended to feed the combatants could be grown, and where a pig farm could be set up as a front. The report submitted by the advance group to Havana on September 11 stated:

The Ñancahuazú property is located in the southeastern region of Santa Cruz province, in a mountainous area with abundant vegetation but little water over the general zone. The property itself has plenty of water. Ñancahuazú is a canyon between the Pirirenda range to the east, and the Incahuasi range to the west. Their highest peaks are on the eastern and western edges. These heights continue southward toward Salta, Argentina. The farm is bordered on the north by the unoccupied Iripití property owned by the same man who sold us the farm, Remberto Villa, who lives on the farm called Terrazas, near Lagunillas, some 20 km from Ñancahuazú; and on the south by the property of Ciro Algarañaz, who raises pigs. The property is 255 km from Santa Cruz by the Santa Cruz–Camiri road and is relatively isolated. It can be reached without going to Lagunillas, which is 25 km from Ñancahuazú, by taking a side route 6 km south of Gutiérrez.

You can only travel on this route across the property called Aguada Grande, owned by Eudol León, a young campesino. Ten persons, all of whom speak Guaraní, the prevalent language of the area, live in this house. León's house is on a hill some 200 m from the road, so you can pass by without being spotted. Barely 3 km from the farm is Algarañaz's house, which is located on the road. This man is the only threat to our work, because he is our nearest neighbor and is extremely inquisitive. During the Paz Estenssoro government he was mayor of Camiri. After we bought the farm we learned that he had said that we would take advantage of the isolation of his farm to set up a cocaine factory. He is interested in selling us some cattle and pigs and therefore keeps good relations with us. He lives in Camiri, where he owns a butcher's shop. On weekends he goes to Camiri and returns on Monday night. Sometimes he stays longer.

In addition, the farm has all the conditions for this type of work but not on a large scale as yet, although we will create appropriate conditions by building a house farther away out of sight, since the present house is visible from the road. The problem, however, is moving people around, because we have to deceive Algarañaz.

The trip from Santa Cruz takes twelve hours in the dry season, in spring. The stretch from Mora to Río Seco becomes nearly impassable and the delay can be as long as two or three days.

The farm has 1,227 hectares and an appreciable amount of timber. In this setting, the plan for concealing our work is to raise pigs and later to build a sawmill.

An important point is that toward the north it is possible to travel to Vallegrande through a thickly wooded, mountainous area; from there on, the woods are sparser. Toward the south one can go over similar terrain to Argentina.[4]

Without establishing any clear coordination with the PCB, since Monje's last pledge was simply to provide four volunteers to join the group instead of the twenty who had originally offered to go; without sufficiently organizing the urban support apparatus and setting up liaison systems that would permit them to maintain contact with the cities of La Paz and Santa Cruz; and without possessing communications equipment for liaison abroad, the group traveled to Santa Cruz in two vehicles after the arrival of Ernesto Guevara in La Paz on November 3. They then went in along a side path to the property on the banks of the Ñancahuazú River. It contained a small, two-room house with a tin roof at which they arrived on November 7 after meeting up with Loro, who was waiting for them there. Up to that time all the activity of the Cubans and the Bolivian support group had gone on without serious incident. They had brought to the base camp a good amount of arms and ammunition, equipment, clothing, and food for the first phase of organization of the training center. They had small radios for nearby tactical communication, a commercial radio, and a tape recorder. They were able to receive and record code messages sent from Cuba in the guise of normal broadcasts, but their communication outside the encampment was limited to the messages that Coco and Loro could take out to Camiri or other population centers only if they remained undetected, a very slow and unreliable method.

The group installed in Ñancahuazú included Che, Pombo, Tuma, and Loro, who initially set about effecting reconnaissance on the outskirts of the property for the purpose of setting up their encampments and depots, in full knowledge that they could not remain in the tin-roof house. The house entailed risks, so they used it mainly as a support point for their supplies. In the first days they set themselves up some 100 meters from the house, in the woods and on the banks of the Ñancahuazú River. They began to dig tunnels for concealing arms and some tins of food, using Algarañaz, who had sold them the property, to constantly bring over supplies. They led him to believe that their intention was to set up a cocaine factory. Only Loro and Tuma were in contact with Algarañaz. When Marcos and Rolando arrived at the encampment on November 20 led by Rodolfo, they found that things had progressed sufficiently so that work could be speeded up. Rodolfo, who was an urban liaison man, returned to La Paz immediately to get in touch with other groups. This made it possible for the group led by Coco and including Joaquín and Urbano to arrive on the 27th. Returning to Camiri on another trip, he brought Ricardo, Braulio, Miguel, Inti, and Ernesto. Until that time, Coco's role remained that of liaison with the outside, since he was already known in Camiri. In fact, he maintained friendly relations with the military personnel stationed there, pretending to be involved in farming in the Pincal zone. Taking advantage of his ease of movement, he was sent to Santa Cruz to pick up Chino, a Peruvian leader who was ready to join the struggle in Bolivia on the strength of conversations he had had in La Paz with the upper echelon, whom he had urged to begin the armed struggle in Peru. When he became convinced that the decision was already taken and that the foco would be set up in Bolivia, he volunteered to come into the group.

Having arrived at Ñancahuazú on the night of December 1, Chino held a long conversation with Che and offered him support, including some fighting men. He then returned to his country so that the vehicle that brought him could make another trip—which occurred when Ricardo, Alejandro, Arturo, Carlos, Moro, and Benigno arrived on December 11, along with a new load of arms and ammunition.

Throughout December the group busied itself organizing the caves and encampments, and doing reconnaissance aimed at preparing escape routes, communication routes between encampments and depots, and paths intended to put any military incursions off the track. On the last day of the year, Mario Monje (Estanislao) arrived to interview Che for the purpose of defining the situation.

THE INTERVIEW

The meeting began with the clarification, meant to allay suspicions, that the movement which Che Guevara intended to organize in Bolivia was part of a much larger scheme, accepted by Fidel Castro, to create an international training base for guerrilla fighters who would be prepared to generate new armed movements in other countries of Latin America. If at first the PCB had got the impression that this was an action in support of the Bolivian liberation movement, it was now plain to Monje that his party would not have any major participation nor a leading role in the coming operations because the objectives exceeded the limits of the party's work. Finally the discussion centered on three basic points:

1. Monje's conviction that the PCB would not enter into the struggle in its own name because the creation of the guerrilla foco diverged from the norms of party activity; to compensate for this, he at first offered to leave the party and join as just another combatant, pledging at the same time to secure the neutrality of the rest of the PCB leaders. Che Guevara responded by saying that Monje should not leave the party structure but rather stay within it and influence it to support the movement led by Guevara.

2. The discussion then turned to who should exercise the political-military command of the guerrilla war. Each man held rigidly to his position. Che refused to hand over the military leadership of the campaign because he felt that in every sense his experience, his ability and his international relationships were a major factor in the conduct of the war. He stated emphatically that he had arrived there in Ñancahuazú, it was his liberated territory, and no one could remove him from it. Monje, for his part, argued the need for a national leadership for this movement, so that it would be capable of winning the support of the people.

3. Concerning links with other Latin American communist parties to obtain their support for the movement that was starting up in Bolivia, there was very little discussion, although an agreement was reached not to disclose information about the presence of Che in Bolivia as yet.

A further point of discussion had to do with any future presence of members of the pro-Chinese sector of the Communist party among the combatants. Monje, who was already aware of the contacts that both Debray and Ricardo had made with the mining leader Moisés Guevara aimed at bringing him into the struggle, stated his firm opposition in terms of the sectarian differences that existed. Che's rebuttal, on the grounds that the cooperation of everyone was needed to gain victory and that the armed struggle itself would produce the leaders, over and above such differences, was not understood by Monje, who found in it yet another reason to refuse support.

The meeting between the Bolivian members of the guerrilla force and the first secretary of the PCB was tense and dramatic. The former were captivated by the prospect of fighting for their ideals and by the role they would play, and they refused to accept Monje's arguments. He outlined the three points he had discussed with Che and made it clear that no accord had been reached. His insistence on claiming the political-military command of the guerrilla war for himself as a matter of principle was not understood by the future combatants. They also rejected the idea of leaving the foreign group to its own fate, insisting on the Latin American character of the revolution and the need to accept the leadership and the military and economic support of people with proven experience. Monje was in agreement that armed struggle was the only path, but in the form of a general uprising, not on the foco model, for which Bolivia did not have the proper conditions.

Monje argued that the guerrilla war should be led by his party and that he as secretary general should have complete command in both political and military terms. Monje's statement to the Bolivians was very clear: "When the people learn that this war is led by a foreigner, they will turn their backs on it and deny it their support. I am certain that it will fail because it is led not by a Bolivian but by a foreigner. You will die very heroically, but you have no prospect of victory."[5]

This opinion of the PCB leader was firmly based on knowledge of national realities. It was not enough to invoke the name of Che to gain the support of Bolivians. On the contrary, this could mean that many organizations would hold back their participation so as not to be in the position of supporting foreigners fighting on national soil. This meeting gave rise to conflicting sentiments within each one of the Bolivians gathered in Ñancahuazú: on the one hand, their loyalty to the party; on the other, their interest in participating in the coming armed struggle, above all because they were under the command of so experienced a man as Che Guevara.

So ended Monje's visit, leaving everyone—Che, the Cubans, and the Bolivians—frustrated and worried about what the PCB rejection of the call to guerrilla warfare could mean. Once the visitors had left, after New Year's Day, activity was resumed to prepare Camp II. The intention was to stay as far away as possible from Camp I and the tin-roof house, since the constant activity in the area was beginning to create suspicion. A visit was even made by a police officer, sent to verify the existence of a possible cocaine factory.

Moisés Guevara arrived at Camp I on January 26 according to plan, together with Loyola Guzmán, a member of the urban support network. The discussion between Che and the mining leader was clear and concise. Moisés Guevara accepted the conditions of disbanding his pro-Chinese group and joining the guerrilla force simply as a combatant, leaving aside international differences. It was agreed that he would come in with his people in mid-February.

Loyola Guzmán received, along with oral instructions, a special document prepared by Che containing "instructions for city cadres," a synthesis of his study *Guerrilla Warfare*, detailing the steps to be followed in order to set up the support network. This document stated in its salient paragraphs:

The formation of a support network of the type we wish to form should be guided by a series of norms that we will state in general terms.

In order to carry out the difficult tasks that have been assigned—and survive—the covert cadre should have the following qualities in a high degree of development: discipline, reticence, evasiveness, self-control, and coolness. It should practice methods of work that cover it from unexpected eventualities.

As much as possible, both the leader of the network and the individuals working within it will have a single function, and horizontal contacts will be made through the leader. The minimal positions for an organized network are the following: the leader, a supply officer, an information officer, a financial officer, an urban action officer, and an officer who will deal with sympathizers.

The leadership of the network will reside in the capital. From that base they will organize the network in the cities which are most important to us right now: Cochabamba, Santa Cruz, Sucre, Camiri—or in other words the rectangle that includes our operations zone.

The development of the network in cities that today are far from our field of action should not be neglected. The support of the population of those cities should be requested, and preparations should be made for future actions. Oruro and Potosí are the most important cities of this type.

Particular attention should be paid to border points. Villazón and Tarija for contacts and provisions from Argentina; Santa Cruz for Brazil; Huaqui or some other place on the Peruvian border; some point on the Chilean border.

For the organization of the supply network, it would help to be able to count on militants who have held a post similar to the activity requested of them now. For example, a grocery store owner who would organize supplies or participate in this section of the network; a transportation company owner who would organize that branch, etc.

The following factories or stores should be organized:

Grocery stores (La Paz, Cochabamba, Santa Cruz, Camiri).

Transportation companies (La Paz–Santa Cruz, Santa Cruz–Camiri, La Paz–Sucre, Sucre–Camiri).

Shoe stores (La Paz, Santa Cruz, Camiri, Cochabamba).

Tailors (La Paz, Santa Cruz, Camiri, Cochabamba).

Auto repair shop (La Paz, Santa Cruz).

Farmlands (Chapare-Caranavi)[6]

As can be seen, these instructions repeat virtually the same concepts found in Che's published work. The difference lies in the application. Loyola Guzmán had serious difficulty keeping up her support for the insurgents as soon as she left the guerrilla war zone. In the first place, once several committed parties had heard about the refusal of the higher echelons of the PCB to participate in the guerrilla war, they began to hold back on their effort and in addition threatened the young liaison woman with explusion from the ranks of the Bolivian Communist Youth (JCB). Later, when operations had begun after the Ñancahuazú ambush, and the military intelligence service had learned from information provided by deserters about the party's link with the southeastern foco and other details, Loyola Guzmán had to go into hiding. Her action was reduced to the minimum, since the guerrilla war was isolated in the area of Ñancahuazú. The impossibility of sending messengers or liaison people, receiving messages or doing anything for the guerrillas, added up to a pattern of defeat that culminated with the capture of Loyola.

RECONNAISSANCE TRIP

With the personnel on hand and with all trace of Camp I removed, February 1 was set for the beginning of a reconnaissance trip.[7] Antonio, Arturo, Camba, and Ñato were left at the base to guard it, to receive any recruits who might arrive, and to conclude some local reconnaissance. Evident in the planning and preparation of this trip were both caution and the attention to detail required for a task of this magnitude. The stated objectives were:

1. To encourage the men to adapt to campaign life (thirst, lack of food, long marches, little rest, etc.).

2. To form a campesino support base or to identify possible areas where the support base of the National Army of Liberation (ELN) could be organized.

3. To become more familiar with the territory under their influence so as to complement information available in existing maps.

Before they left, arrangements were made for alternative rallying points, places to drop messages, and actions to take in case enemy forces showed up, so that the main body and the minimal force left at the encampment could be reunited. The marching column was organized in three groups: the vanguard, consisting of five men led by Marcos; the center, headed up by Che with eighteen men; and the rear guard of six men, led by Joaquín. The entire group consisted of twenty-nine future combatants (fifteen Cubans and fourteen Bolivians).

Reconnaissance itself meant a long, exhausting effort for the guerrilla fighters. Following the course of the Ñancahuazú River, after first trying to take the heights and realizing the futility of the attempt, they arrived after three days at the confluence of the Ñancahuazú and the Grande rivers, which was the first destination of the march without having encountered any inhabitants in the entire area.

Crossing the river was difficult and dangerous because that time of year was not the most favorable. January, February, and March are the rainy season, so the guerrillas had to walk through torrential rains, with the physical and material wear and tear that this meant. After exploring both banks of the river both upstream and downstream without finding the mouth of the Frías River, which is located farther west, they headed for the mouth of the Masicurí River, where on February 9 they made their first contact with a campesino family. They were Honorato Rojas, his wife, and his children. Inti introduced himself to them as the leader of the guerrillas, and convinced Rojas to sell them food and also to give them information about other families in the area. It was here that they confirmed the presence of soldiers farther north. They belonged to Pando 3rd Engineer Battalion, based in Vallegrande and engaged in building the road between Masicurí and Lagunillas. This small complement of troops had a camp at La Laja, 30 km above Masicurí. Because of the distance, the guerrillas dropped the idea of approaching them.

After staying in the area several days, they changed their plan and decided instead to reach the Rositas River, some 20 km to the northeast, where it runs into the Grande River. To achieve this goal, after supplying themselves with food, they began the ascent to cross the San Marcos range without having taken full measure of this obstacle separating the Masicurí and Rositas rivers.

The San Marcos range, which runs from north to south, is truly formidable. It rises abruptly from 600 to 1,800 m above sea level, with rock cliffs and deep gorges. Undoubtedly this wild zone covered with dense tropical vegetation presents favorable conditions for an irregular force to stay hidden and safe for a long time, but in the first place there is a lack of water in the heights, and supply is a problem. There is almost no hunting, and since there are no people settled there, nothing is grown. Perhaps the guerrillas' decision to reach the Rositas River can be explained by the fact that the map they were using was an old copy of a map of Bolivia on a scale of 1:250,000 that had very few topographic details. No doubt this made Che think that there would be inhabitants at the Rositas, as at the mouth of the Masicurí, but this was not the case, as they discovered upon arriving at its banks after ten days of fatigue, hunger, thirst, and efforts to conquer the hills that cost the life of the first Bolivian on this adventure. When Benjamín tried to negotiate a difficult passage in the steep slopes of the bank of the Grande River, the day before the arrival at the Rositas, he lost his footing, fell, and was swept away by the current in spite of the efforts of Rolando, who dove in to rescue him. This first death made an impression on the Bolivians, and Che had to talk to them to raise their spirits and overcome the setback.

After recovering their strength somewhat on the banks of the Rositas River, they sent patrols upriver who found no sign of inhabitants. Facing a shortage of food, and with signs of weakness already visible in the men, and considering that twenty-eight days of traveling had gone by and their absence could be causing concern at the base, where new combatants must have arrived, they decided to start back, crossing the Grande River and continuing along its south bank until they would meet the Ñancahuazú. The vanguard crossed on the last day of February, but a two-day swelling of the river and the lack of contact with Marcos, the vanguard leader, despite the fact that he was carrying radio equipment, made it necessary for the main body and the rear guard to start back on the north bank in order to cross the river at a more favorable place when the waters had subsided.

Walking through the hills once again required a new effort that ended up exhausting the men, who lacked food. Every day they showed greater weakness and fatigue. When they arrived at the Tatarenda water source, which serves the YPFB oilfield, Che sent Inti and Ricardo to swim over to the nearby houses in order to find out if there was any news of the vanguard and to obtain food. The crossing was difficult, and when the emissaries left the shore, the rest waited for more than twenty-four hours before seeing them return. They had found out that the vanguard had gone through on March 5 without incident and that they were carrying sufficient supplies to arrive at the base provided that the trip did not become too long.

This contact with the personnel of the state oil enterprise would set off military action because of the way that both Marcos and Inti acted. Evidently the vanguard—Marcos, Pacho, Loro, Aniceto, and Benigno—after crossing the river with no chance of regaining contact with the main body, chose to change course toward the south in order to find some inhabited area, acquire supplies, and start the return to base on their own from there. When they arrived at the Tatarenda oilfield on March 5, they met Epifanio Vargas, an oil worker, who gave them information about the area and helped them restock their provisions. They left Tatarenda for the south on March 6, along the path leading to Ipitá.[8] Marcos's character came out on this occasion, when he decided to act on his own and did not hesitate to appear before the inhabitants with his men, his arms, and his equipment. This attitude was also to have important effects on later events. For the moment nothing happened, so the group crossed Saladillo Mountain after proceeding in the direction of Ipitá for two days. After traveling a couple of kilometers downriver in search of the main group and not finding any trace of them, they left some signs to indicate they had passed through and then went back upriver in a southerly direction. They arrived at the tin-roof house on the 12th and were received by Antonio.

Meanwhile the main group grew more and more fatigued. On the 14th, they arrived at the mouth of the Ñancahuazú. Although the river was swollen, Rolando volunteered to cross and proceed to the encampment for the purpose of bringing provisions to the rest, since they were consuming their last rations. On the next day the main body began to cross in small groups which were separated by the force of the current. The operation actually was delayed three days, and it cost the life of another man, Carlos, who was swept away by the current. He had been trained in Cuba and was considered one of the most promising Bolivian combatants. Arms, ammunition, and equipment were also lost. The group was weakened and their spirits were very low, although the prospect of returning to camp on familiar roads made their work easier. On the 18th and 19th they completed the march to the encampment, where good and bad news was awaiting them. It was comforting to know that the vanguard was back at the base unharmed, although the explanations made did not satisfy Che.[9] On the other hand, the incursion of a military patrol on the 17th, overhead flights of small planes, the desertion of some men and the capture of another by the army, created a tense and uneasy atmosphere that alarmed the guerrilla leader. The good news was the arrival of Moisés Guevara with his group of seven men, the induction of six others who had already been announced, the return of Chino with two other Peruvians as he had pledged, and the presence of Debray and Bustos, who had arrived with Tania. In fact, the encampment had suddenly become a crowded, risky place which would make world news a few days later since the gears of the military machine, which had been alerted by a whole series of circumstances, were turning.

THE SILVA PATROL

It was by chance that the first news of action by unknown groups reached the Fourth Division headquarters of the army in Camiri. Capt. Augusto Silva Bogado had been sent by the division command to check if Señor Segundino Parada's property, called California, near Tatarenda, was appropriate for lime calcination. It was necessary to verify the existence of ovens and of firewood and water in the vicinity so that production on behalf of the army could begin.

This mission was completed during the entire day of March 9, and at night, Captain Silva was beside the highway, waiting for a vehicle to pass that could convey him to Camiri. He did not have a military vehicle, in keeping with the scant resources of all garrisons in the eastern part of the country. At about eight o'clock, a YPFB van went through and picked the officer up. During the nearly 100-km trip to Camiri, the driver and his helper mentioned, among other things, that some days earlier some "big, bearded men carrying backpacks and arms with foreign accents and with plenty of money" had appeared at the Tatarenda pump station. Through further inquiry Captain Silva learned that initially five men had arrived on March 5 or 6, to one of whom (Benigno) the driver had given a pair of shoes, because he was barefoot. After acquiring supplies they had continued south. On the 8th, according to the driver, two more had appeared. They had gotten soaked crossing the river, and had to dry their clothes and the bills they were carrying with them. The workers estimated that the men were transporting 40 or 50 million pesos. When the officer asked why the men had not been arrested, the workers explained that they were armed, and they said they were geologists from the University of Potosí, doing work for YPFB. Although they were foreigners, one of them at least (Aniceto) had spoken Quechua with the workers, setting their minds at rest.

Upon his arrival at Camiri, Captain Silva immediately went to the division commander, Col. Humberto Rocha Urquieta, to report this matter, which seemed important. On the following day, March 10, the division commander, with part of his general staff and Captain Silva, met with Humberto Suárez Roca, the engineer who was superintendant of the YPFB in Camiri, to coordinate activities aimed at verifying this information and taking necessary security measures. First it was agreed to take advantage of the flight of a company plane to conduct airborne reconnaissance. That same afternoon, the chief-of-staff of the division, Col. Juan Fernández, flew over part of the Grande River with Captain Silva without observing anything out of the ordinary, and stayed over in Santa Cruz. The return flight was made on the 11th, and that time Captain Silva, together with another officer who was accompanying him, managed to see four men on the Grande River beach. The four took cover when they heard the noise of the airplane. With this new information and with a better idea of the configuration of the area, Captain Silva was ordered to travel in a vehicle to Tatarenda, with a corporal and five soldiers to undertake ground reconnaissance. For this purpose he received five submachine guns with 500 cartridges and a 45 pistol with fifty cartridges. When they arrived at Tatarenda, about 8 P.M., the mission learned that engineer Maj. José Patiño Ayoroa, general manager of YPFB, had arrived from La Paz and wished to speak with Captain Silva to coordinate the search.

The meeting in Tatarenda lasted until nearly one in the morning. The workers who had been in touch with the foreigners were called in and all the information verified. The superintendent from Camiri arranged for the worker Epifanio Vargas, who knew the area well, to join the patrol as guide.

At the break of dawn on March 12, the patrol confirmed the information again at the water pump in Tatarenda. The workers told how on the 9th the two men (Inti and Ricardo) had bought and cooked two pigs, which they then placed in their packs, how they had eaten watermelon and corn, had bought canned food and cigarettes, and had crossed back over the river.

With these details in mind, and knowing that the strangers had asked questions about the Ñancahuazú River, Captain Silva left with his group in a YPFB vehicle along the Ipitá highway. They turned onto a footpath leading to the Grande River. The path became impassable at Las Norias, and they continued on foot. At the beginning of the afternoon they found the footprints of five persons who were going toward the west, climbing up to the heights of Saladillo Mountain, an extension of Numaó Mountain. After two days of arduous movement—the patrol did not even have canteens for water—following the descending course of the Saladillo Canyon, and after finding a wild guava plant and observing that the men who had preceded them had eaten its fruit, the patrol arrived at the Ñancahuazú.[10] Exploring this river upstream and down, they found the trail, which continued southward. In the face of his men's fatigue, the lack of provisions, and evidence that the suspects had at least two days' lead, Captain Silva resolved to go out on the highway again, to take another path farther ahead, and to cut the "bearded men" off, since it was clear that they were following the upstream course of the Ñancahuazú. After relaying this news to the division commander, the patrol went along the Gutiérrez-Pirirenda-Tiraboy route, reaching the Ñancahuazú River once again, one kilometer beyond the tin-roof house, and once again finding the trail of the men they were following. They went back on the highway to get to Lagunillas, where Captain Silva was informed by the inhabitants that on the day before, March 11, another military patrol, led by Lt. Col. Alberto Libera Cortez, had left toward the west to reach the Ñancahuazú River and follow its course downstream, in order to meet up with the Silva patrol. Silva then left with his men in the direction of El Pincal. He reached the tin-roof house at 4 P.M. and observed signs of the hurried exit of its inhabitants into the woods when they had heard the motor of the vehicle that was transporting the soldiers. The fire was still burning in the kitchen, and the Toyota jeep that Coco used on all his trips to Camiri was also there. Inside the house Silva found an envelope addressed to Señor Remberto Villa (the guerrillas' supplier) with a note from Coco and the key to the vehicle. There was also another note for Antonio with instructions to get the letter to Villa.

While his patrol rested and prepared something to eat, the officer and the guide Vargas explored the vicinity of the tin-roof house, finding many tracks and recently opened paths, sure evidence of some degree of organization. At that moment, at 5:30 P.M. on March 17, the first shots were heard in the Ñancahuazú ravine.

NOTES

1. The agenda of the Tricontinental listed the following themes:

1. The struggle against imperialism, colonialism, and neocolonialism.

2. Centers of the anti-imperialist struggle on the three continents.

3. Anti-imperialist solidarity of the peoples of Asia, Africa, and Latin America on the economic, social, and cultural fronts.

4. Political and organizational unification of the efforts of the peoples of Africa, Asia, and Latin America in their common struggle for liberation and national reconstruction, peace, and prosperity.

In the Political Declaration it was agreed to display a maximum of combative solidarity with peoples who took up arms against local oligarchies. The General Declaration proclaimed the right of peoples to attain political, economic, and social liberation through the means they deem necessary, and to use armed struggle if they judge that it is needed. The Conference also saw the creation, among other entities, of the Latin American Solidarity Organization (OLAS), which would have its seat in Havana. The Bolivian delegation had accreditation problems because it showed up divided. The delegation led by Mario Miranda Pacheco, leader of the National Liberation Front, an appendage of the pro-Soviet PCB, was accepted. The representative status of the delegation led by Lidia Gueiler, made up of other popular parties, was not recognized.

2. To facilitate the narrative only the aliases of the guerrilla fighters will be used. Their complete identification, including nationality, itinerary, and fate are detailed in Table 1.

3. Debray was following instructions from Fidel Castro on this journey, specifically the order to study Bolivian socio-political conditions for the guerrilla war project (R. Debray, declarations to the Second Department of the army in April of 1967).

4. Pombo's diary (in *The Complete Bolivian Diaries of Che Guevara and Other Captured Documents*, Daniel James, ed. [New York: Stein and Day, 1968]), entry for September 11, 1966.

5. Inti Peredo, *Mi campaña con el Che*, Oscar Crespo V., ed. (La Paz: 1970), Chapter 4.

6. Che's diary, entries for January 15–30.

7. See Map 2.

8. Pacho's diary (*El diario de Pacho* [Santa Cruz, Bolivia: Editorial Punto y Coma, 1987]), entry for March 6.

9. Che's diary, entries for March 19 and 20.

10. Pacho's diary, entry for March 8.

Operations zone: the El Churo Canyon in front; in the distance, the Grande River.

The hamlet of La Higuera seen from the Khara-Khara heights.

Che had to disguise himself in order to enter Bolivia. *Above,* a stop on his trip from La Paz to Ñancahuazú. *Below,* the tin-roof house, the first guerrilla base in the area.

Che discusses events of the day with the rest of his companions.

Above, Coco, Loyola, Inti, and Antonio formed the guerrilla rear guard. This photo made it possible to identify Loyola as the guerrilla liaison. *Below,* guerrillas fording the Grande River.

Left, a military patrol on the Ñancahuazú River. *Right*, the first military units are mobilized in civilian trucks headed toward Lagunillas.

Chapter 7

ÑANCAHUAZÚ AND IRIPITÍ

On the strength of Captain Silva's preliminary information and other intelligence provided by the Criminal Investigation Office (DIC), the Fourth Division command had already taken some measures. For one thing, on March 14, two suspects were apprehended by the police in Lagunillas, in the act of trying to sell a weapon. They were identified as Vicente Rocabado Terrazas (Orlando) and Pastor Barrero Quintana (Daniel). They were interrogated on the spot, and their statements revealed important facts or anecdotes which were relayed to the military authorities. Because of their significance, these statements will be transcribed at length:

Informative statements provided by citizens Vicente Rocabado Terrazas and Pastor Barrero Quintana, contained in the respective book of the interrogation subsection, the literal contents of which are as follows:

In Camiri at 5:30 P.M. on March 14, 1967. A person who gave his name as Vicente Rocabado Terrazas, detained in order to provide his informative statement in response to the following questions:

Q. Identify yourself.

A. My name is Vicente Rocabado Terrazas, 27 years old, single, from Oruro, here in this area temporarily, a mechanic by trade.

Q. Tell us if you know why you are detained in the DIC prison.

A. I think it's because I don't have any kind of documents with me.

Q. Tell us if it was you who sold a Winchester sporting rifle in the town of Lagunillas, to whom, for what price, where you obtained it, and for what purpose.

A. The sporting rifle belonged to me and I sold it to a gentleman who answers to the name of Sabino Villarroel Lino in the town of Lagunillas for 800 Bolivian pesos. I had bought it in the city of Oruro for hunting purposes.

Q. Tell us how long you have been in Luis Calvo Province and what your purpose in being in that province was and what locations you have been in.

A. I arrived in Camiri on February 14, and my traveling companion Pastor Barrero and I headed for Luis Calvo Province, returning on March 11.

Q. Tell us whose orders you were following in going to these places and what the purposes were.

A. In Oruro I was in touch with Moisés Guevara, and he invited me to come to this province of Luis Calvo together with six other men whose names I don't know, for the purpose of getting together with a guerrilla group who were in that place under the direction of a Cuban commandant who uses the name Antonio.

Q. Tell us where you were in Luis Calvo Province and what you observed, and what activity you were engaged in there.

A. I was in the Ñancahuazú area, about 40 km in, and I observed armed individuals there who intended to start a guerrilla war. So far as my activity is concerned, it was strictly to observe and act as a security guard on about fifteen occasions. That was the obligation we all had.

Q. Tell us who is in command of those guerrillas where you were, and how many position points you saw.

A. The main leaders of this guerrilla war are Che Guevara at the top, whom I didn't have a chance to see because he had gone exploring at the head of twenty-five other men. They hadn't returned by the day I left. What I mean is that I learned from what people were saying that he had been exploring in different places in the East for thirty-eight days. I also met two bearded men, Cuban citizens, who used the names of Arturo and Antonio. These two were followers of Che Guevara. I also met an Argentine named Carlos, a leader of the CGP [People's Guerrilla Command]. He had arrived recently, a week before, and was called there by Che Guevara. I also had occasion to meet two Peruvians, one called Chino, and they call him Francisco too, and the other called Doctor. Both of them are big leaders, too. As for the position points that I saw, they are the place I was at, a property owned by Coco, and also the place where the main body of the troops are, which is a huge jungle that doesn't have a name.

Q. Tell us what the owner of the property, this so-called Coco, has to do with these activities and what he contributes.

A. With regard to this Coco, I can say that I found out that he was only an administrator of that property, which the guerrilla leaders have bought, and also he's the liaison guy with the guerrillas and the one that is responsible for bringing them essential items.

Q. Tell us what the aims of these men are and what political doctrine they have, in your opinion.

A. The aims they have are to overthrow the government under the policy and the direct leadership of Fidel Castro.

Q. Tell us if you can estimate the amount and type of arms, and if they have very much money.

A. I can say that I've seen all kinds of arms, and besides that there is a cache of arms of all types that I didn't have an opportunity to estimate the quantity of because it was under ground. I'll also say that I had an opportunity to see the Cuban Antonio handling a lot of American dollars and Bolivian pesos.

Q. Tell us if you have anything more to add to your statement.

A. I have to add that I've made the present statement freely and with no pressure from the authorities, that my whole intention has been to collaborate with the national government, and that I'm ready to keep collaborating to the very end.

He ended here, and after the statement was read to him, he stood by its contents and signed together with the Head of the DIC and the certifying secretary:
(Signed) V. Rocabado—Informant
    E. Vaca Díez—Head DIC
    Detective W. Parada V.—Secretary

Continuing

With the same objective as before, we proceeded to the informative statement provided by Pastor Barrero Quintana.

In Camiri, at 7:00 P.M. on March 14, 1967. A person who said his name was Pastor Barrero Quintana, detained in order to provide an informative statement in response to the following questions:

Q. Identify yourself.

A. My name is Pastor Barrero Quintana, I'm an adult, single, a mason, from Oruro, and I'm here temporarily.

Q. Tell us if you understand why you have been arrested.

A. I've been arrested because I don't have personal documents with me.

Q. Tell us how long you have been in Luis Calvo Province and for what purpose.

A. I have been in Luis Calvo Province for about twenty-five days for work purposes.

Q. Tell us what weapon you brought with your traveling companion Vicente Rocabado.

A. The weapon that Vicente Rocabado and I brought was a 22–caliber sporting rifle, the same one we sold in the city of Lagunillas, and it belonged to my friend.

Q. Tell us if you were carrying out orders from political parties or labor organizations.

A. We weren't carrying out any political or labor order.

Q. Tell us how you participated with the guerrillas who are located in Ñancahuazú, where you have been, and what kind of arms they are bearing.

A. My participation in Ñancahuazú has been agricultural work and guard duty on the roads, and with regard to the arms they're bearing, I've only seen rifles.

Q. Tell us if you remember the names of the top leaders who are in command of these guerrilla operations and what their nationality is.

A. With regard to the top leaders who are in command of these guerrilla operations I have been told that Che Guevara is there. I didn't have the opportunity to meet him because he was not at the place, because he had gone exploring some days before. The second in command is a bearded Cuban called Antonio. There is another Cuban called Arturo, then there is another Peruvian whom they call Doctor. Actually there are a lot of them, with different nationalities.

Q. Tell us what the political allegiance of these men is.

A. I could see that they are clearly communists and under the direct leadership of Fidel Castro.

Q. Tell us more or less how many people there are at that place and what amount of arms you think they have.

A. At the Ñancahuazú post where I was, there were about forty people, but I know from what I've been told that there are many more posts with a lot of people and arms.

Q. Tell us who provides those arms and supplies to these people and with what funds.

A. The only one that I saw bringing supplies was a man nicknamed Coco, and with regard to funds, I suppose they're from Cuba.

Q. Tell us where you met a man nicknamed Coco and what he has to do with the guerrillas' activities.

A. I met this man Coco at a property near Ñancahuazú, and I think he's the liaison guy for the guerrillas.

Q. Tell us if you have anything to add to your statement.

A. Yes, I do, because what we wanted to do was to go to La Paz and tell the authorities, and for that reason we ran away from that area of operations and came to Camiri, on our way to Santa Cruz and La Paz.

Here he ended the present informative statement. It was read to him and he confirmed its contents, signing with the Head of the DIC and certifying secretary. (Signed) Barrero Q.—Informant
      E. Vaca Díez—Head DIC
      Det. W. Parada V.—Secretary

Besides these statements, the DIC supplied the division command with a report on the presence of other suspicious persons in the region, which helped to complete the intelligence picture. This report correctly identified Coco as a liaison, mentioned Tania and her possible links, and clearly pointed to the arrival of Moisés Guevara and his seven men on February 14, indicating where they had stayed and the manner in which they were transported to Ñancahuazú.

On the basis of these pieces of information, Lieutenant Colonel Libera's patrol was assigned to follow the Lagunillas-Itimirí-Yuquı-Quebrada route and to move in on the Ñancahuazú River and search its banks, in order to fill out the details provided by the Silva patrol.

On March 17, at 3 P.M. the patrol came across the entrance to the encampment without being attacked, and continued its advance to the tin-roof house without being aware of Silva's arrival there. Nevertheless, the evacuation caused by Silva's patrol threw the first prisoner, Salustio, into Libera's hands. Armed with a submachine gun, Salustio was trying to lead a mule to safety. Libera cautiously resumed the march and a bit later the group came across Loro, who reacted quickly, fired, wounding one soldier in the leg, and ran into the woods. At about 6 P.M., Libera and Silva met. Their mission was completed, and with a prisoner who could provide additional information, they reported what had happened to Camiri and evacuated the wounded man.

In the guerrilla encampment the events previously recounted were creating a situation of confusion and crisis. Antonio, who supposedly was in command, was on a shopping trip to Lagunillas; the wife of the police chief, who knew Antonio, was surprised to see him at large and advised him that army patrols would be going out to the tin-roof house and the river. This sent him back in a hurry.[1] When the Silva patrol arrived at the house, the guerrillas withdrew to Camp I, where they awaited the arrival of Che, who imposed order and organized things better "in the atmosphere of defeat that reigned."[2]

The original plan to rest for several days after the reconnaissance tour—so as to regain strength, receive and train the new members of the guerrilla force, and improve the supply situation—was thus abruptly changed by the events of March 17, which were the result of Marcos's indiscretion in Tatarenda and of the effective police work in the case of Moisés Guevara and the deserters, which had alerted the army.

This was a decisive moment for the guerrillas, since there was no doubt that the army would act in the next days. Several options were open to them:

—To withdraw without fighting. This would mean that they would be actively pursued, since they had very clearly been detected because of the numerous traces they had left and the information given by the deserters and the prisoner. The army would be unified, and its morale high. This option was further complicated by the fact that if they were in constant movement, their supply problems would worsen. (At that time, forty-seven men were present at the encampment: seventeen Cubans, twenty-four Bolivians, one Frenchman, one Argentine, three Peruvians, and one German woman.) To feed everyone would present a serious logistical problem since there was no support structure.

—To go into combat choosing the place and time meant acquiring experience and, in the case of victory, striking at the morale of the army troops (this in fact happened). By holding the initiative, they would gain a tactical advantage, especially given the fact that there would be encounters in the next few days, since the army was on their trail.

—The third option consisted simply in fading away as a guerrilla force, disbanding, and seeking refuge in the cities to organize the apparatus all over again and recruit new personnel.

This analysis led Che to organize an ambush to initiate combat, taking advantage of favorable terrain and the surprise factor. For this purpose, eight men were assigned to Rolando's command with the mission of ambushing the military forces and inflicting the highest possible number of casualties. The ambush was set up on March 21 and 22, but the troops did not show up. Despite this, the order was given to stay alert and maintain positions.

On the basis of all the available information, the Fourth Division command in Camiri was already aware of the presence of a group of guerrillas at the Ñancahuazú River, although the exact location of their encampment could not be pinpointed because the deserters and the prisoner had not reached it. It was presumed to be between Overa Canyon and the tin-roof house. While arrangements were being made to mount a search operation, Captain Silva, who had remained at the tin-roof house, explored the nearby area and found the site of the provisional encampment with its lookout points some 500 meters upriver. He found the remains of food and materials and, in a cave covered over with a fallen tree, six suitcases with articles of clothing, among them a blue suit with Cuban labels and another from Mexico. He sent all this material to Camiri for evaluation.

Already before, on March 9, with the first news of outsiders in the area, the "Sararenda Plan of Action" had been prepared for the purpose of providing security and controlling the Choreti-Monteagudo-Rosal oil pipeline and the Camiri oilfield. This plan attributed the following probable actions to the guerrilla campaign, which was in an organizational phase, its allegiance not yet established (it was even thought possible that the deposed MNR could be responsible for the guerrilla activity):

—They could commit acts of violence in different areas of the country.

—They could effect terrorist acts and destroy oil pipelines, pump stations, and YPFB camps.

—They could incite the campesinos to join their cause.

—They could create a climate of uneasiness in the country.

The Sararenda Plan assigned military units to provide security and surveillance together with YPFB personnel in Monteagudo, Tatarenda, Lagunillas, Choreti, and Camiri, with the order to effect reconnaissance in those areas and capture guerrillas and suspicious persons.

When the presence of the guerrillas was confirmed, General Operations Order 1/67 was issued on March 21 for the purpose of "locating and destroying guerrilla groups in the region bounded by the Ñancahuazú River, Pampa del Tigre, and the Incahuasi Ranges."

The maneuver consisted in searching the Ñancahuazú River from the tin-roof house to its source with a force made up of four officers, three noncommissioned officers, and fifty-nine soldiers, while another group was to go over the route of the Libera patrol to serve as a barrier on the Ñancahuazú River. This group would have three officers, three noncommissioned officers, and fifty-five soldiers. In order to put together these forces, the division command had to include soldiers from the 6th Campos Infantry Regiment, who had been carrying out administrative tasks and production work and had not even completed their basic military training. In those years (1966–67), the garrisons in the East and South as a general rule had to undergo a short training period of three months and then use the other nine months of their time as draftees in farm labor, construction of living quarters and barracks, and production of materials (railroad ties, bricks, lime, and so forth), so as to create resources to fill such needs of the units as were not covered in the budget. This practice undoubtedly affected the troops' combat ability and also led to administrative irregularities, since in many cases soldiers were rented out as peons to area landowners for the personal profit of the commander. Since the only important mission that the garrisons in the Southeast had was to take care of the advanced military posts on the border with Paraguay and Argentina, they could devote the greater share of their troops, already in short supply, to production tasks. For this reason, virtually every soldier in the region had to be utilized in order to muster the 120 men it was estimated would be needed for the search operation. There was no possibility of sending a regularly constituted unit with its own officers and noncommissioned officers, who would know each other and have mutual trust.[3]

When the hostilities began, the Fourth Division had the following units and strengths:

Military Police Company (Camiri)	81
Headquarters and Supply Company (Camiri)	81
6th Campos Infantry Regiment (Carandaití)	245
11th Boquerón Infantry Regiment (Charagua)	245
1st Abaroa Cavalry Group (Yapiroa)	230
1st Bullaín Artillery Group (Cuevo)	216
Total 1,103	men[4]

The Boquerón, Abaroa, and Campos units each had two advanced military posts on the Paraguayan border, and this limited possibilities even further. For this reason soldiers from the Campos regiment and the military police were used to form the two groups. Proof of the improvised nature of the endeavor came when the operations order and the matériel arrived at El Pincal on March 22. Silva's troops, who had been reinforced so as to constitute one of the two groups, found that they had mortars as support arms. The officers (Amézaga and Loayza) had to spend the afternoon giving instruction in the use of mortars, since the soldiers were riflemen only, with no knowledge of support arms.

At dawn on March 23, the group commanded by Maj. Hernán Plata left El Pincal for the tin-roof house to begin their search operation from there. Arriving at the river, they split into three parts: the first, a vanguard commanded by Captain Silva, with 2d Lt. Rubén Amézaga, Corporals Terceros and Torrico, Sr. Epifanio Vargas, and two soldiers; the center under the command of Major Plata, who followed the first group at a distance of thirty to forty meters; and the rear guard under 2d Lt. Lucio Loayza, where the support arms were transported. When the vanguard had proceeded about 700 meters and was trying to cross a straight section of the river that had on one side rocks about twenty meters high and on the other a small stretch of woods, shots were fired, resulting in immediate losses. Second Lieutenant Amézaga charged toward the bank firing his weapon but was cut down before he could leave the water. The guide,

Vargas, tried to shield himself but was riddled with bullets. After a couple of minutes the firing stopped, and the guerrillas scared the survivors into surrendering. The rear-guard group, who had been kept back by the weight of the arms they were carrying, heard the shots but did not intervene. They halted in order to prevent the abrupt flight of some soldiers who were escaping the ambush.

The prisoners were disarmed, and the guerrillas made them place the corpses on the shore. When one of the guerrillas identified Vargas, the civilian guide, he observed scornfully, "That's the way informers die." (Epifanio Vargas had helped Marcos and the guerrilla vanguard on March 5 when they visited him in Tatarenda. In his diary entry for March 23 commenting on the ambush, Pacho wrote: "Sr. Vargas died. We were at his place on the fifth.") While Major Plata remained with some guerrillas examining the dead, Captain Silva was moved with the wounded and the prisoners to the area of the encampment, for interrogation. The wounded were treated by the guerrillas' doctors, who undertook to indoctrinate them in the aims of the insurgency. They were held prisoner until the afternoon of the 24th. After being set free, they returned to El Pincal and made their report about what had happened.

In the military camp, the ambush had created total confusion. The lack of available units to continue operations made it necessary to wait for the arrival of troops from other garrisons. On the 24th a company of eighty-one men from the CITE Training Center for Special Troops (from Cochabamba) was transported to Camiri, and on the 25th a mixed company, made up of soldiers from the Braun and Manchego regiments, came from Santa Cruz. At the time of the Ñancahuazú ambush, these soldiers were being discharged because their military service was over. Their discharge was suspended, with the predictable reaction of discontent.

The information provided by the officers and soldiers who had been captured was both contradictory and exaggerated. There was talk of forty or more guerrillas, when in fact eight had participated in the ambush. The order was given to hold the position at El Pincal and the tin-roof house, and the presumed location of the guerrilla base was attacked by plane and with mortars. The result of the ambush was discouraging for the army: eight dead, seven wounded, the loss of a large amount of arms and ammunition. The reigning improvisation and disorganization were made painfully evident. The presence of the commanding general of the army, Gen. David Lafuente Soto, in Camiri and Lagunillas on the 24th helped to correct some errors. It was decided to suspend the activities of the Command and General Staff School and the Application School in Cochabamba so as to fill out the general staffs of the units in the area and the ranks of the regimental trainers with the officers freed from school duties. On the 26th, President Barrientos arrived in Camiri. He went immediately to the tin-roof house by helicopter to see the installations that had been found there for himself. On the next day, news of what had happened was officially made public in a communiqué:

In circumstances in which groups of the armed forces were studying the rerouting of the stretch of road between Vallegrande and Lagunillas, in the Ñancahuazú-Lagunillas sector, a group of soldiers under the command of army 2d Lt. Rubén Amézaga Faure, who were doing the road work, was attacked by surprise by unknown groups bearing automatic weapons. The death of Second Lieutenant Amézaga, six soldiers, and the civilian guide Epifanio Vargas, a YPFB worker, were the unfortunate result of this action. After being wounded, they were shot in the most cowardly fashion.

This outrageous, cold-blooded act, committed when members of the armed forces were working to realize the integration of the center of the country with the South, is even more serious because it has brought pain and mourning to the families of the soldiers, workers, and campesinos.

The timely report by survivors permitted a quick reaction with troops of the 4th Army Division, backed up by planes of the Air Force, which dispersed the attackers, causing casualties and taking prisoners. In their flight they left suitcases containing clothing, pieces of equipment, pamphlets on guerrilla warfare and Castro-communist propaganda of Cuban origin, as well as a tape recorder, a portable high-frequency radio, and a jeep.

The prisoners, local inhabitants and surviving soldiers, reported that a large group of persons of differing nationalities, among them Cubans, Peruvians, Chinese, Argentines, Europeans, and also Bolivian Communists, are involved—and that they are supplied with modern automatic weapons and bazookas, none of them of the type used in our army.

The high command of the Armed Forces of the Nation, in accord with the mission entrusted to it in the political constitution of the State and in defense of national sovereignty and the tranquility of the people, has ordered the drastic and immediate eradication of this insurgent foco characterized as a Castro-communist guerrilla war.

The Armed Forces of the Nation, in informing the Bolivian people of these events, appeal to their patriotism and their high democratic and Christian sense, so that they will collaborate in the destruction of these international communist groups, wherever they show up, as the residents of Monteagudo and Muyupampa are doing already on their own.

In the guerrilla encampment, with the knowledge of the general operations order that Major Plata had carried with him, an ambush was mounted upriver in the belief that another army contingent would arrive there. On the 25th, a meeting was held with almost all personnel, and Che again made an analysis of the reconnaissance march, pointing out the exemplary behavior of Miguel, Inti, Pombo, and Rolando. He also urged them to do even better, particularly from that moment on, when clashes with regular forces would demand greater efforts and sacrifices from each of them. He then referred to Marcos, pointing out a series of errors and incorrect attitudes of that veteran who, despite his good qualities, could not control his character. He made note of Marcos's despotic, overbearing attitude and his undisciplined acts that caused the early discovery of the guerrilla enterprise. He accused him of carelessness in his dealings with Epifanio Vargas, resulting in Vargas's service as guide to the army until the ambush of March 23. Given this background, Che had decided to relieve Marcos of his position as leader of the vanguard and third in command of the guerrilla war, and he gave him the choice of returning to Cuba or remaining as a simple combatant. Marcos decided to stay and was assigned to the rear guard. The behavior of the men brought by Moisés Guevara was also discussed in this meeting. Three of them (Chingolo, Pepe, and Paco) were characterized as untruthful, undependable, and clearly not guerrilla material. Two others from the same group had already deserted. The guerrilla leader decided then and there that these men would stay in the group for a time to help set up their new caches and that they would then be dismissed and given some pesos so as to get along as best they could.[5]

The arrival of a coded message from Havana bearing news of the meeting between Fidel Castro and the PCB leaders Kolle, Reyes, and Ramirez raised hopes that they would give all the necessary cooperation with men and measures to invigorate the guerrilla enterprise. They had committed themselves when they learned what kind of project Che had set up. The premature discovery of the International Training Center, however, and the quick action of the army and the police aimed at isolating the area, were to stand in the way not only of PCB support but of all future contact between the political structures and the insurgents.

To gain a clearer picture of the situation, Che sent reconnaissance expeditions in different directions. They identified the presence of troops in the tin-roof house and in the Yuqui (or Yaqui) ranch upriver on the Nancahuazú. Over the radio it was learned that a major military mobilization was mounting to complete the encirclement and destroy the guerrilla foco. The rebel leader discussed these developments with his general staff, and they decided first to ensure themselves of adequate supplies at their site by harvesting corn and sending people to purchase supplies at Gutiérrez (twenty km to the east). They also decided to launch another attack to keep the army busy.

The team sent to pick corn met Red Cross personnel who had arrived there to recover the bodies of those killed in the March 23 ambush, an operation which they had had to suspend because of the state of decomposition of the corpses and the lack of plastic bags for transport. The detail of soldiers who accompanied the Red Cross was required to withdraw to guarantee the work of the mission. At this time the guerrillas showed themselves openly, conversed with members of the Red Cross, and made quite an impression because of their actions and their lack of fear of the army.

The exploration in the area of Pirirenda and Gutiérrez was unproductive.

The guerrillas did not complete their trip, and their intention of laying another ambush on the section between El Pincal and Lagunillas was discarded after radio broadcasts located the guerrilla group accurately in the Ñancahuazú River area and announced major military operations in the next few days.

Taking this news into account, and on the basis of his own estimate of the situation, Che resolved to move north and east to keep the army away from his bases and to attempt to escape the siege. The move was made carefully, close to the tin-roof house, following the course of the Ñancahuazú River so as not to leave a trail. It was not perceived by army troops. The guerrillas set up camp some kilometers downriver, leaving Rolando in command of the reinforced rear guard, which mounted an ambush to stop the army if it pursued them.

In fact, the troops were organizing a more complete operation to search and destroy the guerrilla group. On April 1, following General Operations Order 2/67, the order was given to set up three bases with patrols of company strength, from which reconnaissance could be carried out in different directions in order to identify the location of the insurgents and proceed to destroy them.

—A Company, under Maj. Rubén Sánchez, was to occupy Yuqui.

—B Company, under Capt. Alfredo Calvi, was to occupy El Pincal.

—C Company, under Capt. Raúl López, was to occupy Pirirenda Lake.

—The reserve company, under Capt. Celso Torrelio, would stay in Lagunillas.

This order, which became effective on April 3, did not yield significant results. The patrols found only traces of the guerrilla encampments in Ñancahuazú, confirming the impression that the group had left the area. In accord with this situation, General Order 3/67 was issued on April 7. It restated the plan and assigned new missions to the three companies operating in the area (245 men), who were the entire force mobilized up to that time.

—Major Sánchez's A Company was given the mission to "remain in Ñancahuazú (the tin-roof house) and effect reconnaissance to the north in the direction of Iripití, westward toward the Yuqui River, and eastward toward Tiraboy."

—Captain Calvi's B Company was assigned to "reconnoiter in depth the canyon that leads to the guerrillas' encampment, locating caves, trenches, caches where they presumably have buried arms, materials, and other equipment. When this is concluded, establish a patrol base at the confluence of the Overa Canyon and the Ñancahuazú River and effect reconnaissance in the direction of Pampa del Tigre and Overa Canyon."

—Captain López's C Company was assigned to do reconnaissance in the direction of Gutiérrez-Pirirenda and Tiraboy, and set up a patrol base in Tiraboy.

—Captain Torrelio's D Reserve Company was given "the mission of occupying Gutiérrez and from that place patrolling in the direction of Ipitá and La Herradura."

These units occupied their bases on April 9 and prepared to undertake the required reconnaissance beginning on the 10th.

THE IRIPITÍ AMBUSH

At dawn on April 10, A Company sent three section patrols in the following directions:

—The first section, under Lt. Hugo Gutiérrez Heredia, was to follow the course of the Ñancahuazú River toward the east until it reached the stream where the central encampment was located, in an attempt to find the trail of the guerrilla group and to link up with Captain Calvi's B Company.

—The second section, under Lt. Luis Saavedra Arambel, was to follow the course of the Ñancahuazú River northward, in an attempt to come into contact with the enemy again.

—The third section, under Lt. Remberto Lafuente Lafuente, was to reconnoiter in an eastward direction along the course of the Tiraboy River and meet up with the López Company.

—A reserve section stayed at the base.

The Saavedra and Lafuente patrols left practically together and followed the river bed for about 700 meters until they arrived at the mouth of the Tiraboy River, where the Lafuente patrol turned off. The patrol commanders had been told to advance in the assigned directions for a period of three hours and then to return by a different route.

At 10:30, when the Saavedra patrol had reached the outlet of the Iripití River at the Ñancahuazú it was fired upon from both banks. Lt. Luis Saavedra was killed immediately and three men were wounded, two of whom died within a few minutes. Seven soldiers were captured and four escaped, falling back along the river bed. Significantly, the guerrillas suffered their first combat loss. Occupying a poorly chosen position, Rubio was mortally wounded by a shot to the head. His body was recovered by his companions and taken to the rear guard for burial.

When Rolando informed him of the ambush, Che sent the entire vanguard to reinforce the ten men who had fought—and ordered them to fall back to a prearranged position. Rolando, however, showing great tactical intelligence and a proper appraisal of the terrain and the probable military reaction, decided rather to advance his ambush some 300 meters so as to cause more casualties. Che approved this decision and in the afternoon the second encounter occurred.

As it turned out, the soldiers and the noncommissioned officer who escaped the first ambush fell back to their patrol base in the tin-roof house to report the events to the company commander. After hearing the news, Maj. Rubén Sánchez organized his reserve force and marched toward the ambush site to help the Saavedra patrol, taking with him 2d Lts. Jorge Ayala and Carlos Martins with sixty men. Expecting normal guerrilla tactics, he advanced without taking many precautions. He thought that the guerrillas had carried out a "hit and run" operation, and so Rolando's trick of advancing the ambush was highly successful. All of Major Sánchez's force was ambushed. Second Lieutenant Ayala fell, fighting heroically in an attempt to organize his men for the defense. Major Sánchez, judging all resistance futile because of the unfavorable terrain—they were in the middle of the river and had no way of avoiding the ambush—ordered his men to surrender. Second Lieutenant Martins, who with a small group of soldiers had not reached the "death zone" of the ambush, fell back in disarray.

Meanwhile the Lafuente patrol was arriving at the Ñancahuazú River at this time after completing their reconnaissance, which had taken them longer than expected because of the difficulties of the terrain. When they reached the river, they heard the massive gunfire from the second ambush and immediately headed along the river bed to lend support to what they believed was the Saavedra patrol. They were unaware of the morning's events, since the patrols did not have radios for communication.

Approaching the ambush site, they found terrified soldiers who were falling back without any precautions or any order, some lightly wounded; finally they met Second Lieutenant Martins. After some discussion, they decided to combine their forces, some forty men in all, and go to the aid of the company commander.

Evening had fallen on the canyon when the Lafuente patrol advanced to the site of the second ambush. The guerrillas, carrying flashlights, were recovering the material that the troops had left behind. Lafuente and his men stayed in their positions all night. At dawn when they were getting ready to begin tracking the guerrillas again, they were surprised by the appearance of Major Sánchez and the rest of the prisoners, with their hands behind their heads. After spending the night in the enemy's hands, they were being freed, and were still escorted by some ten guerrillas who were leading them along the river bed. When the officer was preparing to give the order to fire, the guerrillas, aware of the army group's presence, pointed their guns at Major Sánchez and made him order his men to fall back. If they did not, the guerrillas would kill him and all the prisoners. In this situation, Major Sánchez shouted, "Go back, they are setting us free." The regular forces drew back completely.

Over the course of the day the remains of the company arrived at the tin-roof house individually or in groups. At nightfall a detail of soldiers, commanded by Second Lieutenant León, in civilian clothes, recovered the bodies. Two officers, a noncommissioned officer, and eight soldiers made up the total dead. There were thirteen wounded and twenty-three freed prisoners. An appreciable amount of arms and ammunition fell into the guerrillas' hands.

RESULT OF THE OPERATIONS

In the military camp, the evaluation of the operations undertaken thus far was totally negative. In the encounters at Ñancahuazú and Iripití the army had suffered a total of eighteen dead and as many wounded. It had lost arms and ammunition, but above all it had revealed to itself and others its tremendous weakness in men and resources. It could not point to the body of even one guerrilla as proof of its existence.

Immediately after these two encounters, the high command realized that it was faced with a problem that was going to take time and effort to resolve. The solution would not be simple, as with political problems up to that time. When a regiment had been sent to occupy a mining center, a campesino area, or any locale, the mere presence of troops had ended the conflict. The situation in the Southeast was a different story. They were facing an organized and experienced enemy who, in addition to obvious help from abroad, could receive help locally. This enemy required different tactics and techniques, for which the army was not adequately prepared, especially the units of the Fourth Division, who had demonstrated so little military training. It was clear that even troops such as those of the CITE, who participated at Iripití, were not prepared for this kind of operation.

On the other hand a problem of morale was evident among the officers and noncommissioned officers as well as the soldiers. The two operations, with their aftermath of death and panic, had seriously affected the participants. They passed on their defeatist attitude to the units arriving in Camiri in those first days of operations, coming from the 2d Bolivar Artillery Regiment from Viacha (174 men), from the Cochabamba Noncommissioned Officers School (85 men), the Jungle Operations Training Center in Riberalta (CIOS, 71 men), and the 2d Sucre Infantry Regiment from the nation's capital (45 men). These troops were also not used to the kind of terrain they were expected to work in, nor to the hot tropical climate. The terrain also presented a serious obstacle to troop maneuvers. The complete lack of roads made movement difficult. The only viable routes for operations in the area were the beds of the Ñancahuazú River and its tributaries, which were real deathtraps, hemmed in as they were by rocks and abundant vegetation. Movement along the heights was impractical; there was no way to maneuver or observe. Air support could not be adequately used, since there was no way of indicating a line of contact or a front to mark the border between one's own troops and the enemy.

In accord with this evaluation and the need to organize the forces better and gain time in the hope of better conditions, the Fourth Division command issued, on the recommendation of the army command, General Operations Order 4/67 on April 11 at 1900 hours. It displayed a change in attitude by designating the following as the mission of the four companies in operations: "They should be organized defensively, undertaking patrols with a short radius of action in their respective areas, under conditions that will prevent guerrilla groups from obtaining vital supplies. They should isolate the probable area occupied by the guerrillas."

At the same time, orders were issued to the units to carry out adequate training in order to counter negative factors such as the belief that the guerrillas were superwarriors, had long experience in the jungle, and would receive outside support through extraordinary means. This work ultimately bore fruit.

The arrival in the country on March 31 of Gen. Alfredo Ovando Candia, commander-in-chief of the armed forces, who had been in Europe and the United States arranging for the installation of tin-smelting ovens and more military aid, helped to calm spirits.[6] His unquestioned authority over the armed forces, his equanimity, and his gift of command pacified President Barrientos and the members of the high command, who until then had been acting on impulse.

General Ovando decided to organize an Antiguerrilla Operations Command in Camiri and request that the government declare a military zone. He implemented a series of measures that were intended to face the problem squarely. The first news received about the probable presence of Che Guevara (taken from the deserters' statements) was handled carefully. It was not made public, but the intelligence services of other countries (Brazil, Argentina, the United States) were contacted to see if this point could be confirmed.

After the Iripití encounter, the need to manage the entire problem from the upper level was reaffirmed, because of the political and military implications. For that reason it was recommended that the Fourth Division act cautiously and with good judgment.

Military cooperation from neighboring countries was also sought. Col. León Kolle Cueto, the air force chief-of-staff, was sent to Brazil and Argentina to secure logistical support: for the moment, arms and ammunition from Argentina (including FAL rifles) to replace the Mauser rifles with which the Southeast units were still equipped since the time of the Chaco War, and from Brazil, a major shipment of combat rations, which helped partially to solve the troops' supply problems in the operations area. Agreement was also made with these countries to exercise careful surveillance on the common borders to avoid the movement of persons suspected of wishing to join or cooperate with the guerrillas.

Limits were also placed on the statements to be made by military leaders, who were distorting the record with contradictions and exaggerations. For example, on April 1, a high military commander spoke of the existence of from four to five hundred guerrillas, without having any basis on which to make such an estimate, in any case excessive. The decision therefore was made to use the communiqué system, whereby news of events would be released to the public from the commander-in-chief's office, where all information was to be centered.

This position, though advantageous in the sense of controlling and adequately routing information, gave free rein to press speculation. In those days of Ñancahuazú and Iripití the press concocted a spate of alarming and unsettling accounts that shook the consciousness of the nation.

In the political arena, the repercussions of the setbacks suffered by the army took no time in making themselves felt. On the one hand, President Barrientos launched a campaign that was substantial if intuitive in concept, aimed at winning the citizenry over to the side of the armed forces. He thoroughly denounced the international participation in the guerrilla war, even though this still could not be conclusively demonstrated, and the communist effort directed against national institutions. The political parties were asked to take a clear and concrete stand on the situation. This prompted a debate in the parties of the center and right, which ultimately felt obliged to condemn the guerrilla effort, without giving tacit support to the government.

The statements of Dr. Gilbert Flores Barrón, who arrived in Ñancahuazú leading the Red Cross mission to recover the bodies of Second Lieutenant Amézaga and his companions, were cleverly exploited. His phrases—"The guerrillas are young Bolivians and foreigners. They are communist militants. They dress in olive drab. They are in possession of American and European arms. They carry automatic weapons and seek to overthrow the government and implant a communist regime."—were amply reported in the national press as a means of stimulating repulsion among all anticommunist sectors. For his part General Ovando, after an initial inspection of the operations zone, before the Iripití incident, did not hesitate to stress that "the guerrilla movement does not imperil institutional stability. The guerrillas will be defeated," reaffirming these ideas later in a public communiqué. Its text is worth quoting as an expression of the image that the armed forces were trying to create on the political level and as part of the psychological campaign being waged:

1. General of the Army Alfredo Ovando Candia, after completing the mission entrusted him by the nation and the government, reassumed his functions as Commander-in-Chief of the Armed Forces.

2. The guerrillas' area of activity is limited to the quadrilateral included between 19°15' and 19°45' southern latitude and between 63° and 63°55' eastern longitude. Consequently, no guerrilla outbreak has been discovered outside of this zone.

3. The strength of the guerrilla force operating in the "red zone" has not yet been determined.

4. Since the period in Ñancahuazú that resulted in the dead and wounded, of which the public is aware, no new encounters have occurred. Currently action is limited to exchanges of gunfire for the purposes of harassment.

5. The different individuals captured by the army and state security organs are not prisoners, but they are suspected instead of having had dealings with the guerrillas. It should be made clear that none of them were captured in an armed action.

6. In the interest of public calm and as a greater guarantee of the successful outcome of operations, the people are requested not to give credence to the wave of rumors circulating in the country through different channels. A state of calm exists and activities are being conducted normally in the national territory under the guarantee of the armed forces and the state security organs.

7. The morale of officers, noncommissioned officers, and soldiers—and also of the civilians who are voluntarily cooperating in the fight against the guerrillas—is high. The participants have shown a clear desire to avenge the deaths of their companions who were victimized in the sneak attack at the Ñancahuazú Gorge.

8. Guerrilla warfare is characterized by long periods of inactivity. Therefore, the citizenry should not become alarmed by a lack of official communiqués on any given day.

9. The presence of this guerrilla force does not endanger the stability of the country. Since it has been isolated, it will have no effect on day-to-day activity nor on the normal conduct of the national life.

President Barrientos and the commander-in-chief also decided to abandon the announced campesino mobilization that was being readied for the Southeast. The military command judged that the presence of armed campesino groups in the region, especially originating from Cochabamba, could hamper operations or present too high a risk because the contingents would lack military training and because other problems might arise. It was resolved to leave all operations in the hands of regular forces.

The successive ambushes of Iripití, which shocked the public once again, were countered with a hardening of the government stance. The PCB and the Revolutionary Workers' Party (POR) were declared illegal, and forty-one of their leaders, among them Guillermo Lora, Óscar Zamora Medinacelli and others, were imprisoned in the town of Puerto Rico in Pando Department, and in Ixiamas in La Paz Department. This crumbled the political structure that could eventually have given support to the guerrillas.

Within the guerrilla group, the evaluation of the two actions was highly positive. They realized that they had stopped the army with only part of their force, affecting the army's morale and its ability to fight; this augured well for the entire guerrilla enterprise. They also judged favorable the impression made on public opinion, which they felt should be strengthened with new actions. The negative aspect was simply the fact of having been detected prematurely, before they had established the necessary liaison to increase the number of combatants and to assure an adequate flow of supplies. The major problem at the moment related to the need to keep moving. This made it difficult to ensure supplies, since the region where they were located had very little population and very few farming areas.

There were no apparent problems with arms and ammunition, since the matériel captured from the army in fact guaranteed a sufficient supply for the time when the number of combatants would increase. Depots were established to hold everything that had been captured, with the hope of returning for it later.

Everyone's morale was high, despite Rubio's death—judged to be less a sign of the army's expertise than a result of one guerrilla's carelessness, which would serve as a lesson to everyone else.

Although the performance of the air force intimidated the guerrillas at a certain point of the bombing at Ñancahuazú, it was soon dismissed as a risk because it did not affect their ability to operate. The news received over the radio that the United States was sending personnel to Bolivia was thought to be the first chapter of a new Vietnam.[7]

On the strength of this evaluation, Che and his men readied themselves for a new phase of their struggle.

NOTES

1. Pacho's diary, entry for March 16. Che's diary, entry for March 19.
2. Che's diary, entry for March 20.
3. The term "noncommissioned officers" was used generically in the army to designate the ranks from corporal to sergeant.
4. Fourth Division, General Operations Order 1/67.
5. Rolando's diary, entry for March 25.
6. At the time, the post of commander-in-chief of the Bolivian armed forces was held by a military officer, not the president of the nation.
7. Che's diary, entry for April 13.

Chapter 8

A FORCE DIVIDED

The army's passivity after the events of Ñancahuazú and Iripití gave the guerrillas the time they needed to regroup, carry out explorations, and return carefully to Camp II, proving that the troops had not discovered them.

It became clear to the guerrillas that they had to leave the area, not only to avoid contact with the army in unfavorable conditions, but also because of the pressing need to get Debray and Bustos out of the operations zone. Alarmed by all they had seen up until then, the latter were insisting on returning to the cities to carry out other tasks: "The Frenchman stated too emphatically how useful he could be away from here."[1]

The plan of operations outlined by Che ruled out an exit in the direction of Gutiérrez. Everything indicated that the town must be occupied by the army because of its location on the highway to Camiri. He therefore decided to operate in the area of Muyupampa so as to leave off the visitors and then fall back northward into the area that was already known and explored. In any case, before beginning this move, he explained its purpose to his men, observing that they would be entering a zone populated by campesinos, and that it was important to win those people over. Although it could be expected that their first reaction would be fear, he said, and that some would inform the army, they should be treated with care in order to gain their confidence. At the same time, his men should keep the need for supplies in mind, with a view to gaining more freedom of action for the fighting force.

With this advice the guerrilla group set out for the south at dawn on March 16, in the direction of Ticucha, the goal of the first day of March. They left Joaquín behind with the rear guard and the sick, with the specific mission to "make their presence felt in the area to prevent too much movement and wait for the main body for three days, at the end of which he should remain in the area but should not engage in direct combat but rather wait for their return."[2]

This order, correctly interpreted by Joaquín, would, however, result in the definitive separation of the two groups, and would affect considerably not only the fighting ability of the guerrillas but also their morale. They would have no first-hand knowledge of each other up to and including the time that each was wiped out.

It is very difficult to figure out how this could have happened. Aside from the army's plan and its actions, so elementary an error was committed at this point that it casts serious doubt on the military aptitude of the guerrilla leaders. It is normal, even for small-scale operations like short-range patrols, to set up rallying points where everyone can gather in case of an enemy action that requires splitting up. On earlier occasions, such as when they went out on reconnaissance missions and other movements, Che took the necessary care to set up these measures of coordination and control. This time, however, when he was to be separated from nearly half of his force (seventeen men out of a total of forty-seven) for a period of no less than three days and at an approximate distance of 30 kilometers, he did not observe this basic requirement, and the two groups would wander for more than four months looking for each other, sometimes crossing the others' paths with a lapse of only a few hours or kilometers, but never meeting again. No justification for such an elementary error of leadership is found in any of the diaries nor in the statements of prisoners. The only explanation possible is the guerrillas' excessive confidence in their ability and in the ineptitude of the regular forces.

There were reasons for the apparent inactivity of the army in those days. By order of supreme headquarters, important modifications were being made in the units to be used. Also some long-range planning was being done, taking into account the scope of the problem and its probable duration. With that in mind, the decision was made to organize a new unit specialized in anti-guerrilla warfare. With 650 men, Manchego Regiment (until then dedicated to agricultural production in Guabirá, northern Santa Cruz Department) was reactivated so that at the same time it received basic individual training it would take the Ranger course with the support and advice of a training mission from the United States Army. The recently organized unit was filled out with officers from other regiments (the author was transferred from the 8th Braun Cavalry Group in Santa Cruz to this new unit) under the command of Lt. Col. José R. Gallardo and with Maj. Miguel Ayoroa Montaño as battalion commander. The facilities of an old sugar refinery in La Esperanza, 80 kilometers north of the city of Santa Cruz, were rented, and the members of the special forces team (Green Berets), led by Maj. Ralph Shelton and made up of three captains and twelve sergeants—all specialists in combat against irregular forces—were sent there. Irregular-warfare training was also conducted in other units. All of these measures and activities were intended to produce results later.

Meanwhile, the Fourth Division was ordered to adopt measures to ensure the total isolation of the zone where the guerrillas were operating, in order to deny them the option of moving around, to prevent the arrival of new combatants, and to keep them away from sources of supply. Simultaneously the terrain could be adequately analyzed, the civilian population prepared and indoctrinated, and equipment gathered to ensure that operations would go favorably for the armed forces. The equipment included radios, vehicles, campaign rations, ammunition depots, and such.

General Operations Order 5/67, issued by the Fourth Division on April 16 at 6 P.M. reflected these measures. The mission for its companies was:

After reconnoitering the terrain, occupy its areas and organize defensively, gravitating as much as possible toward the possible routes of enemy advance with a view to mounting ambushes and raids, to prevent the enemy from entering areas where there are means of subsistence or to close off any enemy attempt to leave for other operations bases.

The order was for:

—Company E (Pacheco's command) to occupy the Ñancahuazú area.

—Company B (Moreira) to occupy the Yumau area.

—Company C (Oxa) to occupy the Tiraboy area.

—Company D (López) to occupy the Tatarenda area.

—Company A (Lafuente) to occupy Lagunillas and El Pincal.

—Company F (Arnez) to occupy Pirirenda.

—The Vargas group to occupy Overa Canyon. (See Map 3.)

This order, which became effective on the 17th at 6 P.M., coincided exactly with the movement begun by the guerrillas at dawn on the 16th, so that when the troops closed the circle occupying the principal routes of departure from the area, the guerrilla group was already east of the isolated zone, on the Iquira River, outwitting by coincidence the entire military effort.

So it was that the guerrilla force moved south with no difficulty. Over the next three days their contacts with campesinos were not very favorable. The first reaction was cold and timid, since the presence in those areas of army troops just days before had put them on their guard. This region, the border between Santa Cruz and Chuquisaca departments, is peopled by two different kinds of inhabitants: the Chaqueño, a plainsman, and the Valluno, the resident of the Cochabamba and Chuquisaca valleys, who is of Quechua orgin. They have formed a unique, productive society, and at the same time have developed a great affection for their lands and customs. It is therefore hard to establish good relations with them in a short time. On the other hand, they were more accustomed to the presence of the army, which in one form or another represented the most important authority in the region.

Nor was it easy to procure supplies, either for the guerrillas or for the regular forces. A campesino who has some ten goats or an equal number of pigs or four or five head of cattle will be loath to part with a unit, because he will feel deprived and it will take time to renew his herd, so for both sides the problem of obtaining meat was permanent. Although the prices paid by the guerrillas were highly favorable to them, the campesinos, unaccustomed to supply and demand, did not feel very comfortable in those transactions. Despite this, Che's group of thirty men obtained food in Bellavista, Ticucha, and Vides, up to the vicinity of Muyupampa.

There a curious thing happened. The campesinos were informing military authorities in Lagunillas of the presence of this group of guerrillas. This conflicted with the plan and the impression of the Camiri military command, which believed that the guerrillas were surrounded at Ñancahuazú, so they began to assume the existence of another group of guerrillas. While this information was being evaluated, the group continued its movement unhampered. In addition, the Fourth Division, having used up almost all of its forces in the siege operation, took its time to redirect some elements to engage this supposed new group that had appeared southeast of the zone identified as the guerrilla base. Too, information from the campesinos was not always accurate, and at the same time intelligence was coming in from other areas that also indicated the presence of guerrillas, a product of the collective hysteria that had sprung up as a result of the Ñancahuazú and Iripití ambushes.

With greater skill than the army's, a group of children led an Anglo-Chilean journalist, Andrew Roth, to the guerrillas. Roth had heard in Lagunillas that they were nearby and had arranged to be led there so as to see things first-hand. A free-lancer, he tried to interview the leader of the group, but he got only as far as Inti, who assumed that role in all public appearances. At Debray's suggestion, it was proposed to the Englishman that he help Debray and Bustos leave the operations zone under the guise of journalists. In the outskirts of Muyupampa, meanwhile, 2d Lt. Néstor Ruiz, with civilian members of the DIC and the National Public Security Guard, was patrolling and gathering information. Four detectives were detained, disarmed, and then freed by the insurgents. This action prompted Che to get rid of his visitors quickly and leave the town in search of a sheltered place to spend the day—April 20—considering that the army would take no time in showing up.

At dawn on that day the regular troops that arrived at Muyupampa, under the command of Captain Pacheco, detained Debray, Bustos, and Roth and transferred them to Camiri for questioning. Their attempt to get out unobserved had failed.

The inhabitants of the area, meanwhile, were alarmed at the possibility of being attacked by the guerrillas or being caught in the middle of an encounter between the regular forces and the insurgents. They were already organized for self-defense, and they resolved to send a mission to negotiate with the rebels in order to guarantee the security of the people and, above all, to try to mediate between the government and the guerrillas. Once again Inti assumed the role of guerrilla chief, and held a conversation with the delegation of residents. The subprefect of Muyupampa, Justino Curcuy Gonzales; the parish priest, Father Leo Schwartz; and the doctor Mario Cuéllar were the members of the Muyupampa delegation. At eleven in the morning this delegation left for Yango in a pickup truck. Then, walking along a path carrying a white flag, they found the guerrillas about 200 meters beyond the house they were using. Upon the arrival of the guerrilla chief, who was tall, thin, and drawn, like the others, he shook hands with them and the dialogue went as follows:

Father Schwartz: We have come as representatives of the people, who are alarmed by your presence here. They think that you want to come into town.

Guerrilla chief: Obviously our intention is to get to the town to load up with supplies. We suspended an attack because we saw armed civilians.

Father Schwartz: What do you want and what are your motives?

Inti: We have risen up because we are tired of bearing so much injustice. We want to change the current regime because we are the true expression of the poor.

Subprefect: Isn't there any way to end this fighting and reach a pacification? With this fighting the people have become alarmed and they are in mourning.

Inti: Please, don't talk about pacification. That term was invented by Barrientos and we're tired of hearing it.

Dr. Cuéllar: You don't have any sensitivity. I think that you are human beings like us and you have to have compassion for people who are going to die. You yourselves can't be happy with the route you have chosen. You're hungry, thirsty, and tired, when you could be at home in peace.

Inti: You're right, but you know that every prize entails a sacrifice and in every war innocent people are killed. We have taken up arms because we are certain of our ideals and that this is the only way to change the current state of affairs in the country. We have left everything behind. We have among us professionals, doctors, geologists, engineers. Our war will last not one but many years. It is very possible that the majority of us will die, but we are certain that better days will come for the country. We are Bolivians and we come from different parties—the PRIN, the MNR, the PC—and we include Christians and non-Christians. By the way, what happened to the three foreign journalists? They must be in jail.

Subprefect: Right, they're in jail, but they're being well treated.

Inti: They were prisoners of ours. We took them two days ago but we had to set them free because they were hampering our maneuvers. Also we did not let them take pictures.

Father Schwartz: Isn't there any way you can lay down your arms and leave the people alone, since the residents have no connection with you?

Inti: We need to obtain supplies and drugs. We don't want the drugs for ourselves but for the campesinos that are sick and the soldiers from the army that were wounded. We are going to pay the full cost of all of these items. You, Doctor, please, make a list of all that we need: dried beef, rice, beans, flour, lard, antibiotics, sulfa, and other drugs for first aid.

Subprefect: It's hard to get what you're asking for. We have to inform the military authorities about it and it's very unlikely that they will authorize it.

Inti: You have until 6 P.M. today to bring us what we have requested. This will be the meetingplace. If there is any action with the army you'd better not come, and if it's later than we have said, don't even think about showing up in this area.

The army, apprised of this interview, forbade the residents to have any future dealings with the guerrillas and sent an AT–6 squadron to bomb the area where the meeting had been held. The operation only left Ricardo slightly wounded, and did not have any major effect.

On April 22 an encounter occurred on the Coripote hacienda, where the guerrillas were getting ready to start back to Ticucha. They had captured a YPFB van, other vehicles with supplies, and any campesino who came into their vicinity—to prevent information from reaching the army—and had prepared food. The inexperience of Captain Pacheco, in command of the CIOS company, made this operation fail. After having evaded the guerrilla security detail, who had an ambush set up over the road, and having been alerted by the campesinos, the troops went across country until they were close to the hacienda and could observe the guerrillas' cooking-fires and the movement around them. Instead of surrounding the house and waiting until dawn, or at least blocking escape routes, the company began firing on the hacienda house and the fires from a distance of 100 meters or more. This created confusion among the guerrillas and prompted them to move out quickly along the road to Ticucha with the van and six horses they had requisitioned. They were not pursued by the troops, so they arrived at El Mesón at dawn.

On the following day, April 23, the army began to move its troops. Maj. Ives de Alarcón, G–3 (Plans and Operations Officer) of the Fourth Division, who was in Muyupampa, assumed command of all the troops located between Taperillas and Muyupampa on his own initiative in the absence of higher orders.[3] With Captain Pacheco's CIOS company and another company commanded by Capt. Félix Villaroel (President Barrientos's aide-de-camp, who had asked to stay in the operations zone) made up of twenty-four CITE parachutists, twenty-five students from the Noncommissioned Officers School and forty soldiers from the Bolivar Regiment, he arrived at Ticucha at 11 P.M. on the 24th. He learned from the campesinos that the guerrillas had passed through in the early morning on their way to El Mesón with a van and eight horses, and that their strength was between thirty and forty men (in fact, there were only twenty-seven by now). At 7 A.M. on April 25, troop movement began again, and they arrived at El Mesón gorge at 11 A.M., finding the remains of a recently abandoned encampment including warm ashes, baskets of bread, sardine cans, condensed milk, lard, and other supplies that could not be carried, and the disabled van, concealed with branches. Judging that the enemy was nearby, the troops continued their advance, adopting every security measure and putting up front the six police dogs that had been added to the unit, with their respective police trainers.

At 11:25 the dog "Storm" found a trail and rushed in pursuit, followed by his trainer and a civilian guide. They advanced several meters ahead of the vanguard led by 2d Lt. Freddy Balderrama.

The guerrillas were aware of the troops' advance, and they quickly set up an ambush covering a wide stretch of the gorge with about twenty men.[4] Che fired the first shot, surprised by the appearance of the police dog. He missed, but he did set off an exchange of gunfire that killed the dog, the policeman, and the civilian guide but prevented the troops from entering into the area chosen for the ambush. The Villaroel company held the line on the guerrillas while the CIOS company tried to maneuver on the left flank in order to surround them. This action was ineffective because of the unevenness of the terrain and the dense vegetation. The guerrilla group had enough time to fall back in order.

As a result of Storm's sudden attack and the exchange of considerable fire, one guerrilla was gravely wounded and, although he was rescued by his companions, died within a few minutes, leaving an irreparable loss to Che and his men. It was Rolando, who in leading the Ñancahuazú and Iripití ambushes had shown clear signs of tactical judgment and initiative. His spirit of solidarity also came to the fore when he plunged into the waters of the Grande River to try to rescue Benjamín on the reconnaissance journey and when he went ahead alone to the encampment to bring supplies to the main body, which was in a state of exhaustion on the banks of the river. Known to Che since he was a child, Rolando had been his courier in the Sierra Maestra operations, and his death deeply affected the guerrilla chief, who considered the day's operation a failure.

Worn out by the long pursuit, the regular troops stopped to await orders from the Fourth Division, which in view of the situation reported, decided to adopt a new plan, since the presence of the guerrilla group outside the encirclement zone had been confirmed.

One guerrilla had not rejoined the main body after the flight from the Coripote hacienda: Loro, who with his characteristic lack of discipline had not followed instructions and wished to get out of the operations zone, taking advantage of his Bolivian nationality. He headed south toward the vicinity of Taperillas, where he took a campesino's clothes, leaving behind his olive drab uniform and remaining hidden in the area.

On the night of April 27, Sgt. Guillermo Tórrez Martinez and Pvt. Miguel Espada, of the 2d Infantry Regiment, which was garrisoned as a reserve force in this area, were walking on the road conversing, without taking precautions, on their way to a small house nearby. They were surprised by Loro, who left them dead with a burst of automatic fire. He continued to escape in the direction of Monteagudo, secretly followed by a campesino, while others went with the information to Lagunillas. A detail of the CITE, with Maj. Alarcón and Captain Villaroel, went off quickly in pursuit of what was supposed to be a group of guerrillas, wounding and capturing Loro near Monteagudo on the 29th. Loro admitted having killed the sergeant and the soldier in self-defense when they tried to arrest him. He was taken to the Camiri hospital, and his fate is still unknown at the present time. He was operated on at the oil company hospital, and was recovering fully until May 30, when the commander of the Fourth Division, Colonel Rocha, officially reported that the guerrilla, taking advantage of the carelessness of security personnel and aided by outside accomplices, had escaped from the hospital and was presumably headed for the border with Paraguay or Argentina.

Later, stories were circulated to the effect that he had been executed by the army or thrown out of a helicopter alive into the woods, but none of these stories has been corroborated to date. What remains clear is that in heading for Monteagudo in civilian clothing taken from a campesino, Loro was trying to get away from the guerrillas and escape the operations zone.

After these encounters with the troops, the guerrillas, weakened and confused, tried to get out of the difficult terrain where they had sought refuge and to arrive, by way of the heights parallel to the Ñancahuazú River, at Camp II, where they could both find supplies and rest for some days. The army's maneuver and the pressure it had brought to bear had forced the main group to move in a northwesterly direction, far from the area where they could find Joaquín's group. The lack of paths in all the elevated areas slowed them down and tired them out. The delay in reaching their destination exhausted their supplies. At last, on May 7, they managed to reach the camp, finding only a few tins of milk for breakfast. This led Che to send a patrol to the field planted at the tin-roof house. Che was worried about being isolated both from the population and from any support structure. The lack of contact with Joaquín was also a source of concern, since this separation greatly weakened the guerrilla force.

In another vein, given the failure to develop a campesino base, since their contacts with area inhabitants had been futile, Che expressed the opinion that an adequate strategy of terror could at least neutralize the majority, who up until then had not hesitated to give information to the army.[5]

What Che did not know is that the two civilian losses that had occurred up to then had provoked a strong reaction against him, due to a simple fact: the victims were related. In fact, Epifanio Vergas, who had died at the Ñancahuazú ambush, was the stepson of Señor N. Rodas, a resident of the Bella Vista area, while Luis Beltrán Rodas, who died at El Mesón, was also a relative—his grandson. Rodas's family was spread all over the Muyupampa region, so that the death of the two civilian guides set a good share of the population of the area against the guerrillas. Che's visit to Rodas to express his sorrow for the death of Vargas[6] loses all value when one considers that four days later they killed the grandson, whose funeral at Muyupampa caused great public dismay.

Meanwhile, in the military camp, the intelligence systems only then began to understand the problem, from the information obtained from Debray, Bustos, and Loro. When it was discovered that the group operating in Muyupampa was from Ñancahuazú, the operations plan was modified to keep the area under control. Errors were made, such as in the communiqué about the El Mesón action, where the dead guerrilla was identified as Rubio (who had fallen in Iripití) instead of Rolando, but in general a clearer picture of the situation was emerging.

The press presented a touchy problem. With the arrest of Debray and Bustos, the guerrilla war had attracted world attention. Although nothing had been said yet about the presence of Che, the events brought a large number of journalists to the operations zone. Their dispatches, not always accurate, distorted the truth or in some cases provided information to the guerrillas, given the lack of experience of some military leaders in handling press releases or the desire of others for renown.

This prompted the commander of the Fourth Division, with the knowledge of the high command, to declare press censorship in his area of jurisdiction. This measure immediately provoked the reaction of the Press Workers' Syndicate, which, after an interview with the president of the republic and the commander-in-chief, obtained authorization to cover the story with some freedom.

This situation was reflected in the communiqué of April 26, which besides giving information about the clash at El Mesón, clarified relations with the press. The communiqué stated:

1. Units of the armed forces clashed again with red groups that entered into Vaca Guzmán (Muyupampa) in the area called El Mesón.

2. As a result of these actions we suffered two losses, one of them a civilian guide and the other a member of the National Public Security Guard who was leading a police dog.

3. The subversives left two dead in the field, one of whom known by the nickname of Rubio, and understood to be a Cuban national. The other, possibly Bolivian, has not been identified. It was also learned that they had several wounded.

4. In the action six horses that had been stolen in the Vaca Guzmán area were recovered.

5. The Air Force attacked a red detail in the Itimirí area without clear results.

6. The military authority in Camiri stated that it had not declared press censorship, but rather had asked for the credentials of whoever was engaging in journalism in the area, in view of the large number of persons who are identifying themselves as journalists in Camiri and other sites of subversive activity. Some red prisoners captured in action are trying to conceal their antinational activity, shielding themselves in the guise of reporters.

7. Today the different media have been informed that only those press and radio journalists who present their credentials will be given unrestricted access to the sources of information.

8. The Commander-in-Chief's office regrets that the work of the press has been hampered when very justified measures have had to be taken against unscrupulous individuals who have attempted to pass for something they are not, under the protection of the freedom of the press that reigns in the country.

Evidence that the two guerrilla groups had not yet been able to reunite was favorably received, and the units in the area (approximately seven companies) were ordered to intensify their patrols so as to hold the initiative. In these circumstances, unaware of the arrival of Che's group in Ñancahuazú, the armed forces claimed in a press release that they had broken down the guerrillas' supply system, stressing that the lack of food, medicine, and ammunition due to the absence of contacts outside the military zone made the insurgents' situation difficult.

The campesinos' reaction to the armed forces was also considered positive, as could be personally verified by the journalists accompanying President Barrientos on an inspection tour of military posts in the war zone. The fact that civilian deaths had occurred (the guides were from the region), along with attacks and burglaries in the settlements, made a deep impression on the residents, who gave signs of being ready to defend themselves, or at least to denounce the guerrillas' actions to the military authorities.

Despite these favorable aspects, the armed forces felt that they still needed time to replace the troops operating in the region with others from tropical garrisons, better adapted to the geographic area of the conflict. They also needed to improve their supply of arms, means of communication, and transport, as well as the systems of evacuation for the wounded and sick if the guerrilla problem was to be eliminated.

DEBRAY AND BUSTOS

The attempt by Debray and Bustos to escape from the operations area without being noticed, or at least to try to mix with the journalists and the onlookers so as not to fall into the army's hands, failed when they were arrested together with Roth at 5:30 in the morning, which is to say a little over an hour after leaving Che, and sent to Camiri for questioning.

Although at first Debray's status as journalist was apparently accepted, Bustos's situation was jeopardized because his documentation could not withstand the least scrutiny. Debray, however, having his passport in his own name and having been in Bolivia before, could disguise his position as a participant. The first thing that was noticed was that his stay was illegal, since he had not entered the country in February by normal means, but instead through the help of the underground network set up by Tania.

The first public notice about Debray appeared in the press on April 23. He was said to have died in an encounter with the army. This caused a stir in the international press, which immediately linked the presumed dead man with Fidel Castro, noting their great friendship and closeness. To some extent because of this press reaction, the commander of the Fourth Division tried to set up a kind of press censorship that was quickly countermanded at higher levels, as has been explained. Speculation over the fate suffered by the French intellectual and his companions did not in any case let up.

At the very end of April, General Ovando admitted publicly that Debray, Bustos, and Roth had been detained, and he announced that their presumed links with the guerrilla movement were being investigated. He refused any possibility of interviews with those arrested, who were at the time being held incommunicado and questioned.

After several days in Camiri, to avoid the constant harassment from the press, the detainees were transferred to La Esperanza, where the Ranger battalion was training, so that they would be more isolated. At no time were North American personnel authorized to have contact with them. Their security was entrusted to intelligence personnel especially assigned to this task.

The interrogation of the detainees, which lasted more than a month, provided the intelligence service with new insight. In the case of Debray, his extremely lengthy declarations allowed the army to obtain the following information[7]:

—Debray was in contact with Fidel Castro in December 1966 in Havana. Castro informed him of the existence of a guerrilla operation in Bolivia and that it was led by Che.

—Debray would have been able to let the public know that the guerrillas were there, since they had been set up since the end of November.

—Debray entered the country illegally from Chile in mid-February.

—After getting in touch with Tania in La Paz, he traveled by bus with her and Bustos, whom he had met at the same time, to Cochabamba and Sucre, and from there by taxi to Camiri, where Tania, after a meeting with Coco, took them in her jeep to the tin-roof house. They arrived at the encampment in the evening of March 6 and found about twenty men there, the most important of whom were Bolivians and Cubans.

—He had to wait until March 20 to meet with Che, who was returning with another group of men from a reconnaissance trip to the north in the direction of the Grande River.

—The guerrillas had several encampments. Debray indicated the location of the central camp, the encampment at El Oso, and other lesser encampments, where they hid arms and ammunition captured from the army, along with their supplies, in caves.

—The purpose of his visit was to interview Che Guevara. This occurred on March 22 and 23, and the following topics were covered:

1. Che's arrival in Bolivia in November and how he came in disguised, bald, beardless, and with false documents.

2. His intention to stay in Ñancahuazú until he achieved victory or died.

3. There was an exchange of ideas on the theory of guerrilla warfare and the different view each had of its prospects and its dimensions. These differences essentially focused on bases (whether they should be fixed or mobile), the number of fronts (one or multiple), etc.

4. Che explained his project, which was to be continental in scope once certain aspects were tightened up. It was necessary to have a center for the coordination of efforts. The entire action would make North American armed intervention inevitable.

5. How the choice of Bolivia had been imposed on him, since Che felt that Peru would have been better, although possibilities for expansion out of Bolivia into Peru, Argentina, and Paraguay existed. Structures for that had not yet been set up, but the guerrilla chief thought that when his presence in Ñancahuazú was known, other movements would rise up to start the struggle. He would establish communication with them later.

6. The guerrilla foco had lost almost all opportunity of contact beyond the area. It was in a critical situation with regard to food, although it had plenty of money to purchase it.

7. Because of the desertion of two guerrillas from the group led by Moisés Guevara, a serious dispute arose between the latter and Inti, who accused him of bringing in cowards and traitors and blamed him for anything that might happen as a result.

8. Debray did not participate in the Ñancahuazú and Iripití actions, which were undertaken by a small group led by a Cuban. The guerrillas wanted to protect Debray.

9. Debray wished to take advantage of Roth's contacts with the authorities and area residents so as to leave the area.

10. Debray thought that the survival of the guerrilla movement depended on the strategic moves of the army, the political breakdown of the country, the cooperation of bordering nations through their representatives, and the active solidarity of leftist elements in the country.

These long, detailed statements, complemented by those obtained from Bustos, who also cooperated by making drawings of the principal guerrillas, gave the intelligence service a nearly complete picture of the situation and allowed it to determine more precisely the real possibilities that the guerrilla movement had. It was judged necessary to keep the area encircled so as to prevent the guerrilla group from contacts with the outside and also to prevent new members from joining them.

Meanwhile, pressure was being exerted on the government to reveal the situation of the prisoners. Messages interceding for them began to arrive from all over, provoking a reaction from President Barrientos, who accused Debray and Bustos of being participants in the action that was spreading death in Bolivia. He said that they deserved the maximum sentence and asserted that he was ready to ask Congress to restore the death penalty.

A campaign to reject the guerrilla movement and its followers was also mounted in other sectors. Its high point, in addition to several demonstrations and marches in the major cities, was an interview with the president of the republic by the widows and family of officers, noncommissioned officers, and soldiers fallen in Ñancahuazú and Iripití, at which time they submitted a letter to him demanding the maximum penalty for the members of the guerrilla group. Its text read:

Your Excellency:

We who are writing to you, Mr. President, embody the anguish, mourning, and grief caused by criminal adventurists who, trampling on our territory, killed Bolivian citizens who were fulfilling their obligation as such.

The so-called guerrilla war that has appeared in our country is not the product of spontaneous generation, but instead had its origin and takes its momentum in a conspiracy that is known to all. This action of banditry and crime in Bolivia therefore had its ringleaders and intellectual authors. This is so obviously true that the regular forces of our army took prisoners from among the ranks of those who desire our liberation.

Among the assassins of our husbands and sons was Régis Debray, whose unrealistic bent is exposed, for one thing, in his pamphlet *Revolution in the Revolution.* To that must be added without question the application of his ideas: the death of twenty-five men who, before leaving their remains in the cowardly ambush, were the flesh and blood of the struggle of Bolivians for progress.

Mrs. Debray has arrived in our country. She wishes to have her son back and has asked and received the support of intellectual and political groups who tailor their phrases of solidarity to the purposes of propaganda.

If each and every one of those who cry for clemency and freedom for Debray felt in their own flesh the drama that is eating away at us, they would see how far out of bounds they are and how false their pose is. God grant that neither that intellectual nor that politician has to go through such a time of pain and suffering.

Mrs. Debray wants her son back. We say to her that she lost him long ago, even before he arrived in Bolivia. She lost him when he distanced himself from God and his mother to join the pack of criminals without God, without homes, without a flag. She lost him when he was the instigator of cowardly assassinations, when he became the theorist of cowardly slaughters in Venezuela, Peru, and Bolivia.

Now the mother of the idealistic guerrilla should resign herself and realize that her son no longer belongs to her. He will be put before a court that will judge his exploits as a mass murderer.

Our position is uncompromising. We demand that the idealistic guerrilla and assassin Debray be judged by military justice and that he be condemned to the maximum penalty, since his status as a foreigner who has taken up arms against the regular army of our country deprives him of the application of the benefits of our political constitution.

We demand that neither you, Mr. President, nor any civilian or military authority, promote a wave of sympathy that would benefit her political positions and those of her son. She knows the gravity of her son's crimes, and therefore cannot claim justice or freedom.

We ask for the solidarity of the comrades of the officers and soldiers killed in the guerrillas' action in helping us in our fight for liberty and justice in Bolivia. They should act with the conscience of our people and eradicate from the top down and forever the criminals who trampled on our territory.

We ask the national press not to get involved in the premeditated action of the guerrillas' saviors. Would the press be free as it is now, if the Castro-communists imposed their philosophy after their victory through armed violence?

We wish to say to the conscience of the nation and the world that no one, nothing, will silence us. Our desire for justice cannot be bought with money nor influenced by lyrical declarations that try to impose a false direction on our thinking.

The High Military Commanders, thank God, are filled with a high sense of national solidarity, and we know that they will only act with true severity and that benevolence toward criminals will not have any place in the determination of their acts of justice.

We are alert in our fight, stronger than ever, and more determined that any adventurer who steps on Bolivian soil will receive the penalty of justice commensurate with his actions.

With this purpose we express to you, Mr. President, the assurance of our highest esteem.

Julia S. de Amézaga. Prisca C. de Cornejo. Sergio Cornejo. Rosario V. (Widow of) Ayala. Mirna G. (Widow of) Saavedra. Victoria de Soria Galvarro. Yolanda Saavedra de Baluarte. Dr. Primo Saavedra. Ana I. de Amézaga. Celestina de Sanabria. Delia Cornejo. Colonel Rogelio Ayala and Rosaira de Márquez.

The detainees' situation took a new turn when Dr. Flores Torrico agreed to take responsibility for the defense of Debray, despite the threats made against him. In the presence of Debray, who arrived in the midst of a real media event, Dr. Flores Torrico presented a writ of habeas corpus before the Superior Court of the La Paz District against the commander-in-chief of the armed forces and the commander of the army. The court, after due deliberation and in possession of the evidence shown by the armed forces that they were submitting the detainees to the procedures of military justice, threw out the writ, fully validating the military decision to try them before the military court. That decision was expressed in the following document:

Initial Act of Indictment. May 22, 1967. In view of: The prosecution order that runs to 27 pages, record submitted by the Army Command and the summons of the Military Prosecutor which precedes, Criminal Indictment is filed against the aforementioned Salustio Choque Choque, Vicente Rocabado, Pastor Quinteros, Régis Jules Debray, Carlos Alberto Bustos, George Andrew Roth, Carlos Alberto Aidar, Jorge Vásquez Viaña, and Ventura Pomar Fernández, all of whom may turn out to be authors, co-authors, accomplices, and accessories after the fact to the crimes reported, which are defined and penalized by Articles 12, 15, 16, 17, 103, 104, 110, 111, 257, 258, 259, 260, 261, 262, and 296 of the Common Penal Code and Article 78 of the Law of Judicial Organization and Military Competence, in connection with Article 257 of the Military Code and Articles 8 and 24 of the Political Constitution of the State, for the effect of which the legal writs are issued.

Section One: The members of the court will be assembled in what is designated as the emergency zone with the object of proceeding to the deposition of the accused, the investigation of the facts will be undertaken, and the Minister of National Defense consulted so that adequate resources are supplied.

Section Two: In accord with the Prosecutor's Summons, since the guerrilla war is in full activity, to safeguard against the threat to security and public order, discretion is ordered in the investigation of the present case.

The defense lawyer expressed his agreement with this determination, recognizing that at last a decision had been made about how to proceed, allowing him to organize his work in complete freedom.

Another important document relating to the pressures in the Debray situation is President Barrientos's letter in answer to the President of France, Charles De Gaulle, on this subject. Although the communication from the French chief of state was not made public, his Bolivian counterpart's answer received a great deal of publicity. It stated:

Mr. President:

In response to your note of May 5 which I have just received, I must tell you that the fate of the French citizen Régis Debray depends entirely on Bolivian justice.

It is possible that there in France, and in your generous opinion, he may be considered a young and brilliant university student.

Unfortunately here, in Bolivia, we know him only as a meddling subversive gravely implicated in the assassination of twenty-seven soldiers, civilians, and officers of our armed forces, and as a theoretician of violence aimed at destroying institutional order.

The sins of youth cannot serve as a protective veil to lessen outrages committed against humanity, against civil society, and against the life and safety of the citizens of a peaceful population like the Bolivians, who live devoted to their democratic way of life and their internal development, seeking with difficulty to overcome obstacles and remnants of the unjust past that organized bands and mercenaries now persist in trying to make more acute, following orders and interests alien to the life and interest of the Bolivian people.

The justice of my government responds with Christian civilization to the law of bullets, treason, bribery, and crime with which the intruders have challenged the sovereign will of Bolivia, paralyzed development projects, and cut off precious lives, sowing grief, anguish, uneasiness, and rightful indignation.

I think that this unfortunate event will not disturb the good relations between our two nations, and I ask you to admit that if for Your Excellency the first priority is France and the French people, my prime duty is Bolivia and the Bolivians.

Mr. President, please accept the expression of my highest and most cordial esteem.

René Barrientos Ortuño

Against this background, and given the chain of events in the operations zone, the case of the detainees faded from view while all the apparatus of military justice was being prepared so that the trial could be held.

JOAQUÍN'S GROUP (See Map 4)

Since April 17, Joaquín and the rear guard had been separated from the main group, causing Che concern and considerably weakening the total strength of the guerrilla movement. The initial rear guard group, composed of eight men—Joaquín, Marcos, Braulio, Pedro, Polo, Walter, Víctor, and Ernesto—was increased before the trip to Muyupampa with the members of the Moisés Guevara group, who had shown little skill and were considered dead weight, to be dismissed when the situation permitted. They were Eusebio, Chingolo, Paco, and Pepe. When the trip began, Alejandro, Tania, and Moisés Guevara also stayed behind with Joaquín because they were ill, and Negro and Serapio remained as security men. With a total of seventeen combatants, Joaquín, following his orders, remained hidden in the area of Iquira Canyon, outside of the isolation zone set up by the army. Movement was difficult because of the sick and the lack of supplies.

When the time passed for the reunion, the commander of the rear guard began to be concerned. The lack of news did not bode well. Since their position had become difficult because of the constant military activity in the area—a consequence of the pursuit of Che's group after the Coripote and El Mesón actions—both groups were forced to head north toward the Iquira River, crossing each other's paths without meeting.

The presence of troops in Ticucha, Bellavista, Iquira, and Yuqui forced Joaquín to keep his men hidden, assigning pairs to simultaneously look for the trail of the main group and find supplies, which they robbed from the fields, since they were too afraid of being denounced to make contact with the campesinos. The order to "stay in the area at all cost without making any frontal attacks" limited their possibilities of action even further, and as the days went on, everybody grew more uneasy, realizing that severe difficulties must be preventing the reunion of the groups and, above all, that they did not have a specific rallying point.

After a month had gone by in this way, the first incident occurred. Pepe deserted, taking advantage of security negligence. When he headed for the populated area, he was captured by the army in Ití and was killed trying to escape (May 24). One week later, on June 3, Marcos and Víctor, who were on reconnaissance mission, were ambushed by a group of civilians, residents of Ticucha and the surrounding area. They had been organized by the army to participate in operations under the command of 2d Lt. Néstor Ruiz. When Marcos and Víctor refused to surrender, they were killed in combat.

With these losses, Joaquín's group, weakened and disoriented, changed location again, always circling around Iquira Canyon, looking for supplies in the small settlements of the region but avoiding contact with the campesinos so they would not be discovered. The lack of news from the main group made their situation very difficult.

On July 8, a CIOS company that was making a search in the Iquira Canyon area had a brief encounter with Joaquín's security detail, made up of Alejandro and Polo. The two guerrillas had to fall back after an exchange of fire. They were pursued by the troops, who in the afternoon found a series of positions constructed in the Peña Colorada area facing Monte Dorado and on the left bank of the Ñancahuazú River. They had been abandoned by the guerrillas, who had escaped toward the north.

On the next day, another detail that was combing the area, a CITE section, made contact with the group in the central part of Iquira Canyon, engaging in a fifteen-minute combat that caused the death of Serapio and the hasty retreat of the rest of the group, which ran into the heights to avoid pursuit.[8] In their withdrawal the 30–caliber machine gun operated by Pedro played a significant role in slowing the advance of the troops and thus permitting the rest of the group to get away. They managed to escape the danger, although they left part of their equipment, which fell into the hands of the army.

One anecdote came out of Serapio's death. When he fell, he was initially recovered by his companions. The advance of the troops forced the guerrillas to abandon the body, which was found without the beard observed on it when it fell. This led to the belief that since Serapio was beardless, he wore a false beard so as to fit in with the rest of the insurgents.

After these encounters, facing intense activity in the area (as part of the Fourth Division's Cynthia Plan), Joaquín made the decision to move off to the south, in an attempt to find some trace of the main group and some location that would allow his people to rest. They arrived in this way at the house of Zoilo Uzeda in La Tapera, but news of them was obtained by the army in a few hours. Oxa Company was sent in pursuit. Confirming that they had already left Uzeda's house, this unit followed them a distance of 10 kilometers to the south, making contact on July 21 at 8:30 A.M. The group fled in disorder but sustained no losses. Taking advantage of the confusion of combat, Chingolo and Eusebio split off from the group with the intention of abandoning the area on their own. They were captured on the 23rd, 2 kilometers north of Monteagudo, by Maj. Rubén Sánchez, and transferred to Lagunillas for questioning. Their statements made it possible to learn in detail the situation of Joaquín's group and to readjust the deployment of troops to attempt to capture them.

Despite the intense movement of the existing units in the area, however, several days passed before any new, accurate information could be obtained. On August 9, in combined action with Oxa Company of the Campos Regiment, B Company of the Third Division, and 2d Lt. Néstor Ruiz's group of Ticuchans, the guerrilla group was located in the Inao region, east of Taperillas. In this action Pedro fell, together with the 30–caliber machine gun that he had used since they had left the encampment and that on several occasions had been a deciding factor in slowing down the advance of the troops. That was the last contact of Joaquín's group with troops of the Fourth Division. Reduced to nine men and one woman, they abandoned the area, trying to break the army encirclement, only to be wiped out at Vado del Yeso some days later in an operation that will be described later.

Joaquín's insistence on remaining in the area in obedience to Che's order, when Che himself had left the zone, was to be the cause of Joaquín's destruction.

NOTES

1. Che's diary, entry for March 28.
2. Che's diary, entry for April 16.
3. Fourth division, General Operations Report 1/67.
4. Che's diary, entry for April 25.
5. Che's diary, summary for the month of April.
6. Che's diary, entry for April 21.
7. Statements by Régis Debray to the Second Department of the Army, April 1967.
8. Braulio's diary (in *The Complete Bolivian Diaries of Che Guevara and Other Captured Documents*), entry for July 9.

Above, army troops resting in Lagunillas before beginning operations. *Below*, evacuating a wounded soldier in Iripití.

Above, army patrol in Ñancahuazú Canyon. *Below*, transporting soldiers killed in the Iripití ambush, one of the big guerrilla victories.

Above, Régis Debray, the only European guerrilla, during his trial at Camiri. *Below,* Ciro Bustos in his cell.

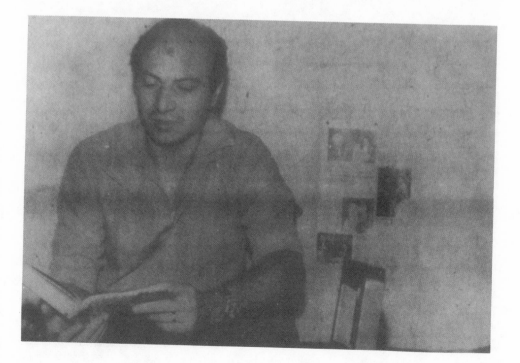

Above, Captain José F. Rico Toro with soldiers from Trinidad Company in the vicinity of Morocco. *Below,* the first guerrilla deserters, Eusebio and Chingolo, after their capture.

Above, the commander of the army, General David La Fuente, congratulating the troops who participated at Vado del Yeso. *Below,* Adolfo Siles, Vice-President of the Government, congratulating Honorato Rojas, who led the guerrillas into the army ambush at Vado del Yeso.

León being interrogated by members of the army intelligence after his capture.

Chapter 9

MOVING NORTH*

Until the end of April, the guerrilla band had not been able to introduce itself to the public in order to explain the reasons for its campaign, although two communiqués were drafted by the Che and his general staff.[1] The first, prepared after the Ñancahuazú ambush and handed to Major Sánchez at Iripití for release to the press, did not arrive because it was confiscated by the military authorities. The second, carried by Debray, suffered the same fate. Due to a leak from the military offices themselves in Cochabamba, however, where a copy had been sent for analysis, a press organ in that city, *Prensa Libre*, put together by an association of independent journalists, gained access to the first document and published it with much fanfare on May 1. That publication, undoubtedly a victory for the press, informed the country of the existence of the National Liberation Army (ELN). It provoked a reaction from military authorities who immediately ordered the prosecution of the editor, Carlos Beccar Gómez, accusing him of being a guerrilla liaison and demanding that he reveal how he had obtained the document. When Beccar refused to name his sources, shielding himself behind the press law, an arrest order was issued, and the procedure was speeded up in the courts. The militant support of all print and radio journalists in Cochabamba and other cities, however, diluted the legal action and prevented the announced arrest from being made. The publication of Communiqué 1 was the only instance when the guerrillas were able to state their position to the country. The text of this communiqué reads:

---

*See map 5, page 272.

TO THE BOLIVIAN PEOPLE: REVOLUTIONARY
TRUTH AGAINST REACTIONARY LIES

The group of usurping gorillas, after assassinating workers and setting the stage for the total surrender of our wealth to North American imperialism, mocked the people with an electoral farce.[2] Now that the hour of truth has come and the people have risen up in arms meeting armed usurpation with armed struggle, that group seeks to carry on its campaign of lies.

Early on the morning of March 23, forces of the Fourth Division based in Camiri numbering approximately thirty-five men under the command of Maj. Hernán Plata Ríos, entered guerrilla territory along the Ñancahuazú River bed. The entire group fell into an ambush set by our forces. As a result of the action, twenty-five weapons of all types fell to us, including three 60–mm mortars with their supply of shells, a good deal of ordnance, and equipment. Enemy casualties numbered seven dead, among them a lieutenant, and fourteen prisoners, five of whom were wounded in the clash and were treated by our medical service as efficiently as our means permit. All the prisoners were freed, after we had explained the ideals of our movement to them.

The casualty list is as follows:

Dead: Pedro Romero, Rubén Amézaga, Juan Alvarado, Cecilio Márquez, Amador Almazán, Santiago Gallardo, and the informer and army guide named Vargas.

Prisoners: Maj. Hernán Plata Ríos, Capt. Eugenio Silva, Pvts. Edgar Torrico Panozo, Lidio Machicado Toledo, Gabriel Durán Escóbar, Armando Martínez Sánchez, Felipe Bravo Siles, Juan Ramón Martínez, Leoncio Espinoza Posada, Miguel Ribero, Eleutero Sánchez, Adalberto Martínez, Eduardo Ribera, and Guido Terceros. The latter five were wounded.

In making public the first action of the war we wish to make clear what the guidelines of our army will be:

Revolutionary truth: our deeds showed that our words were correct. We regret the innocent blood shed by the fallen soldiers, but peaceful roads are not made with mortars and machine guns, as the puppets with decorated uniforms assert. There has not been nor will there be a single campesino who can complain about the way we have treated him or about our way of obtaining supplies, except for those who betraying their class, volunteer to serve as guides or informers.

Hostilities are under way. In future communiqués we will expound our revolutionary position clearly; today we issue a call to workers, campesinos, intellectuals, all those who feel that the time has come to meet violence with violence and to rescue a country sold piecemeal to Yankee monopolies and to raise the standard of living of our people, who grow hungrier every day.

BOLIVIAN LIBERATION ARMY

Communiqué 2, which was not circulated, deals with the outcome of the successive ambushes at Iripití. Several last names are changed or incorrect in this communiqué. Notable in the document, in keeping with Che's theory, is the attempt to implicate the North American army in this campaign and to undermine the military structure with instructions for soldiers. Its complete text reads:

On the morning of 4/10/67 an enemy patrol led by Lt. Luis Saavedra Arambel and made up chiefly of CITE soldiers fell into an ambush. In the encounter the officer mentioned and Pvts. Ángel Flores and Zenón Prada Mendieta fell, and the guide Ignacio Husarima from Boquerón Regiment was wounded and taken prisoner together with five other soldiers and a noncommissioned officer. Four soldiers managed to escape, taking the news to Maj. Sánchez Castro's company base. Reinforced by sixty men from a nearby unit, he came to the aid of his companions and was surprised by another ambush that cost the life of Lt. Hugo Ayala, the noncommissioned officer Raúl Camejo, and Pvts. José Vijabriel, Marcelo Maldonado, Jaime Sanabria, and two more whom we did not identify.

In this action Pvts. Armando Quiroga, Alberto Carvajal, Fredy Alove, Justo Cervantes, and Bernabé Mandejara were wounded and taken prisoner together with the commander of the company, Maj. Rubén Sánchez Castro and sixteen other soldiers.

Following ELN practice, we healed the wounded with our meager resources and we freed all the prisoners after explaining the objectives of our revolutionary struggle to them.

The losses of the enemy army amounted to: ten dead, among them two lieutenants, and thirty prisoners, including Maj. Sánchez Castro, of whom six were wounded. The war booty is proportional to enemy casualties, and includes a 60–mm mortar, automatic rifles, M–1 rifles and carbines, and submachine guns—all the arms with their ammunition.

On our side we have had to mourn one casualty. The difference of losses is understandable, taking into account the fact that in each combat we have chosen the time and place to start, and that the leaders of the Bolivian army are sending green recruits, almost children, to the slaughter, while they invent dispatches in La Paz and then beat their breast at demagogic funeral services, concealing the fact that they are the ones who are really to blame for the blood that is flowing in Bolivia. Now they have stripped off their mask and have begun to call in North American "advisors." That was the way the Vietnam War began—a war that is bleeding that heroic people and is jeopardizing world peace.

We don't know how many "advisors" they will send in against us (we will know how to stand up to them), but we wish to alert the people to the dangers of that line of action initiated by the servile military.

We make an appeal to young recruits to observe the following instructions: when combat begins, throw your weapon aside and raise your hands over your head, standing still at the place where you have been surprised by gunfire; never proceed to the front of the column in marches that enter into combat zones; force the officers—they who are making you fight—to occupy that extremely dangerous position. We will always fire upon the vanguard, with intent to kill. No matter how much it pains us to see the blood of innocent recruits flow, it is an imperious necessity of the war.

NATIONAL LIBERATION ARMY OF BOLIVIA

BACK IN THE ENCAMPMENT

When Che and his companions arrived starving and fatigued at the Central Camp on May 7 after eluding the military checkpoints spread out over the area, they turned to the need to renew their supplies. The stock left at the encampment, a mere eight tins of milk, provided only the meagerest breakfast, although even that was fortifying after the privations they had gone through. To try to gather some supplies, a detail was sent to the tin-roof house to harvest corn from the field there. It returned without supplies and with the news that the property was now a military post and all the corn had been harvested. To secure their stay in the encampment, a patrol was sent under Pacho's command to set up an ambush in case the troops advanced, while the rest filled their bottles with pork lard from a remaining can to prepare a meal, because it was the only food left.

Two soldiers from the Arnez company, garrisoned at Overa Canyon, went unarmed unknown to their commander, along the Ñancahuazú River toward the tin-roof house with the intention of picking corn, with no clear idea of the situation. When they went by in front of Pacho, he tried to stop them and when they reacted, he fired, wounding both slightly and capturing them.[3]

The result of this action was reflected in Communiqué 3, which like the others was not circulated. Notable in this document is the guerrillas' concern over the content of the official communiqués, which with exaggerations and imprecision showed a different picture from what was really happening in the operations zone. Also a threat was laid down to the regular forces, with the intention of slowing down their activity. The text of the communiqué reads:

On May 8, in the Ñancahuazú guerrilla zone, troops from a mixed company under the command of 2d Lt. Henry Laredo were ambushed. In the action said officer and students Ramón Arroyo Flores and Luis Peláez from the Noncommissioned Officers School were killed, and the following soldiers were taken prisoner:

José Camacho, Bolivar Reg.

Néstor Cuentas, Bolivar Reg.

Waldo Veizaga, NCO School.

Hugo Soto Lora, NCO School

Max Torres León, NCO School

Róger Rojas Toledo, Braun Reg.

Néstor Sánchez Cuéllar, Braun Reg.

The last two were wounded when they did not answer the command to halt upon being intercepted in a previous operation. As always, they were freed after the scope and purposes of our struggle were explained to them. Seven M–1 carbines and four Mauser rifles were captured. Our forces were unharmed.

The repressive army issues frequent communiqués announcing guerrilla deaths; blending some truth about their admitted casualties with fairy tales about our own, and, desperate in their impotence, resorting to lies or abusing journalists (who, because of their ideological background, are natural adversaries of the regime), attributing to the journalists all the troubles that are plaguing them.

We state categorically that the Bolivian ELN is the only responsible party for the armed struggle in which it is leading the people, and which can only end with definitive victory, at which time we will require payment for all the crimes committed in the course of the war, independently of the reprisals that the command of our army may judge necessary for any barbarities committed by the repressive forces.

NATIONAL LIBERATION ARMY OF BOLIVIA

Two hours later, two other soldiers armed with M–1 carbines were also captured, and the guerrillas were able to obtain information about the presence and the intentions of troops in the area. Meanwhile a soldier who managed to escape reported what had happened to Lieutenant Arnez, who sent a section patrol to confirm the insurgents' presence in the encampment. The patrol advanced cautiously and managed to enter into the guerrilla deployment, initiating a short combat that ended when the commander of the patrol, 2d Lt. Henry Laredo Arce, fell dead, together with two students (the company was from the Noncommissioned Officers School), and the rest surrendered to the guerrillas, who captured nineteen men and, most importantly, obtained something to eat from the supplies the soldiers were carrying. Freeing the prisoners at dawn, the group undertook a withdrawal northward toward Iripití to get away from the Army reaction, which took no time in coming.

In fact, about 10 A.M., after a bombardment and the machine-gunning of the main encampment by the air force, the Arnez company, reinforced by the Lafuente company that had arrived from Yuqui during the night, entered the guerrilla redoubt without encountering resistance.

Che was forced by the weakness of the guerrilla band to make the decision to approach the unexplored inhabited area east of Ñancahuazú. He decided to head toward Pirirenda to get closer to the Santa Cruz–Camiri highway, where it would presumably be easier to obtain food, although at higher risk.

In the area of Pirirenda Lake they found some cultivated fields and took over the house of Chicho Otero, where some of them had been on an earlier occasion. After so much privation, they overate and became seriously ill. After filling up on pork, corn, squash, cheese, coffee with sugar, fried food, and the like, they were sick and in need of rest. Most had severe intestinal disturbances.

LA MANGA AND CARAHUATARENDA

Their presence on the Tiraboy hacienda was quickly reported to the army by area residents. With the available troops (a significant portion of the force was still in the Muyupampa sector, trying to search out and destroy

Joaquín's band) a task force was formed under the command of Lt. Col. Augusto Calderón from sections of the Noncommissioned Officers School, the CITE, the Braun, and the Fourth Division command. Arriving in Tiraboy at dawn on May 14, they traveled toward La Manga and managed to push the guerrillas toward the east with air support. Although the military dispatches claimed to have made contact with the guerrillas, the fact was that they had only seen them from a distance and had not managed to inflict any damages on them. The guerrillas remained basically hidden in the vicinity of the hamlet of Pirirenda, where they used their time to rest and eat, since the residents had left their homes upon learning that the guerrillas were there.

They took full advantage of those days—when the army in its disorientation was unable to locate the group—to prepare food and hide stores of it, so that when they got back into action they were stronger and in better spirits. Walking in a circle around Pirirenda to the sawmill of Bruno Manfredi, they found a good amount of supplies that improved their logistical situation.

The action of the military, after several days of inactivity, was limited to a continuing search of the area with no success. That allowed the group to move westward and arrive at the Ñancahuazú River once again on the 24th. Although there was no apparent reason for this movement which in effect put them at some distance from the inhabited area, it was probably due to a new attempt to make contact with Joaquín (although no mention is made of that in any of the diaries that have been seen). After scouring the banks downriver and even passing through the encampments used on the reconnaissance trip, they arrived at the Saladillo River and followed it to its sources. Then they crossed the mountain of the same name and descended again toward the highway.

To the surprise of the military authorities, who thought the group had been definitively expelled from the area and disbanded,[4] the incursion into Carahuatarenda was carried out on Sunday the 28th with the typical mobility of the guerrilla force. It must have been intended to both cover their needs and score a publicity coup. The incursion began with the intention of secretly obtaining some supplies, but when the guerrillas were discovered by several campesinos, they had to take them prisoner and then take control of the entire settlement, closing off both ends of town and simultaneously cutting off the Santa Cruz–Camiri road. Among the vehicular traffic detained in this action were two jeeps and two trucks. At night the group abandoned the settlement in two vehicles making their way to Ipitacito. After removing all the items from a store there, they headed for Itaí, another small community, this time off the highway. They continued toward Espino, thus threatening the Yacuiba–Santa Cruz railroad.

In a single day, thanks to the mobility gained with the use of vehicles, the guerrillas had occupied three small towns, extending their radius of action outside the zone where the army was hunting for them and making an important psychological impression on the residents.

EL ESPINO AND MUCHIRÍ

The operation set up to pursue them was again entrusted to Lt. Col. Augusto Calderón, who with two motorized companies (one from Méndez Arcos Regiment and the other from Colorados Regiment), reached the vicinity of El Espino on May 30. Arriving at the El Cruce fork, the Colorados company was sent on the eastward road to the railroad station of the same name, while the Méndez Arcos company took the northward fork to arrive at the rail line some kilometers farther ahead. A patrol from this company detailed to search the road that goes into the rail line was ambushed. Two men died—2d Lt. Eduardo Velarde and Pvt. Wilfredo Banegas—and four were wounded. Strangely, the rest of the company did not pursue the guerrillas, who withdrew calmly with the confiscated jeep, which was used on several trips to carry their equipment to the north, along the right side of the rail line.

With a company of Boquerón Regiment that had arrived as a reinforcement the night before, Lieutenant Colonel Calderón's troops began an intense search of the area in an attempt to find the guerrilla group. The existence of several paths opened by the oil company in the region in its task of exploration facilitated motorized movement. The vanguard of the Boquerón company was hit by a grenade fired by Camba, which exploded over the hood of a truck, wounding the commanding officer, 2d Lt. Max Siles and three soldiers, and killing the guide, Señor Alejandro Saldías. Again the pursuit came to a halt, giving the insurgents time to withdraw at their ease, abandoning the jeep and taking refuge in the woods.

These new setbacks for the regular forces, although accepted as part of the price to be paid for the type of war that was being waged, forced the command to take steps to correct mistakes and to achieve the destruction of the enemy in a shorter span of time. With the aim of ensuring a better command operation, the commander of the Fourth Division, Col. Humberto Rocha Urquieta, was replaced by Col. Luis Antonio Reque Terán. Some days earlier, the army command, displeased with the conduct of the campaign, had sent a recommendation to the Fourth Division to the effect that the operations should be considered in terms of irregular warfare, and tactics and maneuvers appropriate for that kind of war applied, instead of the procedures of conventional warfare. This recommendation was made as a result of the difficulty observed up to then at the higher levels in adopting a mode of operations that clearly required different ideas and approaches.

This change of command, together with the change of command of the Eighth Division (Col. Joaquín Zenteno Anaya for Col. Roberto Vargas

Claros) effected a few weeks before, gave more confidence to the high command and subordinates because of the professional prestige of the new division commanders—who, with evidence that the operations would cover the jurisdictions of both units, began to coordinate their plans immediately. The jurisdictional limit between the Fourth and the Eighth divisions was marked by the course of the Grande River.

Here the guerrillas undoubtedly lost sight of the importance that staying in the forefront of the news could have for their image, and the effect it could have on the military deployment. After the military reverses of Ñancahuazú and Iripití, having shown an extraordinary ability to cover distances and sufficient aptitude for eluding military checkpoints and siege formations, when they arrived at the rail line, they had in their hands the opportunity to stage a raid that would have had an incalculable effect as both spectacle and propaganda.

If they had stopped one of the passenger and freight trains coming from Argentina every other day in that tourist season, they would have exposed the vulnerability and weakness that could prevent the government from guaranteeing free transit and the normal activities of the citizenry. Furthermore, by threatening this communication route, they could force a wide military deployment, tying up important forces in this passive effort and preventing their use in the pursuit of the rebels. Their complete failure to discern these consequences, and their ignorance of the socio-economic reality of the region, led the guerrillas instead to abandon the area and take cover again in the woods, where their presence created no problem and their supply difficulties worsened.

For its part, the high command, conscious of the importance of what was happening, asked the government to suspend traffic on the Yacuiba–Santa Cruz railroad, believing that halting a train with hundreds of passengers and considerable freight could be a tempting objective for the guerrillas. This measure was kept in force for eight days, until it was certain that the guerrilla group had moved away from the rail line.

The executive branch was at this time facing other problems that were social in nature but had unmistakable political connotations. A teachers' strike had paralyzed schools, and unrest had been stirred up in the mines by a series of demands that were hard to deal with immediately. Under pressure from these activities and other, covert ones, President Barrientos resorted to decreeing a state of siege throughout the entire nation. This strengthened the position of his government, as did the declaration of an early winter school vacation, intended to undercut the striking teachers. A few days later, in view of a new outbreak of political tension and the threat to declare some mining centers "liberated territories," forces from the army violently occupied the Catavi and Siglo Veinte districts, provoking bloodshed and a public reaction that continues even today. This occupation—known as the "San Juan Massacre" from the date when it occurred,

St. John's Day, June 24—has become a milestone in the social struggles of the country, although responsibility for what happened has never been clarified, nor have the charges against the armed forces been substantiated.

EL CAFETAL

None of this had any significance or effect in the operations zone. The captured campesinos who led the guerrilla band to the Grande River, abandoning the rail line, conveyed this information to the army, which could therefore be almost certain that they would try to cross it in order to penetrate in the direction of the Rositas River. To block this possibility, Trinidad Company was sent to the north bank under the command of Capt. José F. Rico Toro, so that they could effect a search out of Abapó with the order to locate and destroy the guerrilla group. Carrying out the orders, the commander of the company filed the following report:

When we were scouting the enemy following the north bank of the Grande River, we were surprised by automatic fire coming from the south bank in the area of El Cafetal, which caused the death of the runner Antonio Melgar; the wounded were machine gunner Eladio Arias Garnica, and a third soldier, not seriously, since he was only hit by rock fragments caused by a bullet ricocheting. Locating the reds' position, my unit concentrated mortar and light arms fire on the enemy, assuming we caused four casualties according to shouts of pain heard in different parts along with verbal orders to move them back to the rear guard.[5]

In these circumstances the division command ordered Méndez Arcos Company to move along the south bank of the Grande River and make contact with Trinidad Company so as to catch the enemy between two fires and destroy them.

Later Trinidad Company reported that its reconnaissance had determined that the reds were heading west and that the company was returning to Abapó due to supply difficulties. Méndez Arcos Company was doing the same, and thereby a good chance was lost, according to the division command, to finish off the guerrilla group—"since this unit with a strength of 158 men, equipped with light machine guns, 60–mm mortars, and rocket launchers, with personnel from Beni Department, was in a position to get their bearings, march, and attack at night."[6]

This action was also considered negative for the guerrillas, since "firing without rhyme or reason"[7] only served to alert the army, particularly with an obstacle like the Grande River in the way. Che's annoyance lessened somewhat when news of the army casualties came through, because in this way "the rhythm of clashes with deaths" was maintained.[8] He was still concerned, though, less because the official communiqué incorrectly listed guerrilla deaths and mentioned Inti among them than because it gave pretty accurate facts about the international composition of the guerrilla band. This showed that the army intelligence service was already obtaining precise information not only from prisoners but from some other sources that allowed them to learn what was happening in detail.

THE CYNTHIA PLAN

Meanwhile the new commander of the Fourth Division, Colonel Reque Terán, was reorganizing his general staff and restructuring his forces, taking into account the organic units of his division and the companies added as reinforcements. This made it possible to stop the current practice of operating on the basis of independent companies and to create battalions instead. They would have commands and proper support facilities that would not only streamline the transmission of orders and the coordination of efforts, but also simplify the task of the Division Command, which was having a difficult time directly commanding ten or twelve subordinate units.

Three infantry battalions were organized with available resources, in compliance with General Operations Directive 8/67, issued on May 23 by the army general command. It imposed on the Fourth Division the mission of surrounding and wiping out the enemy groups stage by stage and in order, and established three areas of operations.

Until that time, during Colonel Rocha's command, the Fourth Division had operated with the following units and strengths:

Organic Units:

Company (−) of Campos 6th Infantry Regiment	64
Company (−) of Boquerón 11th Infantry Regiment	46
Company (−) of Bullaín 4th Artillery Group	17

Reinforcements:

Battery (+) of Bolívar 2d Artillery Regiment	164
Company (−) of Manchego 12th Infantry Regiment	63
Section of Braun 8th Cavalry Group	37
1st CITE Company	67
Noncommissioned Officers School Company	85
CIOS Company of Jordán 9th Infantry Regiment	71
Section of Sucre 2d Infantry Regiment	45

Parachutists (specialists)	24
Total	693 men

That was the strength of troops employed up until then—the end of May—to meet the problem posed by the guerrilla war. In addition, in the second half of May, the following units and strengths arrived in Camiri to join the fighting:

2nd CITE Company	81
1st Ranger Company (from Méndez Arcos 24th Infantry Regiment)	82
Colorados Company (from Colorados 1st Infantry Regiment)	81
Toledo Company (from Max Toledo 23rd Infantry Regiment)	81
Ingavi Squadron (from Ingavi 4th Cavalry Regiment)	81
Trinidad Company (from Ballivián 2d Cavalry Regiment)	158
Total	564 men

With all of these forces, the Division Command prepared the "Cynthia Plan" and put it into effect on June 15, organizing the reinforcement units in two battalions, the 1st and 2d Infantry battalions, at the same time forming the 3rd Infantry Battalion with the organic contingents (putting together forces from the division units) and taking into account considerations of discipline, supplies, experience, and morale for this organization.

The Cynthia Plan basically involved splitting the division's territorial jurisdiction into operations areas called A, B, and C, and destroying the enemy stage by stage and in order. The plan was to carry out the task first in area A, and then to transfer resources to area B so as to proceed in the same way.

To initiate operations in area A, the maneuver included:

First Phase: Initial occupation of the main encampment and the tin-roof house at Ñancahuazú and establishment of a mobile defense system in these areas, with the goal of providing security for the operations to be undertaken within area A.

Second Phase: Simultaneously with the first phase, probably the escape or reinforcement routes of the reds would be occupied, closed up, and cut off.

For this operation the two first phases were the responsibility of the 1st Infantry Battalion, under the command of Col. Augusto Calderón; the third phase, of the 2d Infantry Battalion under Maj. Rubén Sánchez, and the 3rd Infantry Battalion was kept in reserve, under Maj. Ives de Alarcón.

When this operation was beginning, the main guerrilla group was located on the banks of the Grande River, crossing this barrier in a northerly direction and leaving the operations area of the Fourth Division, which in order to carry out the mission assigned to it had had to enter into the jurisdiction of the Eighth Division.

When the Eighth Division maintained that it should direct operations because the guerrillas had entered into its area of responsibility, the following units were transferred to its jurisdiction in the second half of June:

Trinidad Company, June 24.

Manchego Company, June 24.

Braun Squadron, June 24.

CITE Company, June 26.

Ingavi Squadron, June 30.

This reduction of forces made it necessary for the Fourth Division to rework the Cynthia Plan, and the deployment with which the clearing of area A was begun on July 6. In that operation, encounters related in Chapter 3 were made with Joaquín's group, which had remained in the area, resulting in the guerrilla losses of Pepe, Marcos, Victor, Serapio, and Pedro; the capture of the deserters Eusebio and Chingolo; and the definitive expulsion of Joaquín's group from the area.

NORTH OF THE GRANDE RIVER

The Eighth Division of the army had been following with interest the movement of the guerrilla group since it left the Ñancahuazú encampment (see Map 6). From the onset of hostilities, details from Manchego 12th Infantry Regiment and Braun 8th Cavalry Group had been sent to reinforce the Fourth Division. These units had been participating with their share of blood and sacrifice. With evidence of the movement north and with the surety that the guerrillas would cross the Grande River to get away from the Fourth Division military deployment, which was seriously hampering their efforts, plan began to be made and measures taken to confront the problems that would arise when the guerrilla band entered the jurisdiction of the Eighth Division.

The scant organic forces did not permit big operations. Aside from the 8th Cavalry Group and the 12th Infantry Regiment, the division had Warnes 10th Infantry Regiment in San Ignacio de Velasco, which was carrying out cover missions near the Brazilian border and could not be used in these operations, and Pando 3rd Engineer Battalion, a technical unit that would have to stop work on the Vallegrande-Masicurí-Lagunillas road to undertake security missions within its jurisdiction.

The division still had the 2d Ranger Battalion (the 1st Ranger was Méndez Arcos 24th Infantry Regiment, garrisoned in Challapata, which had already assigned a company to the Fourth Division) in antiguerrilla training at La Esperanza with the support of United States Army Special Forces. It would be ready to operate at the end of September.

When units of the Fourth Division crossed the Grande River to operate in Eighth Division territory, the corresponding arrangement was made, resulting in the transfer of several units and of responsibility for conducting operations from that time on, while the Fourth Division was to continue searching out Joaquín's group.

From the beginning of the antiguerrilla operations in March, the Eighth Division had adopted some precautions, notably the following:

—On March 18, following instructions from the army command, the 3rd Engineer Battalion was instructed to "organize surveillance and alarm posts on the major paths that lead to the Masicurí River from the south, and to capture any unusual individual discovered in the area."

—On March 16, it reinforced the Puerto Camacho military post No. 10 on the Grande River, with a section of the 8th Cavalry Group given the mission of "organizing surveillance and alarm posts on the major roadways and paths that lead from the south to the Grande River" and "patrolling between Abapó and the mouth of the Ñancahuazú."

—On April 10, it organized a mixed force of company strength, made up of a section of the 12th Infantry Regiment, a section of the 8th Cavalry Group, and a section of marines from the naval force to move from Masicurí southward, under orders from the 3rd Engineer Battalion, following the upriver source of the Ñancahuazú River to operate in coordination with units of the Fourth Division.

—On April 12, with news of the events at Iripití, it ordered the detail that was marching south to halt on the heights of Saladillo Canyon and to lay ambushes in depth above the Ñancahuazú River (this operation was unsuccessful, because the guerrilla band, instead of heading north, headed west and south to go to Muyupampa).

—On June 5, it reinforced the Abapó military post, which was in the charge of the naval force, with a section of the 8th Cavalry Group assigned to operate in the area.

All these preliminary operations allowed the Eighth Division to ready itself for the encounter with the guerrilla group. The experience gained by the Fourth Division in the first two months of fighting was assimilated, and extensive reconnaissance of the terrain was undertaken by land and air, so that everyone would be familiarized with the area where he would have to operate.

The first armed combat involving the Eighth Division took place in Piraí, 5 kilometers west of the town of La Florida, on June 26.

As it turned out, after crossing the Grande River on June 15, Che's group headed for the Rositas River and moved up its course, having found some residents who took them to the junction of the Mosqueras and Morocos Rivers. There they captured three civilians who identified themselves as pig dealers. It became clear in the interrogation that they were police officers asigned to the Postrervalle zone to make inquiries for the army. They were freed on the next day, but were warned not to show up in the area again.

This was the time when the guerrilla group made the most contact with the campesinos residing in the area. Che acted as dentist at that time, extracting molars from several sick people. The appeal for volunteers to join the fighting did not yield any positive result. The men refused to commit themselves. Only one, Paulino, agreed to serve as their guide, and Che decided to use him as a courier, sending him to Cochabamba to take the four communiqués written thus far by the ELN, which had not been circulated (except for the first, and that only in part), along with messages to be sent to Cuba.

Communiqué 4 was intended to counter official reports that continually listed guerrilla casualties, although no bodies had been produced. In one of them, covering the clash with Trinidad Company in which an exchange of fire had been made from one bank of the river to the other, they had gone so far as to state that Inti had died. To correct that information, this communiqué was written:

Communiqué No. 4

In recent reports, the Army has admitted some of its casualties, sustained in advance guard clashes, assigning us, as usual, a good number of dead whom they never exhibit. Although we lack reports from some patrols, we can assert that our casualties are very few and that we suffered none in the recent actions admitted by the army.

Inti Peredo, in fact, is a member of the command of our Army, where he occupies the post of Political Commissar. He commanded recent actions. He is in good health and has not been touched by enemy bullets; the false report of his death is a clear example of the absurd lies spread by the Army in its inability to fight against our forces.

As regards the announcements of supposed combatants from other Latin American countries: in the interest of military secrecy and of our watchword, revolutionary truth, we will not give out figures but only explain that any citizen who accepts our basic program aimed at the liberation of Bolivia is welcomed into revolutionary ranks with the same rights and obligations as Bolivian combatants, who naturally make up the immense majority of our movement. Any man who rises up in arms for the freedom of our Fatherland deserves and receives the honorable title of Bolivian, no matter where he was born. That is how we interpret true revolutionary internationalism.

BOLIVIAN NATIONAL LIBERATION ARMY

The courier would later be detained by the army, and the attempt to establish some kind of communication was destined to fail, leaving the guerrilla movement completely isolated.

After resting, the group started up again, well supplied. They marched west in an attempt to reach Florida. They had information that this was a small town there where they could establish more contacts. Crossing the Corralones Range, they reached Piraí, a small hamlet on the bank of the river of the same name. Coco and other guerrillas went ahead to Florida to purchase supplies, arriving at the grocery store at four in the morning and persuading the owner, Doña Bella, to sell them granulated sugar, loaf sugar, and thread. They questioned her about the presence of soldiers who had arrived in the area on the same day, and she replied that there were a number of them. Then they left for Piraí carrying their purchases in a bag.

In fact, with information about the guerrillas' movement along the Rositas and Morocos Rivers, the Eighth Division command had foreseen that they might come out into the nearest towns, so it covered both with troops. In the case of Florida, Captain Juan Castillo Figueroa, who since the 5th of that month was reinforcing the Abapó military post with a section of the 8th Cavalry Group, was ordered on June 24 to gather available troops and undertake a movement from Abapó to Florida with responsibility for their own transportation in order to organize ambushes in the area, including Piraí.

The difficulties began with organization. The Abapó company was made up of a section of the 8th Cavalry Group, a section of the 12th Infantry Regiment, a section of the 8th Regional Agricultural Detachment, and a section of the naval force. This kind of unit, lacking good training, with disparate members who did not know each other, badly armed with only Mauser rifles and not a single automatic weapon, of course also lacked radios and all other means of communication. It was unable to transport itself, failing to find civilian vehicles in the area for requisition, so it had to travel by train from Abapó to the Curiche station. From there it walked to Florida, a distance of 30 kilometers, arriving in the town on the evening of the 25th. It was the intention of the company commander, after resting his troops outside the town, to begin reconnaissance and prepare ambushes on the 26th. At dawn, Captain Castillo learned that the guerrillas had been in town a couple of hours before, purchasing supplies, and had headed for Piraí.

In search of better information, he assigned a patrol of three men in civilian dress, under the command of Lt. Walter Landívar of the military police, to verify the presence of the guerrillas on the route from Florida to Tejería and La Piedra. Another patrol, commanded by Sgt. Hernán Andrade of the naval force, was sent along the Florida-Piraí route. These patrols were to come back to Florida by 2 P.M. Their delay in returning forced the company commander to go out in search of the enemy, leaving a section in Florida for security. He assigned a section under the command of Capt. Guillermo Vélez and naval force Lt. Francisco Mariaca to the vanguard with the mission of occupying Piraí, while another section, with 2d Lts. Marcelo Soruco and Victor Encinas, was to reach La Piedra.

Meanwhile, in the guerrilla encampment located in a house outside of Piraí, with the information Coco had brought about army troop movements in Florida, an ambush was laid on the approaching road, although the terrain was not favorable for this type of action, being flat and only partly covered. Its surface was sandy and easy to maneuver on, and, with no commanding heights, it was inappropriate for defense. The bed of the Piraí River, dry most of the year, presented no barrier, and its banks were smooth. Lieutenant Landívar's patrol was detained when it arrived at the Piraí and its members identified. This provided more information about the troops.

At the moment when the foremost elements of the vanguard were nearing the guerrilla position, they were ambushed. Three soldiers fell dead and two were wounded. The rest of Captain Vélez's section took positions immediately and engaged in combat with the guerrillas, who were being reinforced at that point by personnel that were coming to relieve those manning the ambush. Captain Castillo ordered Second Lieutenant Encinas to maneuver around the right with two squads and Second Lieutenant Soruco to maneuver around the left with two other squads, to try to cut off the guerrillas' retreat. The advance was slow, and the rustling of vegetation alerted Che and his men, who withdrew hastily.[9] The resolute and aggressive action of the troops had taken its toll on the guerrillas: Tuma, wounded in the abdomen, died when they were attempting to operate on him, and Pombo, wounded in one leg, virtually had to be dragged, slowing down the movement of the rest.

At night contact was lost. The lack of any means of communication forced the company commander to order Second Lieutenant Encinas to go on foot to the Río Seco station 40 kilometers away, to communicate with the division in Santa Cruz over the railroad telegraph in order to ask for help in evacuating the dead and wounded and to report on the situation.

At dawn on the 27th, when the company was getting ready to resume pursuit of the enemy, Lieutenant Landívar showed up with the members of his patrol and reported that they had been freed by the guerrillas, who at about 3 A.M. had left Piraí for an unknown destination. A section under

Captain Vélez was assigned to La Tejería, where there was evidence that the guerrillas had passed through. The troops remained stationary for the next few days until they could receive new information about the insurgents' activity.

In point of fact, this procedure should have been followed since Ñancahuazú. The troops undertook short-range patrols and deployed some civilian elements to obtain information, at the same time that an effort was made to establish contact with all the residents of the area. When sufficient information was received about the location of the guerrillas, the nearest units were deployed in order to make contact and join combat. The risk of these operations was that the troops could be ambushed as they were being deployed, since they were leaving the initiative to attack or not in the hands of the guerrillas, depending on the situation, the terrain, and other factors.

The guerrilla band, now made up of twenty-five men, headed slowly north, intending to approach the Santa Cruz–Cochabamba highway and the inhabited zone along it. The situation became difficult because they had not been able to reestablish contact with Joaquín's group and their strength had been reduced. They were weak and sick, and they had not been able to recruit even one additional combatant.

The campesinos avoided contact with them; when detained, they agreed to sell their products and eventually to serve as guides, but with no enthusiasm, arousing the guerrillas' suspicions as to the information they would give to the army later.

At this stage of activity, there was evidence that the guerrilla push had been slowed down, and that the majority of national opinion opposed the guerrilla action—which in any case had not managed to affect the lives or the activities of the populace. The problems with miners and students had also been dealt with. The government and the armed forces therefore felt sufficiently optimistic and sure of themselves to state publicly, with all available evidence, that the guerrilla war was being led by Che Guevara and had been organized and supported by the Fidel Castro regime. This brought the problem to a level of worldwide prominence.

NOTES

1. Che's diary, entries for March 27 and April 14.
2. "Gorilla" is used colloquially and ideologically in Latin American Spanish to designate military leaders who exercise reactionary political power.
3. Che's diary, entry for May 7. Pacho's diary, entries for May 7 and 8.
4. Fourth Division, General Operations Order 1/67.
5. Fourth Division, General Operations Order 2/67, p. 12.
6. Fourth Division, General Operations Order 2/67, p. 40.
7. Che's diary, entry for June 10.
8. Che's diary, entry for June 12.
9. Che's diary, entry for June 26.

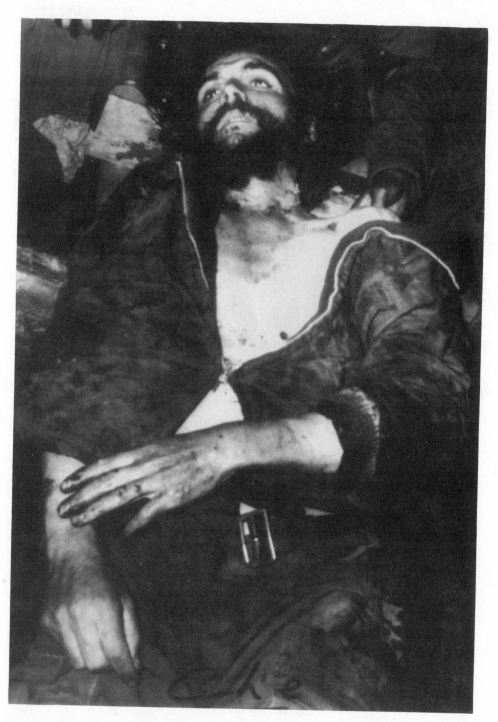

Che's body upon arrival at Vallegrande.

Above, General Alfredo Ovando being briefed by Captain Celso Torrelio in La Higuera on October 10. *Below*, President Barrientos congratulating the members of Ranger-2 B Company.

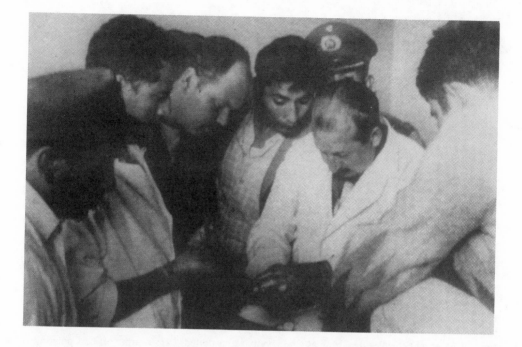

Above, a CIA agent, known as González (third from left), was present at the autopsy of Che's body. *Below,* Colonel Zenteno conversing with officers of B Company.

Above, CIA agent González departing as Che's body is transported. *Below*, army officers pointing to impact marks on the body.

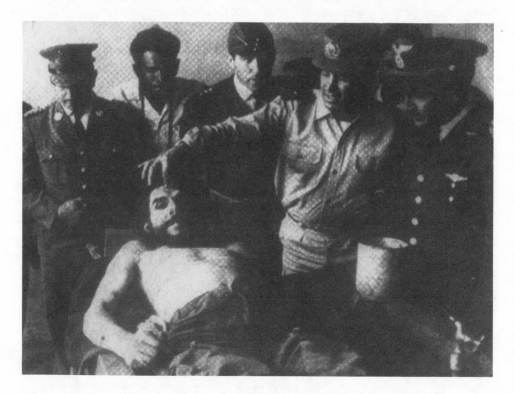

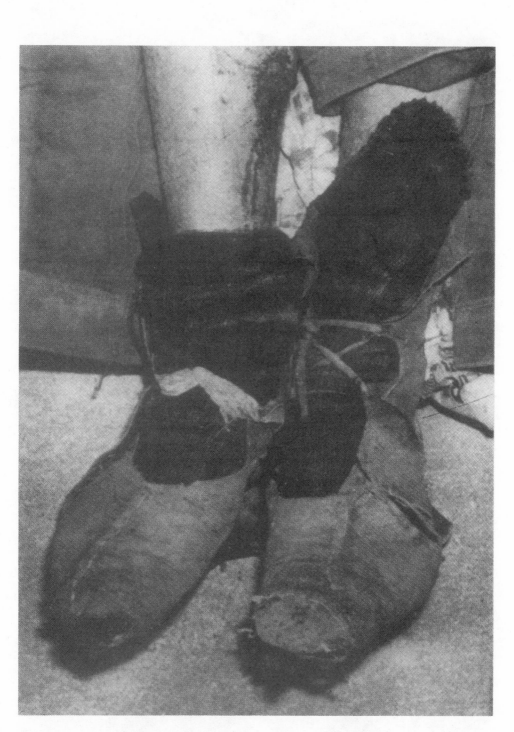

The guerrillas had to make their own shoes due to the scarcity of resources. Note the wound on Che's right calf.

Above, Che's body was transported by helicopter from La Higuera to Vallegrande. *Below*, Che's carbine was disabled by the impact of a projectile.

Chapter 10

NO WAY OUT

GUERRILLA WARFARE IN BOLIVIA: WORLD NEWS

The decision to make public Che's presence and his leadership role in the
Bolivian guerrilla war was calculated for maximum impact. The procedure
used was the simplest possible. Up to that point, the end of June, Debray
was dominating press coverage, as the date for his trial neared. News of
encounters and combats with the guerrillas received less media attention,
not only because the army was no longer at a disadvantage, but because
of that special characteristic of the press of our time, its constant hunger
for sensationalism and novelty. Debray's pose as enfant terrible and a
victim of circumstances had to be revealed. What better way than to portray
him as the man who reported Che's presence to the army? And Che's
capture or death was a matter of time, according to military analysts, given
the guerrillas' situation.

Accordingly, the commander of the Fourth Division, Col. Reque Terán,
was authorized to submit a photocopy of Debray's statements to the defense
lawyer, Dr. Walter Flores, who had made repeated requests to see tran-
scripts of the interrogations to which the defendant had been subjected.
In this way the lawyer, not the armed forces, would be the one to reveal
Debray's role as an informer.

Things went as planned. On June 29 in Camiri, Dr. Flores revealed to
the media the information given by his client, notably that he had gone to
Ñancahuazú to interview Che, that the meeting had been held on March
20, and that the guerrilla chief had explained his theory of the creation of
the continental foco and his intention of staying in the jungle for ten years
if necessary to create it or die in the attempt. Through this means, details
were made known about Che and the Cubans' entry into the country, as
well as about their organization and their links with the Castro government.

This news had a great impact on public opinion. Although there had been discussion of Ernesto Guevara's presence in Ñancahuazú for several weeks, officially nothing had been said. The only time that any Bolivian military authority had mentioned the subject was on the occasion of the Conference of Intelligence Chiefs of American Armies, held in Bogotá in mid-May, when Col. Federico Arana Serrudo, G–2 (chief of intelligence) of the army general staff, asserted that there was "evidence pointing to the possibility that the Cuban Ramón, leader of the Bolivian guerrilla war, is Che Guevara himself. Almost all of the workers and students involved in the Bolivian guerrilla band have been trained in Cuba, which they visited for different purposes."

This statement, carried over the broadcast media from press agency cables, did not make much impression or cause commentary. It was only after Debray's confession that the military authorities, beginning with the commander-in-chief, began to discuss the subject and state that the guerrilla band would be destroyed despite the caliber of its leader and the foreign aid received for its organization. The military chiefs took this opportunity to stress once again the international nature of the movement, its dependency on Castro-communism, and the need to stand up to it in defense of "our national values."

Also significant for the Bolivian government and the armed forces was the solidarity of regional governments and their rejection of this intervention. As a result of the release of news about Che's presence in Bolivia, relations between the intelligence services were improved, particularly with Brazil, Argentina, and Paraguay, the countries closest to the operations zone. It was decided to undertake a surveillance action on the borders.

All of this led to renewed interest in the Bolivian situation on the international level. A large number of internationally known journalists were attracted to the country, of the type who were used to covering the most important events. The Debray trial threatened to become a cause célèbre, to the discomfort of the members of the War Council.

On the domestic level, the confirmation of Che's presence at the head of the guerrilla band had several effects. For one thing, it bolstered the anticommunist stance of the government, which thereby had a splendid opportunity to exploit the nationalist sentiment of the people. President Barrientos's denunciations and charges against Prime Minister Castro and Cuba grew louder, and he went so far as to state unequivocally that the national will would prevail over foreign intervention.

The situation was delicate for the political parties. In view of the evidence of Cuban interference in the guerrilla war, their possibilities of action were limited. To back the guerrillas meant agreeing with Castroism and submitting to its plans, a position that the majority of parties were not willing to take, simply because that meant distancing themselves from their very base of support, the people, who intuitively opposed anything coming from abroad. All that was left to political organizations was silence, which smacked of complicity, or direct statements against the intervention, which did not necessarily lend support to the government. This was the course chosen by the majority. Only some marginal political groups decided to offer lukewarm support from underground for the Ñancahuazú fighters. It was only rhetorical support, since nobody even attempted to join their enterprise, which by this time everyone thought was condemned to resounding failure.

On the tide of this nationalist sentiment, demonstrations were organized on the initiative of the armed forces in all cities of the country, to back the national cause. Thanks to efficient planning, they attracted large crowds who rejected Castroism and its envoys with chants and signs and offered their support to the military in its fight against subversion. Civic organizations responsible for getting food, clothing, and delicacies to the soldiers were created as a way of demonstrating public support for their effort. All these events had considerable repercussion in the ranks of the military, building up morale.

Within the officer corps, official confirmation of what was already known internally made everyone feel that the guerrilla problem had until then served to lay bare the weaknesses and errors of the military, which had cost lives, and that a great joint effort was necessary to end the Castroite threat. A spontaneous commitment was needed from the military to carry on the fight resolutely until the defeat of the main exponent of guerrilla warfare on the continent was obtained.

But the guerrillas did not let up. After the Piraí ambush, they headed north, seemingly in order to reach the paved highway that runs from Santa Cruz to Cochabamba. This forced the Eighth Division to adopt a plan to protect the major towns in the area. The very length, however, of the stretch of road under its jurisdiction—Santa Cruz to Comarapa, 250 km—made an efficient cover action impossible. The division command faced the typical dilemma of this kind of war: they could either protect all towns in the area with small forces, lessening effectiveness to provide apparent security, or maintain a strong mobile reserve force ready to act as soon as exact information of the enemy's whereabouts was obtained.

An intermediate solution was adopted. Ingavi Squadron, divided into four platoons, was assigned to San Luis (km 50), La Angostura (km 60), Petacas (km 70), and Bermejo (km 80). This deployment without vehicles was simply dissuasive. In no case would they be ready to meet any reaction, save for a local reaction. Farther west, the 3rd Engineer Battalion, a company of Manchego Regiment, and a section of the Braun Group, in addition to a company of Ustariz 13th Infantry Regiment (recently arrived as a reinforcement from Cochabamba) were all assigned to the area of responsibility of the recently organized ATI-3 (Infantry Task Force 3) in Vallegrande, under the command of Col. Constantino Valencia Oblitas. As in the case of Ingavi Squadron, Ustariz Company was divided into groups of twenty men to cover Comarapa, Samaipata, Mataral, and Mairana. The company commander, Lt. Juan Vacaflor Alfaro, set up his command post in Samaipata.

THE SAMAIPATA RAID

The guerrilla group reached Peña Colorada and found the town nearly deserted due to the fear inspired by their campaign.[1] This did not favor their plans. They kept moving until they arrived at Alto de Palermo at the beginning of the afternoon. The reception there was similarly uninviting, so by nightfall they reached the paved highway at a place called Las Cuevas, where they set up a temporary base.

Information about the guerrillas' presence in the area had been reported to military authorities at about 8 P.M. They sent the information on to Vallegrande, to the ATI command, whose jurisdiction it was. The ATI, however, was unable to communicate with Lieutenant Vacaflor, due to the lack of radios and the faultiness of the state telegraph system, which at that time functioned only irregularly. For this reason Lieutenant Vacaflor's section would be quite careless, aside from taking some routine precautions.

After several vehicles had been detained on the highway, six guerrillas (Ricardo, Coco, Pacho, Aniceto, Julio, and Chino) left in a truck loaded with sugar on a mission to obtain supplies and medicine in Samaipata and to return to the provisional base at Las Cuevas, where the rest remained preparing food. Arriving at a truck stop at 11:45 A.M. on July 6, they got out and took Lieutenant Vacaflor by surprise at a snack stand, where he was in the company of two members of the public Security Guard and a sergeant from his unit. At the same place they found a Gulf Oil pickup truck, which they immediately requisitioned for their withdrawal. Pacho got into the driver's seat. After buying cold drinks for the Gulf Oil men and some curious villagers, and talking about their objectives, they took the officer and sergeant hostage and left two guerrillas to guard the highway. The rest headed to the school where the troops were billeted, three blocks away. They made the sergeant identify himself to the sentry so that he opened the door, and the rest of the guerrillas rushed in to overpower the soldiers. One of them, Pvt. José Verezaín, resisted and fired upon the group. He was cut down in front of the others, who then ended their resistance.[2]

Reduced to nine soldiers, the troops were disarmed. Their five Mauser rifles and one Bruno light machine gun were loaded into the pickup. Keeping Lieutenant Vacaflor hostage, the guerrillas went to a grocery store and pharmacy where they obtained a considerable amount of food and medicine, although they did not find the medications ordered specifically by the guerrilla leader for his asthma, because Samaipata is a small town, essentially a rest stop for travelers from Santa Cruz and Cochabamba and a small commercial center for the campesinos of the area. Although Samaipata is two hundred years old, its progress has been very slow. This was why the pharmacy-grocery carried only commonly used medications. Because of the altitude (approaching 2,000 meters) and dry climate, asthma was not a very common disease for the inhabitants. In this respect, the incursion was a failure.[3]

Although they had the inhabitants and the troops under their control, the tension of the moment, their reduced strength, and the possibility that other troops were nearby made the guerrillas behave somewhat recklessly, rushing through their shopping and committing some errors. After paying for their purchases, they set off in the pickup and got onto the highway in the direction of Santa Cruz to return to Las Cuevas, where the rest of the group were waiting for them. A couple of kilometers outside of Samaipata, they left off Lieutenant Vacaflor and the sergeant, after taking their documents, shoes, and money, and disappeared into the night. When they returned to the provisional base, at 2 A.M., they began marching south to get away from the highway, without correctly evaluating the effect of their action.

In fact, their raid on Samaipata made a considerable impression on the military, since it showed the vulnerability of the deployment adopted and the inefficiency of the small military posts spread along the highway and in other towns. Trinidad Company, which was acting as a motorized reserve at Santa Cruz, was sent, near dawn on July 7, on a mission to "go to Samaipata to neutralize the red details that are active in that area, make contact with the Vacaflor Company, and act decisively to reestablish order; deal vigorously with all suspicious persons, who should be locked up."

Setting up its base in Palermo, 17 kilometers from Samaipata, Trinidad Company did reconnaissance in the area, finding signs of the reds' withdrawal to the south, which removed any danger from the Cochabamba–Santa Cruz highway. Subsequently, the unit was transported to Quirusillas, arriving on July 12. They renewed the search for the guerrilla group without finding their trail, and so they were brought back to Santa Cruz on July 20.

The most important repercussion of the Samaipata raid was felt in the civilian sector. The paved highway was a vital route for the national economy. A high percentage of the vehicular traffic bearing tropical products (sugar, rice, corn, wood, alcohol, and so forth) to the altiplano area of the country travels on it, as well as countless passengers. The insecurity created by the raid had a psychological effect that was not duly exploited by the guerrillas.

If within a few days they had made another raid on the highway, at any town, the political effect of the action would have been catastrophic, for they would have exposed the inability of the military to secure a major artery. The decision to withdraw to the south and leave the highway can only be seen as an error, since confirmation of that movement permitted the Eighth Division to relax its efforts to control the highway and deploy its forces in other directions, rather than keeping them tied up in a security mission.

On the other hand, Samaipata would have been an ideal place from which one of the guerrillas, properly instructed, could have shed his beard and uniform and left the area for one of the cities, be it Cochabamba or Santa Cruz, to reestablish contact with the urban support network. A rallying point on a highway or in some other place could have been designated in order to pick up the outside liaison later. None of this was done, and leaving this opportunity behind, the group marched south, where once again they were faced with the supply problem, the campesinos' wariness, and above all Che's malady. He kept growing weaker without medication.

The press had plenty of material for several days. The disparity of reports was astonishing. While some residents spoke of seventy or forty guerrillas participating in the Samaipata action, all of them insisted that they had seen Che personally directing the operation. Pacho was probably mistaken for Che, being the most striking of the group and resembling the guerrilla chief to some extent.[4] This action meant more propaganda for the guerrillas than all of the combats that had occurred up until then, but its effects ended immediately because it was not followed up with other similar actions.

THE NEW MILITARY APPROACH

After evaluating the Samaipata events and confirming the main group's move south, the army general command made preparations to thwart once and for all any possibility Che had of meeting up with Joaquín again. It therefore became necessary to reorient the action of the two divisions involved in operations so that they would be able to coordinate efforts, since there was evidence that the area adjacent to the Grande River was where the encounter could occur.

Simultaneously with this effort, when the guerrillas were pushed south away from the paved highway and from the possibility of receiving support from outside of the operations zone, their supply situation became difficult. The Parabano and San Marcos zone did not offer much in the way of resources, and they were being forced to keep on the defensive and on the move, further complicating their ability to recruit supporters and to disperse without entering into combat.

It became important to the military command to limit guerrilla action to the least populated zone, where the effects of their probable raids would make little impact on public opinion, due to the lack of communications.

Keeping the guerrillas isolated and continuing intensive patrols to keep pressure up on the enemy were the priorities.

A result of this thinking was Operations Directive 13/67, dated July 28, which gave the Fourth and Eighth divisions this mission: "With the resources currently assigned, make an effort to destroy the reds in their operations zones in the shortest time possible, especially in order to reduce the guerrilla operation zone."[5] To fulfill this mission the army command set up the following phases:

First phase: Simultaneously, both major units would eliminate the more advanced nucleuses at Yerba Buena and Monteagudo to guarantee the Cochabamba-Samaipata–Santa Cruz and Sucre-Monteagudo-Camiri cross routes and the Santa Cruz–Abapó-Charagua-Boyuibe longitudinal route.

Second phase: Fourth Division. After occupying and closing off probable escape routes east and west of the Ñancahuazú River, comb from south to north to clear the zone, particularly the Oso [Bear] Camp, until reaching the Grande River.

Eighth Division. Reduce the guerrilla zone through combing and cleanup from north to south until reaching the Vallegrande-Postrervalle–El Filo–Piraí-Florida cross route.

Third phase: Once the deployments of the major units have joined together again and the enemy has been isolated at Mosquera, destroy the reds in the area with a specialized Ranger unit.

This general plan, with some variations, would be carried out until the Ranger–2, Manchego Regiment—currently receiving training at La Esperanza—was in readiness. Once Ranger–2 entered into operations, it would definitively bring the guerrilla problem to an end.

CORRALONES AND MOROCOS

The information received in the Eighth Division command in Santa Cruz after the Samaipata raid showed clearly the guerrilla movement south, which fit perfectly into the plan conceived by the army command to limit the operations zone to the banks of the Grande River. When the insurgents' presence in the vicinity of Piraí and Florida was confirmed, Trinidad Company was activated once again. This most-accomplished and best-armed of available companies was transported by vehicle to Florida, a movement that ended at dawn on the 24th of July.

Meanwhile, in the interest of coordinating action, the Fourth Division commander was invited to Santa Cruz, where after a complete briefing it was suggested to him that he commit part of his forces to the Rositas–Morocos River area to act as a force of containment vis-à-vis Trinidad Company, which had the mission to "first reach Piraí and then continue along the La Oscura–Morocos–Rio Rositas route, attempting to make contact with the guerrilla forces and push them to the south, where Fourth Division forces are operating in coordinated fashion."

Along the same lines, the Eighth Division ordered the Abapó military post to organize ambushes in the Florida and Piraí areas, undertaking limited-range reconnaissance.

With the expectation that the Fourth Division would succeed in stationing a unit on the Rositas River, Trinidad Company began its reconnaissance out of Florida, obtaining the information that the guerrilla group could be found on the slopes of Durán Mountain. A request for air support to force them to move and abandon their positions was honored with a twenty-four-hour delay, since the available planes, two T–6s, were in Camiri.

At nightfall on July 26, Capt. Rico Toro split his company into two columns: one section, under the command of 2d Lt. José Rivera Sundt, was to march along the Florida-Piraí-Durán Mountain route and join up by the following noon with the rest of the unit in Corralones, to serve as a force of containment at the guerrillas' rear, in coordination with the maneuver that the main body would undertake in order to push them in toward Río Seco–Pampa de los Torunos and Corralones Canyon.

The movement was accomplished during the night, and near noon on July 27, the guerrillas were spotted from a distance. Some mortar shells were fired to slow their movement down, while a section commanded by 2d Lt. Fernando Galindo undertook an outflanking maneuver from the left, an action that could not be completed because the terrain was so uneven. When the vanguard of the main force was reaching the guerrilla position, it was ambushed. The civilian guide Armando Cortez Espíndola was killed and Pvt. Jesús Gutiérrez Malele was wounded.

Despite that setback, the troops continued their advance. The guerrilla group had to withdraw without being able to recover anything from the corpse and the wounded man because of the nature of the terrain and pressure from the troops.

The loss of contact with the guerrillas, and the guide's death, halted Trinidad Company's progress. They also needed time to regroup their forces, since the section sent with second Lieutenant Rivera had stopped at Durán Mountain without reaching Corralones, failing to complete the maneuver conceived by the company commander.

When he reported events to the Eighth Division command (via the Fourth Division, because his radio could only communicate with Camiri), Capt. Rico Toro requested air support for dawn on the 28th, so as to keep up the pressure on the guerrillas. This part of the terrain was perhaps the only one that lent itself to the use of air support, since the characteristics of the terrain, its vegetation and cover, made it possible to coordinate land-air operations. In other sectors such as Ñancahuazú, Rositas, or La Higuera, this option was limited by the difficulty of drawing a clear line between the regular forces and the enemy.

In the case of the Trinidad Company request, this support was late in coming and turned out to be ineffective. Meanwhile the company, taking advantage of a canyon, moved along until it reached the junction of the Mosquera and Oscura (or Suspiro) rivers without incident. It rested there.

Up to that point, the afternoon of July 29, Capt. Rico Toro's unit was sure that the maneuver provided for by the two division commands was being carried out. The Eighth Division had sent a radiogram to Camiri at 9 A.M. on the 28th, with this message:

Section III 452/67: Since reds are hemmed in by Rico Toro Company five km south Durán Mountain, suggest detail of your unit proceed north direction Rosita Canyon–Morocos Canyon–Oscura Canyon to coordinate action.

On July 30 at 10:30 A.M. Trinidad Company was alerted to this effect in the following radiogram:

Section III 461/67: For coordination purposes a Fourth Division company is to leave 1500 today; proceed along Rositas River branch off Mosqueras, northerly direction. Take precautions to avoid clashing with own troops.

This radiogram arrived in the unit addressed after the Morocos clash. As it turned out, a woman residing at the junction of the Mosqueras and Oscura rivers (which empty into the Morocos, a tributary of the Rositas) had reported that two leagues below her house there were troops numbering approximately sixty men, whom she herself had seen. Acting on this information, Capt. Rico Toro ordered a section—once again under the command of Second Lieutenant Rivera, and with precise instructions to carry out the mission assiduously—to move along the river until they met and engaged those troops.

The guerrilla group, marching south, had decided to continue in that direction, but they took precautions not to be seen, since they were all certain that the campesinos would run to inform the army of their presence. Abandoning the roads and paths they knew, they looked for an exit onto the Rositas River and arrived there on the afternoon of July 29. Although he knew their position was poor because they were in an exposed place, Che ordered his men to camp right there, given their exhaustion. He instructed them to get up at five in the morning to continue their movement.[6]

The Rivera section began its movement at four in the morning on July 30, and traveled in the specified direction without encountering major problems. When they arrived on the north bank of the Rositas River, at approximately 4:30 A.M., the point men spotted a campfire on the other bank. Ignoring the noncom Miranda's opinions to the contrary, Second Lieutenant Rivera mistakenly thought that the fire could only belong to their own troops, with whom he had been ordered to make contact. So without waiting for dawn or verifying the identity of those who were near the fire, he went to the head of his men and crossed the river, lighting the way with a flashlight, which was observed from the guerrilla encampment, where the light and the sight of people approaching caused confusion. Moro, wrapped in a blanket, was making coffee at the fire. When he asked, "Say, who is it?" the officer did not hesitate to reply, "Trinidad Detail," causing the guerrillas to react immediately. They began to fire and organize for the defense, while they saddled up the horses they had and tried to gain time. The rest of the Rivera section stayed on the river bank firing upon the guerrillas in the encampment.

Trinidad Company, following some thirty minutes away, speeded up their advance when they heard firing. A bit farther on they came upon a messenger sent by Miranda to report on the happenings at the Rositas. A few minutes later, occupying the north bank, the company commander ordered the Monzón and Galindo sections to maneuver along the two flanks while the center launched a frontal assault under his command. The company's rapid action caught the guerrilla group trying to organize its retreat and forced the members to run in several directions, abandoning equipment and animals. Leaving the vanguard and rear guard (twelve men) to contain the troops, the rest drew back hastily. The troops' clash with the guerrillas was violent and aggressive. The Galindo and Monzón sections managed on several occasions to outflank the guerrillas and threaten them with encirclement, causing them to draw back even farther.

In one of these actions Ricardo fell wounded. When Arturo, Raúl and Pacho were trying to rescue him, Raúl fell dead from a shot in the mouth, and Pacho was wounded in the buttocks. With great effort, abandoning Raúl's body, they managed to rescue Ricardo and transport him until they met up with the main body, but efforts to save his life were futile, and he died near midnight.

These two losses affected Che and his men deeply because for the first time they had been surprised, followed, and hunted down vigorously by army troops; two combatants had died, diminishing their ranks even further; and the situation had become difficult for the rest. Undoubtedly Arturo was most affected of all. He was deeply grieved by his brother Ricardo's death, and he disturbed the others to the point that they could not figure out how to console him.

The pursuit lasted about fourteen hours, after which time the exhausted troops had to regain strength. Among other things they captured were ten packs with the guerrillas' personal effects, seven hammocks, ammunition, a bag holding first-aid materials, a radio, and a tape recorder, without which the guerrilla group was no doubt even more isolated. In addition, they captured explosives, detonators, supplies, and the horse that Che had been riding.

Trinidad Company's action took its toll on the army. Four soldiers died, three of them from wounds received in combat and the delay in obtaining a helicopter to evacuate them. Four were wounded, among them 2d Lt. José Rivera Sundt.[7] The evacuation of dead and wounded had to be effected by light aircraft from Abapó and Florida.

On July 31 the Abapó military post reported: "Today 0730 hours Maj. Ives Alarcón arrived this Garrison with five officers, five NCOs and 96 soldiers."

The Fourth Division was just now sending the unit that was to operate out of the south. This company relieved Trinidad Company, which was transferred to Santa Cruz and after some days to its base in Beni Department, where it was demobilized. This concluded its participation in the antiguerrilla operation.

ENCAMPMENTS AND DEPOTS

From its command post in Camiri the Fourth Division had taken the necessary steps to comb the area, in keeping with the Cynthia Plan. They were unable to complete the first phase—total elimination of Joaquín's group—but they did push him toward the Grande River, where he would meet destruction. In that attempt, the actions of Yuqui, Iquira, and Iñao, already recounted in Chapter 3, were carried out. They resulted in seven casualties for that insurgent group.

The 2d Infantry Battalion, under the command of Maj. Rubén Sánchez, would continue searching for Joaquín's group in the regions of La Tapera, Monteagudo, and Iquira until they were certain that no guerrillas were in the areas under their jurisdiction.

To carry out the second phase of the army general command's directive, the 1st Infantry Battalion under Lt. Col. Augusto Calderón was entrusted with this mission: "While monitoring the fords over the Grande River, covering the Tiraboy–La Manga–Pirirenda regions, and controlling the La Herradura–Gutiérrez-Tatarenda line, initiate an offensive maneuver in four directions converging with these operations on the enemy's 'Bear' encampment."

The units and missions specified for the 1st Infantry Battalion were:

—CIOS Company: Maneuver along the Yuqui and Frías rivers until reaching Iripití ravine and making contact with A Company of the Third Division.

—Toledo Company: Maneuver in the direction of main encampment–Bear encampment in coordination with the 2nd CITE Company.

—Second CITE Company: Maneuver in the direction of tin-roof-house–Rubio encampment—Bear encampment in coordination with Toledo Company.

—A Company, Third Division: Maneuver in direction Manfredi Sawmill–Ñanca-huazú River–Iripití Ravine until making contact with CIOS Company on the Frías River.[8]

This plan was based on two assumptions:

—A map of probable caches left by the guerrillas, drawn by the prisoner Roberto Bustos, alias Pelao.
—The supposition that some guerrilla group left behind as a security force was still in the area.

To facilitate the units' mission, the prisoners Chingolo and Eusebio were taken along with the 2d CITE Company and Toledo Company, respectively, although in point of fact they knew little about the location of caches, having been used more for transport between the tin-roof house and the main encampment than to build and conceal depots. Beginning the maneuver, the units converged directly on their destinations without encountering resistance. The careful search began to yield results on August 6 when the 2d CITE Company found the first depot at Las Piedras Brook, and the following day Toledo Company located the Bear encampment depot. Then the 1st NCO School Company, which formed part of the reserve in Lagunillas, received an additional report about another cache near the main encampment. They traveled there to search the area and found it on the 9th. Subsequently, the 2d CITE Company discovered the depots at the Clinic and Elevator encampments, thereby striking a heavy blow at the guerrilla force. The army took a large portion of their supplies and at the same time recovered all of the arms captured by the guerrillas at the Ñancahuazú and Iripití ambushes.

All of the material was transferred to Lagunillas and Camiri to be inventoried and then exhibited to the press, to show in concrete fashion the results of the military operation and to make the public feel that the guerrilla band was ever more endangered. The inventory taken by the army of the encampments showed the following results:

Las Piedras Brook (2d CITE Company)

  9 Garand M–1 30–caliber rifles

14 Mauser 7.65–mm rifles

  2 sawed-off Mauser 7.65 rifles

  4 PAM 9–mm submachine guns

  3 Solothurn 9–mm submachine guns

  4 GNSP (uniformed police) submachine guns

  2 Thompson 9–mm submachine guns

  2 Brno 7.65–mm light submachine guns

1 American 60–mm mortar

8 60–mm mortar shells

144 30–caliber cartridges

117 9–mm cartridges

211 7.62–mm cartridges

34 submachine-gun magazines

25 ammunition belts

7 plastic canteens

20 pairs of boots (new)

20 shirts (new)

1 30–caliber carbine

At Bear Camp (Toledo Company)

2 Brno 7.65–mm light submachine guns

2 9–mm Schmeisser submachine guns

14 Mauser 7.65–mm rifles

9 Solothurn 9–mm submachine guns

14 Mauser bayonet blades

10 grenade launchers

30 rifle grenades

31 60–mm mortar shells

142 hand grenades

2,000 7.65–mm cartridges

26 dynamite cartridges

3 slow fuse rolls

17 magazines

Near the Main Camp (1st NCO School Company)

1 115–volt electric generator

Documentation including the key to name code and other communications codes

Clothing

Equipment

Some women's clothing

At the Clinic and Elevator Camps (2d CITE Company)

1 Box of hypodermic syringes

3 Medical bags with a variety of medications

1 Complete case with geometric compasses

Graph paper

12 Pairs long-range binoculars

1 Portable radio

3 Notebooks with a variety of information

1 leather case with documentation

Shoemaker's material

1 Air gauge

2 Bandoleers with 10 clips

2 Small axes

1 Box of soap

Books in French

One part of the Fourth Division mission was accomplished. In the interest of locating Joaquín's group, a new combing of the area was effected with all available units. No new traces were found, however, and it was decided to maintain the current deployment in anticipation of an eventual return by the guerrillas to Ñancahuazú.

ABORTED RETURN TO ÑANCAHUAZÚ

Unaware meanwhile of the results of the Fourth Division's efforts, and with no news of Joaquín, the guerrilla group kept moving south very cautiously after the Morocos combat. They intended to reach the Grande River and decide from there which direction to take.

In the assessment that preceded this decision, the lack of communication with the outside and the reduction of the guerrilla force under Che's command to only twenty-two men showed through clearly. The losses they had suffered could not be replaced, since efforts to add new combatants had been futile. Given the time that had gone by since Paulino was sent as a messenger to Cochabamba, and the lack of response through agreed channels (preestablished messages, disguised as personal messages on commercial radio stations), the guerrilla chief realized that the attempt had failed and that the presence of more-combative and somewhat more-experienced army units jeopardized the prospects of the movement.

Taking all this into consideration, Commandant Guevara gave careful instructions: a patrol made up of Benigno, Julio and Ñato should travel to Ñancahuazú to obtain medications from the cache, find out if there was any news of Joaquín, and assess the military situation in the area to weigh the alternative of returning to that zone so as to evade the pressure from the army. This patrol would go accompanied by other elements who would return in stages from different parts of the route to inform the main body of whatever news they picked up. Rallying points were carefully set: the house of Epifanio Vargas—the guide killed by the guerrillas at Ñancahuazú—in the vicinity of Tatarenda; a stream leading to the Grande River, known from the earlier trip; Honorato Rojas's house in Masicurí; and lastly, the Ñancahuazú encampment. The eight patrol members—three

who were to go as far as the Ñancahuazú and five to return—were urged
to act with the utmost care and avoid army ambushes.

That night, August 8, just after Che had given his instructions, two events
occurred that had an important effect on the guerrillas:

—The army announced it had found the insurgents' caches at Ñancahuazú. When
the guerrillas heard the news over the radio, the mission of the patrol took on
even more importance, since if all the caches had been found, the guerrilla band
would have to fall back solely on the scant resources they were carrying with
them.

—In the dispute that subsequently arose in the guerrilla encampment over their
general situation, the first open splits between Bolivians and Cubans came to
the surface.

In fact, up to that time relations among the members of the fighting
force had been kept on a more or less normal level, but the evident air of
superiority assumed by the Cubans because of their experience, military
rank, and close relationship with Che, had begun to cause frictions with
the Bolivians present, who did not very willingly accept that treatment.
They themselves were natural rebels—the proof was their participation in
the guerrilla war—and were not willing to let themselves be ordered around
by just anyone.

In a difficult situation like the one the guerrillas were going through,
when the psychological effects of the operations were undermining their
strength, and the army's permanent pursuit was creating an atmosphere
of insecurity, it was natural for these latent differences to break out and
for disagreeable incidents to occur.

Months earlier, Che had had to muster all his authority to check Marcos's
excesses, and to contain the continual theft of food and the minor squabbles
among the guerrillas.[9] On this occasion, though, the situation was more
critical, because of the very position of the guerrilla band. It was the first
time that the entire group debated the situation of the fighting force, that
the state of affairs was bluntly analyzed, and that they were asked to decide
whether to go on to the end—the end in question was not clearly explained—or to abandon the struggle. Although after Che's speech everyone
decided to go on, it was obvious that some Bolivians, such as Camba,
León, and Chapaco, could no longer be fully trusted, not only because
they were not very enthusiastic, but also because they were showing some
signs of unbalance.[10] As for the Cubans, they too were questioning the
future of the guerrilla war, but Che's authority and his conviction that
everything would improve in the future prevailed. It is important to point
out how great hopes were raised in the guerrillas with small details. The
occupation of the mines in June was considered almost a guarantee that
the government would fall. When its effects dissipated and the problems

with the miners were resolved, disappointment set in. To support and encourage that miners' movement, Che drafted Communiqué 5, which likewise did not reach the public because by that time the guerrillas had no way of sending a message to the outside, their communication lines having been broken. The text of this message read:

Comrades:
Once again proletarian blood is flowing in our mines. In an explosion several centuries old, slave blood sucked from the miner has alternated with blood spilled when so much injustice causes the outbreak of protests. That cyclical repetition has not varied in the course of hundreds of years.

Most recently, the rhythm was broken provisionally and the insurgent workers were the basic factor in the triumph of April 9. That event brought the hope that a new horizon was opening up and that finally the workers would be the masters of their own destiny, but the dynamics of the imperialist world showed those who cared to look that in the matter of social revolution there are no halfway solutions. Either you take all the power or you lose the gains made with so much sacrifice and so much blood.

The armed militias of the mining proletariat, the only element of strength at the beginning, were joined by militias from other sectors of the working class, militants from other classes, and campesinos, who were unable to see the essential unity of interests and entered into conflict, led by antipopular demagoguery—and finally the professional army reappeared with a lamb's fleece and a wolf's claws. And that army, small and hardly noticed at first, was transformed into the armored fist raised against the proletariat—and into the surest accomplice of imperialism. That is why they approved the military coup.

Now we are recuperating from a defeat caused by the repetition of working-class tactical errors, and we are patiently preparing the country for a profound revolution that will change the system in its roots.

False tactics should not be repeated. They may be heroic, but they are also sterile, plunging the proletariat into a bloodbath and thinning their ranks by depriving us of their most combative elements.

In long months of fighting, the guerrilla war has thrown the country into confusion, caused the army a great number of casualties, and demoralized it, while suffering hardly any losses; in a confrontation of a few hours, that same army sweeps the field and struts over proletarian corpses. The difference between correct and erroneous tactics is the difference between victory and defeat.

Comrade miner: don't listen to the false apostles of mass struggle, who interpret it as a dense, frontal attack by the people against the oppressor's weapons. Let's learn from reality! Heroic chests are of no use against machine guns; against modern demolition weapons, barricades are useless, no matter how well built. Mass struggle in underdeveloped countries with a large campesino base and extensive territory should be undertaken by a small, mobile vanguard: the guerrilla army, based in the midst of the people; it will gain strength at the expense of the enemy army and will capitalize on the revolutionary fervor of the masses until it creates the revolutionary situation in which state power will crumble at a single blow, well aimed and well timed.

Make no mistake: we are not asking for total inactivity; we recommend, rather, that forces not be jeopardized in actions with no guarantee of success, but pressure from the working masses should be brought to bear continually against the government, because this is a class struggle, with unlimited fronts. Wherever there is a proletarian, he has the duty to fight to the extent of his capabilities against the common enemy.

Comrade miner: the ELN guerrilla force awaits you with open arms and invites you to join the underground workers who are fighting beside us. Here we will rebuild the worker-campesino alliance that was broken by antipopular demagoguery; here we will turn defeat into triumph and the sobs of proletarian widows into a victory hymn. We await you.

BOLIVIAN NATIONAL LIBERATION ARMY

The news of political events, agreements, the withdrawal of parties from the government coalition, strikes, and such—routine in the political life of the nation—also gave hope and encouragement to the guerrillas, and this showed how little the guerrillas knew of Bolivian affairs. These kinds of tensions were felt every day in Bolivia, but that did not necessarily add up to change.

The only communication with the outside, the reception of coded messages from Cuba by radio, was yet another source of hope, although no response could be made. A typical case related to Message 38 sent by Fidel Castro, which was received by Che, taped, and decoded before the Morocos combat.[11] His opinion was requested on the advisability of opening another front with thirty or forty men; the possibility was mentioned of opening it at Apolo, La Paz Department. Che was informed that a group of twenty-three men was being prepared in Cuba—all of them students with scholarships on the island, belonging to the communist youth and the Spartacus group—to join the struggle. Similarly, scholarship students that were in the U.S.S.R. and Czechoslovakia were being encouraged to join the struggle under the guidance of the ELN. This kind of news would appear to be very positive, but seen realistically, it was a simple illusion of support that would not materialize, since by then it was clear to those outside that the guerrillas' chance of success was remote. Despite all of this, the guerrillas' state of mind was not the best when it was confirmed over the radio that all of their caches had been found and confiscated by the army. The delay of the exploration group in returning began to worry them all, and in order to get closer to the rallying points, they marched to the Grande River, reaching it on August 17. Occupying the stream designated in advance as a rallying point, they prepared to wait, remaining there four days and clearing paths for an exit toward the west.

The presence of troops in Tatarenda was confirmed on August 23 when the guerrillas detained two hunters who spoke in captivity about the military deployment and reported that patrols of soldiers were going out in groups of twenty to fish on the river. Acting on this information, the guerrillas decided to set up an ambush to inflict casualties on the army, but the operation came out badly. Antonio attacked the first elements not of a group of fishermen but of a patrol of C Company, Third Division, that was doing reconnaissance on the banks of the Grande River. The soldiers' quick reaction to protect themselves, and the support they received from the rest of their squad, forced a guerrilla withdrawal to the west. They disappeared into the woods when the rest of the section, under the command of 2d Lt. Luis Dorado, crossed the river and pressed the search.

In desperation the guerrillas looked for an outlet that would afford them protection within the zone, which was intensively patrolled by the army. The steep banks of the Grande River continually cut off their route. Added to this was concern for the prolonged absence of the patrol assigned to the Ñancahuazú encampment since August 9, of which no news had been received. They were forced to wait for the patrol in the region without moving too far away.

Thirst was a constant problem, since there was no water in the heights where they were organizing their defense. They were obliged to shift position frequently and often suffered privation.

Only on August 27, after nearly twenty days of absence, did Benigno, Ñato and Julio show up, and the news they brought was discouraging. They had found troops at Tatarenda and Yumao, as well as at all the occupied encampments, from which the caches had been removed, leaving the group without medications, documents, and ammunition. The psychological effect of all this hit them all hard, including Che, who reflected it in his diary in the summary for the month of August, calling that the worst month of the whole war. With great effort they continued their advance to the west until on September 1 they reached the stream that runs near Honorato Rojas's house, where less than twenty-four hours before a military operation had been undertaken that would be a heavy blow to guerrilla operations. The search for Joaquín's group would come to an end in the way Che and his men least expected, and the error of not adequately setting a rallying point would be paid for in blood.

VADO DEL YESO

In mid-August the Eighth Division, seeing the need to coordinate operations better and to speed up the destruction of the guerrilla group within its jurisdiction, put into execution the so-called Parabano Plan, which laid down two points as its objective:

Dependent units of the Eighth Division and reinforcement units, with the regular contingents at hand by 0400 hours on 16 AUG 67 will seek to destroy the reds in A Zone (north) of their operations zone in the least time possible, advancing from north to south starting at the Samaipata–Santa Cruz cross-route, first reducing the guerrilla operations zone through combing and clearing up to the Vallegrande-Postrervalle–El Filo–Paraí-Florida cross-route and then, in coordination with the Fourth Division and specialized units, reducing the reds in the isolated area.

To carry out this mission, troops were stationed on the Cochabamba–Santa Cruz highway, and began southward movements in the directions of Angostura–Loma Mansa–La Paliza; Bermejo–Las Juntas–El Filo; Samaipata-Quirusillas-Postrervalle; and Vallegrande-Lajas–Masicurí Bajo, covering at the same time Morocos-Florida and Abapó. So by August 20, the first part of the mission was accomplished: the guerrillas' operations zone was effectively reduced, limiting them to the banks of the Grande River, since the units, in their movement south, found no evidence of the rebels' presence. Removing the risk to transit on the Santa Cruz–Cochabamba highway and the Santa Cruz–Yacuiba rail line served to calm public fears and to lessen the guerrillas' impact on activity in the region.

In these circumstances there occurred the ambush at Vado del Yeso.

On August 29, Capt. Mario Vargas Salinas of the ATI–3 from Vallegrande received the order from Col. Constantino Valencia Oblitas, unit commander, to transfer to to the Masicurí military post to take command of that post and the one at Lajas, which was under the command of 2d Lt. Pedro Barbery Arzabe. Having arrived in Lajas, Captain Vargas was organizing two committees of civilians to send them south in search of information, according to Colonel Valencia's instructions, when Pvt. Fidel Rea arrived. He had been assigned for some days to the Grande River. His report was important and substantial: at about noon that day, when he was fishing in the Masicurí River, he was approached by Honorato Rojas's son, a twelve-year-old boy who had been told by his father to "warn the soldiers that three bearded men had arrived at his house." Private Rea immediately marched the 30 kilometers to Lajas to inform his superiors, even leaving his weapon and equipment behind.

Quickly organizing the available troops, the two officers, three NCOs, three students from the NCO Military School, and thirty-three soldiers (seventeen from the 12th Infantry Regiment and sixteen from the 8th Cavalry Group, all from the class of 1966)—a total of forty-one men—left for the south to confront that guerrilla group.

The march was accomplished quickly and efficiently with a short stop at Vado de Arenales. They reached Vado de Morón, located some 8 kilometers from Honorato Rojas's house, at three A.M. on August 31. Reinforcing his vanguard, Captain Vargas continued his movement toward the Grande River, taking advantage of his men's knowledge of the area, until he was a scant 500 meters from the Honorato Rojas farm at dawn. At that moment they spotted Rojas's wife, who was coming along the path in their direction with her small children. In conversation with her, the troop commander confirmed the information about the guerrillas' presence. Four more had arrived at her house the night before, but she didn't know why, since they spoke only with her husband. A few minutes later Honorato Rojas himself appeared, bringing some things for his wife. Rojas's information was clear: the guerrillas had asked him to help them cross the Grande River in the direction of the south on that night of the 30th, but he had stated that it was dangerous at night, so they had agreed that he would show them a ford in the afternoon of the following day, which is to say that day, the 31st. Judging this a shining opportunity to defeat the guerrillas, Vargas convinced Honorato to lead the guerrillas, if they really did show up in the afternoon, to the nearest ford, at the junction of the Masicurí with the Grande River, so that the soldiers would have the upper hand. Accompanied by Rojas, he went over to Vado del Yeso, where they finalized details of the the operation to be carried out. He then took leave of the guide so that he could go back to his normal tasks.

Captain Vargas adopted a simple deployment. He left Sergeant Barba on the north bank of the Grande River with six men so that they could position themselves to the rear of the guerrillas when they appeared, and he took his main force to the south bank, where they occupied ambush positions from 6:30 A.M. on, choosing each position carefully and urging his men to remain absolutely silent and motionless as they waited for the guerrilla group to appear.

After the Iñao encounter of August 9 when Pedro had fallen, Joaquín and his group had chosen to head for the Grande River following the course of the Frías River, crossing to the north bank in search of some evidence of Che's group. When they failed to find signs that it had gone by, they tried again to move into the Ñancahuazú zone, where they hoped to meet up with the other group. Weakened by the continual pressure from the troops, fearful of letting the campesinos see them and denounce them, they made the mistake of approaching Honorato Rojas's house, where they had been in February on the occasion of the reconnaissance trip. Inexplicably, they asked his help to find a ford when they could have attempted the river crossing on their own. This indiscretion would prove fatal. On the afternoon of August 31 they went back to Honorato's house. According to plan, he led them to Vado del Yeso, explaining that they could cross there and they could find a path that would lead them toward the Ñancahuazú (see Map 4). Reaching the shore of the river, they paused a few minutes while they observed the south bank and some footprints that the troops had not covered up, but suspecting nothing, they took leave of the guide, who left quickly, and they began to cross.[12]

Meanwhile, the troops in ambush stoically withstood the heat and the bugs all day. At 5:20 P.M. a sentry advised Captain Vargas that movement could be seen on the other shore. Word was passed on to everyone to stay alert and await the signal to open fire. Braulio was the first to enter the water. Holding his weapon at chest level, he made it to shore and, after scanning the surroundings and not discovering the presence of the soldiers, he made signs to the rest to follow him. When the foremost elements were about to get to land and the last were entering the water, Captain Vargas gave the signal to open fire. A short volley followed, while the guerrillas threw down their packs and tried to find cover or to escape by floating with the current. Second Lieutenant Barbery and one soldier located Braulio and cut him down, while from the other bank Sergeant Barba blocked any retreat. A part of the troops moved along the shore to prevent the flight of any of the insurgents. In this way Polo, who had moved some 600 meters downriver, was eliminated. Two survivors, who had been marching in the rear guard, hid behind some rocks. Sergeant Barba forced them to leave their shelter and cross the river to Captain Vargas's position, where Ernesto tried to resist and was cut down, while Paco surrendered easily, becoming the only survivor of the group. Tania, whose body was swept away by the waters, could only be found three days later. Negro, the Peruvian doctor, was found on September 3, and a difference of opinion about his death arose between the Eighth and the Fourth Divisions. While Colonel Zenteno attributed it to the Vado del Yeso action, Col. Reque Terán insisted that Negro had managed to elude the ambush, riding the current, and had later run into Toledo Company which was deployed on the 31st to support the Eighth Division at Vado del Yeso. What is clear is that Negro's body was given by Toledo Company to the Fourth Division for identification and burial, thereby liquidating Joaquín's group and striking a hard blow at the guerrilla movement.

The news impact of this was significant. For the first time the army could show the press the results of an operation that was successful because of the number of casualties, while only the death of Pvt. Antonio Vaca Céspedes was to be mourned. Army morale was raised and strengthened, and a short-term end of the guerrilla war could be glimpsed.

Transporting bodies to Vallegrande was a hard undertaking. Some horses were obtained in the vicinity so as to reach the highway access in Masicurí Alto, where vehicles could be used.

Captain Vargas's decision to act with speed and vigor, and his perseverance in keeping the ambush for twelve hours, bore fruit. Those who had up until now ambushed the army were paid back in kind.

As an example and as a reward, the president of the republic promoted Capt. Mario Vargas to the rank of major and 2d Lt. Pedro Barbery to the rank of lieutenant there in the operations zone, and this action was spoken of favorably in all units. The identification of the three Cubans (Joaquín, Alejandro, and Braulio) and of the Peruvian (Negro), in addition to Tania, served as tangible proof of foreign participation in the guerrilla war. Among the Bolivians, Ernesto was listed as a student in Cuba. Moisés Guevara, the mining leader, was a member of the Marxist-Leninist Communist party and had brought Paco with him. Polo was one of the first to join up, recruited by Coco, and he even traveled in December to Viacha to take leave of his family before joining the ranks definitively on the 19th. Walter had joined on January 2, also brought in by Coco.

Discussing the overall situation, the commander-in-chief, Gen. Alfredo Ovando Candia, very clearly stated: "The armed forces are striking a series of hard blows at the Castroites, fundamentally because we have gained experience and we are carrying out a series of tactics aimed at destroying the enemy. Their fighting ability has been blunted, they are reduced to their minimal force, and now it will be hard for them to face the armed forces."

In effect, the time when surprise and initiative were in the hands of the guerrillas was over. They now amounted to a pursued and reduced force that had no way of leaving the operations zone in the face of a siege that was closing in daily. Although they could hide temporarily because it was difficult for the military to locate so small a force in so vast a territory, at some point they would have to become visible and make contact with the campesinos to supply themselves, and that would surely mean information for the army, since by then it could count on full campesino support for the regular forces.

THE OLAS MEETING

Meantime in Havana they were carrying out one more step of the plan aimed at unifying hemispheric guerrilla movements. In the first half of August, a meeting of the Latin American Solidarity Organization—OLAS—was held. Several aspects of the meeting were related to the guerrillas in Bolivia:

—In the opening speech, the Cuban president Osvaldo Dorticós, sent "Special greetings, a message of admiration and affection to our brother in combat, Commander Ernesto Che Guevara, wherever he is." By then, the Bolivian government had already made Che's presence official; Debray's and Bustos's statements were proof of it. Nonetheless, Cuba still refused to admit as a fact the presence of Che and a group of Cubans fighting in Bolivia. Possibly the military victories of recent days made the guerrillas' patrons doubt their chances for victory.

—The Bolivian delegation was considered disastrous. It was made up of Aldo Flores and Ramiro Otero of the PCB, Mario Carrasco of the PRIN, and Ricardo Cano of the FLIN (National Liberation Front, the political arm of the ELN), who took positions opposing the guerrilla war. Flores, who tried to pass as a representative of the ELN, was denied accreditation by the Cuban hierarchy, so that the "Bolivian" guerrilla forces had no one to speak for them.[13]

—In the closing speech of the OLAS, Fidel Castro made no mention of Che or the guerrilla war in Bolivia, despite the fact that Che had been designated "Honorary President" of the conference.

—The theory approved at the conference, although it reaffirmed the Tricontinental concept that revolutionary war should be the goal of all progressive forces and admitted the existence of conditions all over the Latin American continent that made this possible and justifiable, also ambiguously stated that in certain countries conditions were not immediately evident. Apparently the intention was to anticipate the defeat of some guerrilla focos, among them the Bolivian.

Despite these assertions, it was felt necessary to issue a document expressing support for the Ñancahuazú struggle in some way, and so a resolution was drafted and approved stating:

The First Latin American Solidarity Conference declares its fervent revolutionary solidarity with the guerrillas fighting in Bolivia, who with their victorious appearance have created new conditions for the struggle of all peoples of Latin America. These auspicious battles have begun in Ñancahuazú and they show that a new path has been opened for the long-suffering and rebellious people of Bolivia, which will lead them to complete victory. Against the intervention of the Green Berets, Yankee soldiers, and interventionists at the service of imperialism and dictatorship, the peoples of Latin America must rise up.

With regard to this situation, the First OLAS Conference declares its full support for the heroic Bolivian guerrilla movement and urges all revolutionary forces of the Latin American continent to commit themselves to a vast campaign in their respective countries, so that their solidarity will become practice. It should be remembered that this is the most effective means to reinforce armed struggle wherever it appears and to prepare necessary steps for initiating one of the highest forms of struggle in those countries where this phase of revolutionary action has still not been reached. Our destiny is closely tied to the destiny of the Bolivian people. Our peoples must be assured that our lands will be bases for solidarity and struggle and never bases for aggression.

None of this had any influence on the remaining guerrilla group, which—now reduced to only twenty-two men—learned about the extermination of Joaquín's group over the radio. The news, at first received with disbelief, was assimilated little by little from the proofs that were presented daily—identifying members of the group, reporting statements by the survivor, Paco, and bearing other details that made Che and his men see that more than four months of searching (since April 17) had ended tragically and that from then on they were left to their own devices.

This situation was reflected in a breakdown of morale in the group, who urgently needed food, medicine, and rest to recover their strength. Perhaps at this point they should have discussed the advisability of going on with the project, which obviously was taking on negative aspects with each passing day. Instead, on the one hand they clung to a kind of tenuous hope that the news was not true, that Joaquín or some of his people were still in a position to rejoin them; on the other hand, the terms of the bitter, distressing debate that took place on the night of August 9 in the vicinity of the Rosita River were still in the air. So many differences came to light and so many things had been said there that a breach was created between Cubans and Bolivians. Perhaps for that reason no one said anything and everyone quietly accepted Che's decision to remain for some days in the region of Masicurí and the Grande River. The area had a scattered population and some cattle, so supply problems could be easily solved, but the presence of troops would force them to begin moving again after two brief skirmishes.

NOTES

1. Che's diary, entry for July 6.
2. Pacho's diary, entry for July 6. Inti Peredo, *Mi campaña con el Che*, Chapter 7.
3. Che's diary, entry for July 6.
4. Pacho's diary, entry for July 7.
5. See Map 7.
6. Che's diary, entries for July 29 and 30.
7. Of the two H–19 helicopters available for use in operations, one had been provided for a Border Commission inspection that was evaluating the Chovoreca case, and the other was located in Camiri for repairs and could not leave because of prevailing bad weather.
8. To compensate for the withdrawal of the units that were transferred to the Eighth Division at the end of June, and at the request of the Fourth Division for more strength, on August 2 three companies (A, B, and C) belonging to the Third Division of the army arrived at Camiri. They had been organized, prepared, and trained in Villamontes to participate in the operations. Although these units did not enter into any combat, they displayed efficiency, discipline, and above all aggressiveness. The total strength of the three companies was 260 men.
9. Che's diary, entries for February 25, February 26, March 22, August 8. Rolando's diary, entry for March 25. Pombo's diary, entry for May 14. Pacho's diary, entries for February 25, August 8, September 15 and 16.
10. Che's diary, entry for August 19.
11. Che's diary, entry for April 14. Message No. 38. Documents captured by the army.
12. Honorato Rojas Vaca was rewarded by the army by being incorporated into the service roster with the rank of sergeant, assigned to Manchego Assault Regiment in Guabirá–Santa Cruz, where he was also given a small plot of land on which to build a house. At dawn on July 14, 1969, nearly two years after the Vado del Yeso ambush, he was assassinated with two revolver shots as he was sleeping, apparently as reprisal for his participation in the counterinsurgency.
13. Message No. 39 from Fidel Castro to Che, August 26. Archives of the General Command of the Bolivian Army.
Che's diary, entry for September 5.

Drawings of guerrillas done by Bustos: Pombo, Urbano, Ricardo, and Chino.

Thanks to these drawings the army was able to identify the guerrillas: Mora, Andrés, Nato, and Pacho.

The remaining portraits: Marcos, Pedro, Negro, and Chapaco.

Photographs of the Cubans on the false passports they used to enter Bolivia: Alejandro, Urbano, Antonio, and Moro.

Benigno, Joaquín, Tuma, and Marcos.

Braulio, Miguel, Ricardo, and Rolando.

Chapter 11

LA HIGUERA

The troops that had carried out the successful ambush were replaced on
September 1 by another company, detached by ATI–3 from Vallegrande
with the mission to occupy Vado del Yeso and to keep up surveillance in
the area in the expectation that the guerrilla group would show up there.
A reinforced section under the command of 2d Lt. Guillermo Román
Carranza arrived at a place called Yajopampa near Honorato Rojas's house
on September 3 at about 2 P.M. after ten hours of marching. They adopted
a peripheral security formation while they rested and cleaned their weapons.

One of the sentries saw men approaching at 3 P.M. and called out, "Some
gentlemen are coming." Because of the distance and the growth on the
path, he didn't realize that they were the guerrillas. In fact, a group of
guerrillas under Inti's command was on its way to the houses at Yajopampa
intending to get supplies. Sgt. José Ortiz reacted quickly, simply firing his
weapon at the group without thinking of any other response. Initially the
guerrillas took cover behind the buildings, but the soldiers tried to surround
them, moving to one side. The guerrillas then drew back, killing Pvt. Benito
Velasco and wounding Pvt. Fanor Lino. The nature of the terrain precluded
any quick pursuit, and contact was lost; but the soldiers had prevented
them from obtaining supplies.

With this confirmation of the guerrillas' presence in the Masicurí area,
the commander of ATI–3 sent another company to keep up the pressure
on Che and his men. This unit, called Tiger Company, led by 2d Lt.
Eduardo Galindo Grandchant, was made up of Manchego Regiment draftees from the 1966 class, who had completed their military tour of duty
and had been participating in counterinsurgency operations since April,
initially in the Fourth Division, where they were sent as a reinforcement
through June 24. Then they had returned to the jurisdiction of the Eighth

Division. The unit had carried out missions in Abapó and Florida, was sent to Samaipata to begin the Parabanó operation, and finally was incorporated into ATI–3 at Vallegrande beginning September 1.

On the 3rd, this unit was detached to Yajopampa to coordinate its action with Second Lieutenant Román, whom they joined in Lajas. They received the latest briefings and continued their march to the last point where the guerrillas had been seen. Arriving at the junction of the Masicurí and Grande Rivers, they patrolled the area, engaging in combat on the 6th with Urbano, who was coming in advance of the guerrilla group so as to carry out an order to call off an ambush that the insurgents had laid on another path.

The clash came as a surprise to both sides. No casualties resulted, and though Second Lieutenant Galindo did not realize that the guerrilla group was divided and that his men had taken a position between the two groups, he maneuvered so as to surround them. This took him out of the danger zone, but he also lost contact with the guerrillas. Although he kept up the effort to pursue them for four days, he advanced slowly because of the precautions he took to avoid being ambushed. At that point a notable event occurred. This unit found Tania's body on the 7th and requested a helicopter to transport it to Vallegrande. That same day the president of the republic, Gen. René Barrientos Ortuño, showed up at the post, and decided to stay with the troops for twenty-four hours and accompany Second Lieutenants Galindo and Molina on the patrols they were running in the vicinity in search of the guerrillas' trail. The presence of the chief executive with the troops near the area where the guerrillas were operating was later made known to the public, who appreciated this gesture of the general's as a true sign of his character. It was encouraging for all units to see him share the risks with officers and men with no additional security.

After the first week of September, there was again no news of the guerrillas. It was assumed that they had moved westward up the Grande River, but since their location could not be determined, the deployment was modified. The Galindo company and Braun Squadron—which was also in the area under the command of Second Lieutenant Lara—were withdrawn to Vallegrande to be used when the enemy's position became known.[1]

During these days the guerrilla group made small advances along the course of the Grande River, crossing it several times because of the difficulty of maneuvering on its banks. Internal tensions flared up again, and uncomfortable incidents took place among some of the guerrillas. This forced Che to speak with the Bolivians individually and to take a tough attitude with the Cubans, in an attempt to pull the group back together. Fights over food, arguments over assignments, and other problems created a tense atmosphere that worsened with the difficulties of the route and the lack of prospects for the future.[2]

DESTRUCTION OF THE URBAN NETWORK

In La Paz, agents of the Ministry of Justice, after a thorough investigation of the documentation and photographs found by the army in the caches at the camp, made a roundup of everybody who was thought to be involved in the guerrillas' urban support network. The capture of Loyola Guzmán, clearly identified in several photographs with the major figures of the guerrilla band right at the Ñancahuazú camp, dealt a severe blow to what little remained of the structure that had provided the guerrilla movement with some backing in the cities.

Loyola Guzmán, twenty-five years old, a philosophy student at the Universidad Mayor San Andrés and a member of the Bolivian Communist Youth, tried to commit suicide by jumping from the fourth floor of the ministry building when she was being interrogated, but a tree broke her fall and she was not seriously injured. Under pressure from university people, who thought her arrest unfair, all the evidence held by the government was made public, and she was allowed to be interviewed by the press and by the leaders of the students' union. In their presence, she publicly admitted her involvement in clear and precise terms: "I am fully conscious of my situation. I am in this situation out of conviction. Despite the error that I have committed, since many documents have gotten out that can be used by the authorities to arrest many people, I hold to my ideas. Although this is a blow to us, the struggle will go on, even if many more people must die." In view of all of these clarifications, no one could do anything more for her, and she was handed over to civilian justice to be tried with other detainees.

PROOFS OF CUBAN INVOLVEMENT

Continuing the offensive aimed at destroying any possibility of support for the guerrilla movement, and also at exposing foreign influence upon it, President Barrientos and the commander-in-chief, General Ovando, held a press conference at the Government Palace on September 22 at which they showed foreign correspondents and local journalists all the evidence available to date demonstrating that the insurgency was being led by Commandant Guevara, who had the backing and participation of members of the upper echelon of the Cuban Communist party, and that Castro's involvement in Bolivian domestic affairs was a proven fact. The abundant documentation and available photographs made it possible to establish:

—That Ernesto Guevara entered the country using Uruguayan passports numbered 130220 and 130740, issued in Montevideo on December 2 and 22, 1965, under the names of Ramón Benítez Fernández and Adolfo Mena Gonzales.

—That for that purpose he had shaved his head and beard to change his appearance. Photographs of the entire process of change were shown.

—This was substantiated by comparing the fingerprints on the passports with those on Che's draft card, which had been supplied by the Argentine government.

—Joaquín, Braulio, and others were clearly identified as members of the Cuban army with a display of the passports they had used to enter Bolivia.

—At this time two offers made by President Barrientos in the previous days were made official. The first regarded guarantees extended to all Bolivian members of the guerrilla force who laid down their arms, "since it is well known that they are disillusioned because they are not receiving the pay that was offered to them and also because they know that they are not gaining anything with this human slaughter ordered by Fidel Castro." (This impression was taken from some of the statements made to the army by Paco, the survivor of Vado del Yeso, and by Daniel and Orlando, who had been enlisted for the guerrilla operation by Moisés Guevara.) The second offer had to do with the ransom set by the government for the capture of Che Guevara dead or alive, preferably alive, at 50,000 Bolivian pesos (approximately $4,200 U.S.). The commander-in-chief closed the news conference firmly and securely, stating, "The victory of the armed forces is near and those who managed to get out of Vietnam, the Congo, and Peru will die in Bolivia, which is as always a cradle of liberty."

At the time this press conference was being held, Foreign Minister Guevara Arze was presenting the same documentation and proofs at OAS headquarters in Washington, D.C., for the purpose of demonstrating Cuban involvement in Bolivia and demanding sanctions that ultimately were not applied by the international organization, which took only a lukewarm position on the matter.

DEBRAY'S TRIAL

In Camiri, after a long process of preparation and waiting, combined with picturesque and absurd goings-on, the long-awaited trial of Debray, Bustos, and the others accused began on September 25. The withdrawal of the defense lawyer, Dr. Walter Flores, made it necessary for the court to name Dr. Raúl Novillo public defender for the Frenchman. For his part, Bustos hired Dr. Augusto Mendizábal Moya as his defense lawyer, while the Bolivians on trial were given Dr. Arturo La Fuente as their public defender. In addition, relatives of those fallen at Ñancahuazú, constituted as civilian litigants, hired Dr. Manuel Morales Dávila, and relatives of the soldiers ambushed at Iripití hired Dr. Adalid Herbas Castro, who together with the attorney general, Col. Remberto Iriarte, completed the roster needed to begin public proceedings.

After being captured and presented to the press, Paco voiced heavy attacks against Debray and accused him of bearing arms at Ñancahuazú and having been in touch with the major guerrilla leaders at all times, thus forming an integral part of the group. When the accused was asked about this, he only stated that he used weapons for hunting and that all of this would be discussed at the trial.

When the proceedings began, the attorney general enumerated in his opening statement all the proofs that existed of foreign participation in the guerrilla movement and then asked that the maximum sentence provided by the law, thirty years in jail, be applied to Debray and Bustos. For the Bolivians he asked for lesser sentences, because they were obviously sorry for what they had done and had alleged that they had been deceived. Although this was only the first chapter of a trial that was expected to last several weeks, it made a strong impression on the public, who avidly followed the events in far-off Camiri, which became an important focus of the international news. But the impact of the trial had to give way to other, more important news originating in the operations zone when it was announced that in a clash with the insurgents on the 26th, the army had inflicted new losses on the guerrilla band, among them Coco Peredo, who until then had been considered the Bolivian head of the movement together with his brother Inti.

LA HIGUERA

On September 16, Che abandoned the Grande River and proceeded along the La Pesca River in search of high ground and also supplies (see Map 8). The guerrillas thus entered a new geographic area differing from the one they had been operating in up to that time. With elevations as high as 2,000 m, vegetation was sparser and virtually nonexistent on the peaks. Only the canyons and ravines offered good cover. On the other hand, the population was denser. In nearly all the small valleys there were communities devoted to agriculture and cattle-raising, so that there was no way the guerrillas could fail to be observed. It was a fact, however, that the military deployment had not yet reached those communities because it was concentrated more in the east, on the banks of the Grande River and those of its tributaries that had been favored by the guerrillas up until then: Ñancahuazú, Masicurí, and Rositas.

The decision to move westward and then to the north was made despite the fact that Che himself thought it probable that the army was allowing them to move so that it could trap them in an area more suited to its maneuvers.[3] To prevent the campesinos from denouncing them, they captured and took with them everybody they met. They set as their destination the community of Los Sitanos up the La Pesca River. The caravan—for the guerrilla movement had turned into that—was made up of twenty-two fighters; their animals, including cows and mules; and campesino prisoners. They arrived at the hamlet of Los Sitanos on the night of the 20th, occupying the entire town immediately and cutting the telegraph line that came in from Vallegrande, although that line had not been operating for a long time. The search for food and clothing in the little general store did not produce much, and they set out again in the direction of Alto Seco, some four leagues away, a place where the cart track from Vallegrande ended and where only small vehicles could get through. En route they crossed the Piraimirí River and found the houses along its banks deserted, because people preferred to leave rather than to face them. The entry of the group, preceded by the vanguard at dawn on September 22, was effected without major incident and the small town of 300 inhabitants remained in the guerrillas' hands for nearly twenty-four hours. This occupation of the town had important consequences, for it was the first occasion that the guerrillas remained for a fairly long time in a village and tried to obtain volunteers for their ranks. After cutting the telegraph line linking the town with Vallegrande, and preventing the inhabitants from leaving for any other place, they searched all the houses and then set about preparing their meal. They set up their command post in an abandoned house 200 m outside of town. At the two stores they bought the entire stock of clothing (trousers, shirts, and some pairs of shoes), but this did not cover all their needs. To the campesinos, who very rarely saw this type of entertainment, it was all a novelty. Che's entry, riding a mule, constantly looked after by his men, made them realize that he was sick and that all the guerrillas showed him great deference, but the truth was that most of the campesinos had never heard of the guerrilla chief, and had only had news that foreign "communist bandits" were present in the area, so their natural reserve as rural people increased in the circumstances. The guerrillas' demand to see the mayor was not heeded. They were told that he was not in Alto Seco—he had left the day before. It was, however, very clear—the entire population knew it—that when news came that the guerrillas were coming into town, the mayor had gone into hiding in a neighbor's house and would stay there for the length of the occupation of the town.

In reprisal for the absence of this authority, the guerrillas confiscated all the merchandise that he had in his store, answering his wife's complaints by saying that if her husband was the mayor, he was in the pay of the government, so "let his president pay for these purchases."

All day the inhabitants of Alto Seco remained alert and afraid. Departures from the town were closely controlled. In the area of the cemetery, where the cart track came in, trenches were dug and barricades posted. The pickup truck that regularly ran from Vallegrande to Alto Seco did not arrive that day although it was expected, and this made everyone more nervous.

At night the order was given for all male inhabitants of the town to meet at the school for a talk with the guerrillas. The account by one of the campesinos present describes the conversation:

Roberto, Coco Peredo [it was really Inti] began the session stating that he had brought them together to inform them of their goals. "You may believe that we are crazy to fight the way we're fighting," he said. "You call us bandits, but we are fighting for you, for the working class, for workers who earn very little while the military has high salaries. You work for them but, tell me, what do they do for you? You don't have water here, you don't have electricity, the telegraph isn't working. You are abandoned, like all Bolivians. That's why we're fighting."

Nobody dared to speak; the campesinos kept quiet. The guerrillas were pointing their rifles at them menacingly—they wanted to humiliate us.

Peredo concluded indicating that all those that wished to were welcome to join the guerrilla movement to keep fighting until Barrientos was toppled.

Then Che spoke: "We want you to come of your own volition. Not by force. We don't use force. Everybody who wants to join will be well received." Turning to another point, the guerrilla chief stated:

The Army says that they killed Joaquín and other comrades of ours, but that's a lie; it's all army propaganda. The bodies they showed at Vallegrande came from the cemeteries. It's a lie; they haven't killed guerrilla fighters, and I can assure you of it because just two days ago I was in touch with Joaquín.

Che ended his statement saying:

We will continue fighting in every country to free ourselves of North American oppression. You have heard about Santo Domingo; it's a country just like Bolivia. There the Americans went in and killed many campesinos who were seeking a better life. The same thing is going to happen here. That's why we're fighting.

The guerrilla chief's words were met with total silence. No gesture was forthcoming from the campesinos, no expression that might indicate what they were feeling. Earlier only the schoolmaster had asked about socialist doctrine and whether they would be fighting within towns. The others present, more astonished than frightened, were simply trying to assimilate what they had heard. They knew nothing of Joaquín or Santo Domingo, nor of the Americans, so their understanding of everything that had been said was reduced to two expressions that they did know—"Army" and "Barrientos"—and the fact of the matter was that in that area, both were accepted and the president in particular was considered to be a friend. Therefore reactions were silent and even hostile.

After the meeting, one young campesino approached one of the youngest guerrillas, an almost beardless boy called Pablito, and asked him if it was worthwhile joining up. The response in Quechua, given quickly before the others could hear, was blunt: "Don't be a fool, we're all washed up and we don't know how to get out of here."

Early in the morning on the 23rd, the guerrilla band left the hamlet in small groups. They took a campesino as a guide and headed west toward the Santa Elena River and the hamlet of Loma Larga, where they arrived at dawn on the 24th after staying hidden during the day in an orchard near the river. All the inhabitants of the area left their houses and disappeared when they showed up.

In Vallegrande on the afternoon of September 22, the ATI–3 command had received the news that the guerrillas were in Alto Seco. Lacking troops to send in that direction, the commander, Colonel Valencia, had to arrange for Manchego Company and Braun Squadron, which were in Masicurí, to be transported to Vallegrande to receive new orders. The troops arrived in the city on the evening of the 23rd and left near midnight in two directions. Braun Squadron under the command of 2d Lt. Alfredo Lara followed the Vallegrande-Pucará–Alto Seco route, and Manchego Company was ordered to occupy Pucará under the command of 2d Lt. Eduardo Galindo. By the 24th, with this deployment, the insurgents' chances of proceeding north toward Vallegrande were cut off. Simultaneously the commander of the Eighth Division in Santa Cruz, seeing that the guerrilla group had abandoned the Grande River area, decided to transfer his command post to Vallegrande so as to be closer to the action. He also moved Manchego Ranger–2 Regiment, which had completed its training with the American mission in La Esperanza, to Vallegrande so that it could be used in the final stage of the fighting, which was drawing near. The 650 men were sent at night on the 25th, arriving at their destination mid-morning on the 26th. With these forces, the division commander, Colonel Zenteno, began to plan the next moves together with his general staff in Vallegrande.

Meanwhile Braun Squadron reached Alto Seco and verified that the guerrillas had left the area. Nevertheless they held to their ambush positions on the outskirts, but on the 25th they received orders to withdraw to Pucará to allow Second Lieutenant Galindo's company to advance to La Higuera. There was information that the guerrillas had headed for the Grande River rather than to continue along the Alto Seco–Pucará road. That same information was also transmitted to the Fourth Division so that it would use its resources to reinforce the towns west of the Grande River in Chuquisaca Department, which were under its jurisdiction, in order to prevent the guerrillas from leaving the area. Accordingly, the Fourth Division detached CITE–2 Company to monitor Padilla and Villa Serrano.

On September 26 at 6:00 in the morning, the Galindo company began its movement toward La Higuera. At 11:00 they reached the Khara-Khara heights, from which the hamlet of La Higuera could be observed from a distance of some 3 kilometers.

After leaving Loma Larga, the guerrilla group reached El Pujio on the

25th and went on through Trancamayo and Abra del Picacho at dawn on the 26th. From there, taking no special precaution and not even waiting for twilight, they moved to the hamlet of La Higuera and occupied it at about 10 A.M. A quick search of the houses revealed only a telegram from the authorities at Vallegrande in the mayor's house. It stated that any news regarding the guerrillas should be reported immediately. By disconnecting the telephone, the insurgents thought they could prevent or at least delay the report of their presence in the area. In conversation with the mayor's daughter, Coco Peredo seemed friendly and cheerful, full of life. Although he was spent with fatigue, he made a good impression. Che kept out of the way. He did not speak with the inhabitants (mostly women) who had stayed in town, and he remained surrounded by some men who apparently were his bodyguards, holding on to the two mules that the group had with it.

The guerrillas were in a hurry to leave La Higuera in order to reach a nearby town one league to the north, called El Jagüey, by following the bridle path that goes along the heights in the direction of Pucará. This movement by the guerrillas in plain daylight through an open area with no vegetation and with considerable population cannot be explained. It was logical to suppose that their presence would be detected. The radio news reported their every move with only a few hours' delay, and the army certainly had to be making plans to cut off their route. They were thus running a high risk. Despite all of these factors, at 1 P.M., the vanguard, made up of Coco, Benigno, Miguel, Julio, Aniceto, and Pablito, started moving again while the main body remained in the hamlet. Half an hour later, when the rest of the guerrilla band was getting ready to leave, shots were heard, indicating without a doubt a clash with the soldiers.

As a matter of fact Second Lieutenant Galindo had observed from the Khara-Khara heights the movement of the first men from the guerrilla group, who were marching toward his position. Accordingly, he quickly organized an ambush on the path. Given the distance maintained between each man, it was difficult to ambush the whole vanguard, and at the same time it was not possible to wait for the main guerrilla body, since the troops' positions would be visible due to the lack of covering foliage. So combat was initiated against the vanguard when it came into the ambush zone. After the first shots, as the guerrillas drew back, Second Lieutenant Galindo ordered his troops to advance in pursuit. When they reached La Higuera, they found that the main guerrilla body had abandoned the hamlet and had gone into some canyons that feed into the Grande River. Redeploying, they recovered the bodies of those who had fallen in the ambush— Miguel and Julio in the heights and Coco farther down, where he had been taken by Benigno in an attempt to rescue him while he was still alive. What had happened was that Coco, wounded, had been transferred to the rear guard but had been hit again by the soldiers' fire. They wounded Benigno at the same time, and he was forced to leave Coco's by-then-lifeless body. Benigno retreated with Aniceto and Pablito to La Higuera, where Che was waiting with the rest of the men. Letting the mules go in an attempt to throw off their pursuers, Che ordered the group to go into the canyon that runs westward toward the Grande River. They managed to get some kilometers away and enter San Antonio Canyon, moving some distance into it until they found a safe place to spend the night.

In the confusion of combat two other men had disappeared: Camba, who had so often asked to be freed from the guerrilla movement, and who had been promised he could leave after La Higuera, and León, who left his equipment and ran into another ravine so as to get away from the group. These defections amounted to another hard blow to the guerrillas, who were left without a vanguard and were forced to stay in the area with the problem of the Doctor and Chino, who were very sick and weak, thus hampering movement. After picking up the guerrillas' bodies, the Galindo company was ordered to withdraw to Pucará while the Lara squadron occupied La Higuera and tried to find the guerrillas' trail. News of the combat at La Higuera prompted the Eighth Division command in Vallegrande to immediately detach part of the Ranger–2 in order to keep up the pursuit.

First all light vehicles were assembled (the Pucará road did not permit truck traffic) to transport a company. Capt. Celso Torrelio Villa's A Company was given this assignment and was to enter the operations zone that same night of the 26th. When Captain Torrelio reported personnel problems in his unit, the mission was shifted to B Company, under Capt. Gary Prado, who said he was ready to take it on. The orders were as follows: "After motor transport to Pucará, march on foot from there to Vado del Oro at the Grande River and close off the guerrillas' escape route."

Beginning their movement at dusk, B Company reached Pucará at 9:30 P.M. After checking for new developments and hiring a guide, they marched along the Pucará–El Tolar–El Quiñal road at 11:30 toward their destination at Vado del Oro. After several hours of marching along a narrow mountain path, with his troops fatigued (B Company had traveled from Santa Cruz to Vallegrande the night before), the company commander ordered a halt at El Quiñal to wait for morning. Starting up again and arriving at San Antonio Canyon, they learned at Señor Francisco Rivas's house that his dogs had barked a good deal that night in the direction of the canyon, indicating the presence of strangers there. Since San Antonio Canyon led into La Higuera Canyon, a search of the area was undertaken. It ended in the capture of Camba, after a brief resistance. He surrendered to the soldiers after his ammunition was spent. When he was interrogated by the commander of the Ranger battalion, Maj. Miguel Ayoroa, and the S–2 (battalion intelligence officer), Capt. Raúl López Leyton, together with the company commander, the prisoner said he did not know where the rest of the group had ended up. He said that he had been separated from the rest the day before in La Higuera and had not been able to find them. Asked where the rallying point had been set, he stated that Che had not set one, and that was why he was lost. The search of the canyon produced nothing else, but in point of fact Che's group was 200 meters above, listening closely to everything that was going on and fearing that they were going to be discovered at any moment.[4]

León, the other fugitive from the guerrilla group, arrived at nightfall on the 27th at the house of a campesino named Tomás Peña, where he got a change of clothing. He tried to make it to Pucará, leaving his weapon behind. He was judged suspicious by a highway service work detail in the area, and was detained and handed over to the troops in Pucará. From there he was sent to Vallegrande.

The guerrilla band, now reduced to only seventeen men, was in a very tough situation. Although there were only two army units in the area where they were operating—Ranger–2 B Company under Captain Prado with 145 men, and Braun Squadron under Second Lieutenant Lara with 37 men— their patrol activity in all the gorges and canyons kept the insurgents on tenterhooks on September 28, 29, and 30. The guerrillas were locked into a little ravine, unable to light a fire to cook their scant food supplies, and lacking water, which could only be brought at night when some men took the risk of going down into another canyon that had a small brook with bitter water. They constantly listened to the radio news and no longer doubted that Joaquín's group had been eliminated. Their efforts to find an exit from the area always came across the presence of troops, and this increased their discomfort. This state of mind was reflected in everything they did, and it made some members of the group think that the end was near. Morbid thoughts possessed the minds of most of them. An entry from Pacho's diary will give us an idea. The quotation comes from October 1:

Surrounded.—We started out the day walking. Soon after we camped we heard fire from automatic and semi-automatic weapons; it seemed they were coming from the canyon. At 9 A.M. a plane flew over us, apparently looking for information by radio. Fernando asked me for a cigarette and asked me to put together a clip for his pistol. He has the pistol in his hand as if he had to decide to kill himself before being taken prisoner. I am in the same frame of mind. 9:25 A.M. Pombo is on guard, I'm cleaning my weapon. We have few bullets, have food in our packs but can't cook it. The water is now very far away, given the distance we walked in the night. Only the sound of birds can be heard. The campesinos have left their homes. The night walk was like walking through hell: thorns on the trail stick into our feet because we are wearing sandals, and into our legs, and there are thorns on the sides at head level; it was terrible. Only Fernando's commanding voice gets people to walk. The guerrilla operation is slow because of men like Chino; we make tracks when we walk. Besides the tension of the moment, I dream sleeping and awake of T. and E. [his wife and son]

Nevertheless it was to be army decisions that would give the insurgents a breather. The Eighth Division command in Vallegrande, concerned over the lack of news of the guerrillas after September 26, ordered Captain Prado's B Company to search the area comprising Vado del Oro–Ocampo–Porongo–El Fuerte (following the course of the Grande River) where it was to link up with Florida Company, which was undertaking the same mission from the south, and CITE–2 Company, Fourth Division, which would come from Villa Serrano to prevent the guerrillas from crossing the river and entering Chuquisaca Department.

The operation was accomplished flawlessly. B Company combed both banks of the Grande River until they reached El Fuerte; results were negative. After exchanging briefings with the units mentioned, they went up through El Estanque–El Pujio–Trancamayo to Abra del Picacho, where they set up a patrol base on October 4 to continue searching the area. The First Section of the company, under the command of 2d Lt. Germán Venegas stayed at El Quiñal, near La Higuera, searching through the adjacent canyons, with the mission of preventing the guerrillas from moving north.

Parallel to this mission, the division command replaced Braun Squadron with Ranger–2 A Company under Captain Torrelio, which set up its command post in Pucará on October 2 and detached two sections with 2d Lts. Carlos Pérez and Eduardo Huerta to La Higuera to keep watch on the area where the guerrillas were presumed still hiding, in the absence of any information indicating they were in another sector. Before being relieved, Braun Squadron sustained a brief skirmish with a guerrilla patrol, which fled and left behind a pack with first-aid materials and some supplies, confirming their presence in the area.

Ranger–2 A and B companies and Florida Company, Sixth Division, assigned to the Eighth Division, kept up their search operations on October 5, 6, and 7 from their bases in La Higuera, Abra del Picacho, and Loma Larga without finding anything.

COMBAT AT EL CHURO CANYON

At 6:30 A.M. on October 8, 2d Lt. Carlos Pérez, commander of the First Section of A Company at its base at La Higuera, received word from the campesino Pedro Peña that while he was irrigating a small potato field at El Churo Canyon, a tributary of San Antonio Canyon, he saw a group of seventeen men pass by. After advancing some meters farther up, they had set up a kind of camp and were staying there. The campesino had waited until dawn to go to La Higuera in order to inform the army.

Second Lieutenant Pérez assembled his troops and part of Second Lieutenant Huerta's section, and headed toward the area immediately. Making radio contact with Captain Prado at 7:00 A.M. according to previously established procedures, he reported the event to him and asked the captain to reinforce his operation, since he did not have support arms (60–mm mortars and machine guns). The commander of B Company agreed and proceeded immediately to the area with a section of riflemen, two 60–mm mortars, and a 30–caliber Browning machine gun. Upon arriving at the high ground near El Churo Canyon, he made contact with Second Lieutenants Pérez and Huerta and, after evaluating the situation, assumed command and adopted a plan appropriate for the terrain.

El Churo Canyon, some 300 meters long, feeds into San Antonio Canyon after merging with La Tusca Canyon. Since the guerrillas might have moved in the time elapsed since the campesino saw them, Captain Prado ordered the troops of A Company to enter through the upper part of El Churo Canyon while the Third Section of B Company, under the command of Sergeant Huanca, were to do the same on the upper part of La Tusca Canyon until both canyons were searched. In order to prevent the guerrillas from escaping if they were still inside, he set up the command post and the blocking position with mortars and machine guns at the confluence of the two canyons. The starting positions were occupied by 12:30, and the search operation began. The first shots were fired immediately.

Since dawn the guerrilla force had heard the troop movements, but they had not decided on a course of action. During the night, when Chapaco and Willy were moving into the area, they thought they saw a light moving along the canyon. Although it disappeared momentarily, Che did not investigate. It was the campesino watering the potato field. When he heard noise from the guerrillas, he put out his lantern and kept still. At 2:30 A.M., the guerrillas decided to stop at the headwaters of El Churo Canyon, since they were all weak and fatigued and were uncertain about which direction to take. Just before daybreak, the individuals who went out on reconnaissance—Benigno and Pacho to the right, and Urbano and Ñato to the left—returned with the news that there was a movement of troops on the heights, which the guerrillas had hoped to reach.

The first men of Second Lieutenant Pérez's section were already occupying positions. At that time the guerrilla band had two options. They could retreat downstream to a more convenient position, where the soldiers had not arrived. This meant they would be turning back toward San Antonio Canyon, where they had stayed for several days, and moving away from the high ground where they had hoped to break the encirclement. Or they could stay in the position they held, in hopes that the army would not discover them, as had been the case in the last few days. A quick scan of La Tusca Canyon showed them that it did not come out onto high ground, so Che decided to remain at El Churo in order to avoid returning over the same route at night for the purpose of breaking the siege. Accordingly, they organized the defense taking great care not to be detected by the army. Although they made contingency plans, the guerrillas did not set a rallying point in the event that they were separated. The band divided into three groups. The vanguard—Pombo, Inti, Darío, and Ñato—covered the upper part of the canyon; Che remained in the center, hidden in the most sheltered part of the canyon; and the rear guard—Chapaco, Moro, Pablo, and Eustaquio—were sent beyond the confluence of the canyons, and thereby outside of the encirclement organized by Captain Prado.

When it became clear that the army was mounting a careful operation, it was too late to attempt to get the main group out, so at the time that the first soldiers of Second Lieutenant Pérez's section sought to enter the upper part of El Churo Canyon, Inti, Pombo, and Urbano began firing, killing two men and halting the movement momentarily. Shots were exchanged as each force tried to maneuver into better positions. The troops had in effect cut off the exit to high ground but were prevented from moving into the area of the canyon.

With the evidence of the guerrilla presence at El Churo Canyon, Captain Prado, at the same time that he ordered Sergeant Huanca to speed up the search at La Tusca, ordered the machine gun and mortars to be pointed toward the point of confluence in order to hold off the guerrillas' certain attempt to break the siege through that area. In fact, before the Huanca section could complete its mission, the first attempt to break through was made and repulsed with mortar and machine-gun fire—one burst of which wounded Che in the right calf, destroyed his M–1 carbine at the chamber, and pierced the black beret that he was wearing. The guerrillas were obliged to retreat into the canyon, where they occupied new positions.

The situation was difficult for Che's group. The advance of the troops on the upper side had been checked, but they themselves were confined to a stretch of some 200 meters of the canyon that had sufficient covering vegetation but did not offer good options for getting out. The slopes, in addition to being steep, rose to open fields where the men could be seen readily. In order to reinforce the blockade, Captain Prado transferred two squads of Company A under Second Lieutenant Huerta's command toward the confluence of the canyons to await the Huanca section, which was still moving slowly along La Tusca Canyon, effecting a thorough search. Another attempt to break the siege was repulsed, and Chino was wounded, taken to a small cave, and left alone there.

A pause in the fighting ensued. The commander of B Company took advantage of it to contact his base at Abra del Picacho over his short-range PRC–10 radio. He described the situation so that from there Second Lieutenant Totti, who had remained in command, would inform the 8th Division headquarters in Vallegrande that contact had been made with the guerrillas, that there was fighting, and that since casualties had already been suffered, a helicopter was needed for evacuations. The request was made allowing for the time required for this support to take effect, considering some thirty minutes of flight time from Vallegrande. When this news was received at the division headquarters, the dispatch of two T–6 airplanes with napalm bombs and machine guns was authorized so that they could provide support to the troops involved in combat. Within a few minutes the planes flew over the area and requested instructions as to where to bomb. The situation at the time made air support impossible: distances were very short and the terrain too uneven for the bombing to be effective, and the risk for the troops themselves was very great. For this reason, Captain Prado informed the planes that it was not possible to use them, and they returned to their base at Vallegrande. The LS–4 helicopter piloted by Maj. Jaime Niño de Guzmán that arrived at the locale attracted fire from the guerrillas at the same time that it was receiving smoke signals to land in the vicinity of the command post. In view of the risk of its being hit, it was agreed to reroute the helicopter to La Higuera, where it would land and await instructions. A Company was ordered to recover its two dead and send them to La Higuera for transportation to Vallegrande.

Meanwhile, Sergeant Huanca had concluded his search of La Tusca without finding anything. He received an order from Captain Prado to move into the lower part of El Churo with mortar and machine-gun support, so as to continue on upward to meet Second Lieutenant Pérez's section and thus clear out the canyon. Sergeant Huanca's leadership in this operation was aggressive and brave. Positioning himself at the head of his men, he pressed on with great energy into the interior of the canyon, where a blockade set up by Antonio and Arturo tried to prevent his advance. With great courage, Sergeant Huanca attacked the position using hand grenades. Although he lost one man and had two others wounded, he broke the resistance, causing the deaths of Antonio and Arturo and thus facilitating the advance of the rest of the troops.

It was at that moment that Che, aided by Willy, caught alone in the interior of the canyon since his other men could not come to his aid, tried to escape through a corridor up the side, climbing carefully toward the top where he thought they could slip away toward another canyon. Their movement was being observed, however, by two soldiers guarding the command post and the mortar pieces, who let them advance until they were a meter away and demanded their surrender, advising the company commander, who was 15 meters away, "Captain, there are two here. We have captured them." They were brought to the position of Captain Prado, who looked at the guerrillas and asked Willy, "Who are you?" "Willy," he answered, and then clarified his identity as Simón Cuba from Huanuni. "And you?" he asked the other, who replied, "I am Che Guevara." Taking out a copy of Bustos's drawings, the officer compared the features and then asked him to stretch out his left hand, on the back of which he observed clearly a scar which had been indicated as an identifying mark. Satisfied with the identity of his prisoners, he ordered them to be transferred to the command post located some 20 meters below, and seated under a tree, where their hands and feet were tied to prevent any escape attempt. At the same time, he ordered Private Ortiz, his assistant, to pick up all the guerrillas' equipment—arms, packs and knapsacks, and even a pan with some eggs—and to keep it all intact so that it could be inspected later. Leaving the prisoners under guard, he radioed Che's capture to his base, so that the 8th Division could be informed of it, and then he went to the canyon to continue combing the area.

Inti's group tried again to approach the center of the canyon, no doubt for the purpose of rejoining Che, about whom they still knew nothing, but they were repulsed and fell back to the left, where they accidentally found a break in the encirclement that allowed them to move some distance out of the area and avoid combat.

At dusk the canyon was clear, but since there was not enough light, the company commander decided to withdraw his men from the area to avoid errors during the night. Leaving some troops blocking the exits, he drew back to the hamlet of La Higuera, two kilometers away, to rest and regroup his forces. The bodies of Antonio and Arturo were removed from the canyon, and taking the prisoners Willy and Che, the latter leaning on a soldier, they began to move toward La Higuera at dusk. At the first height, they met Maj. Miguel Ayoroa, the battalion commander, who came from Pucará upon learning of the operation, and Lt. Col. Andrés Selich, commander of Engineer Battalion No. 3 at Vallegrande, who had come in the helicopter sent by the division headquarters.

Captain Prado informed both superiors of developments in the operation, and they all made their way toward La Higuera, amid the curiosity of many compesinos who had come to the heights from all the surrounding communities to learn the outcome of the combat.

The entry into La Higuera became almost a procession, since three wounded soldiers of B Company and a dead one were being carried on improvised stretchers, in addition to the two guerrillas who had died in combat. Then came Che and Willy walking in the midst of a security guard, and then the rest of the troops who had fought that day. The village school was used to confine the prisoners and deposit the bodies. The helicopter had left for Vallegrande at dusk carrying the bodies of the first two soldiers of A Company who had died at the onset of the fighting; its return was expected at the first daylight hour so that the evacuation of the wounded soldiers could be continued. Establishing a command post in the telegraph operator's house, Captain Prado sent the complete report of the day's events to the division headquarters, as follows:

X2 to X8, 082030–OCT–67

While making search of El Churo Canyon, which leads into San Antonio Canyon, with A Company (-) and B Company (-) at 1300 we clashed with main red group with these results:

Our casualties:

A Company
   Dead: Privates Mario Characayo, Mario La Fuente, Manuel Morales
   Wounded: Private Beno Jiménez
B Company
   Dead: Pvt. Sabino Cossio
   Wounded: Pvts. Valentín Choque, Miguel Tablada, Julio Paco

Enemy casualties:

Dead: Arturo and Antonio
Prisoners: Papa (wounded) and Willy

Presume more casualties inside canyon. Due to late hour and difficult terrain, impossible to effect search and recovery over sharpshooters' resistance. Will continue operation tomorrow.
Captured arms, equipment, and important documentation.
Lt. Col. Selich making inventory.
Request helicopter at earliest hour at Higuera to evacuate wounded; it should bring M–1 ammunition and linked ammunition for light machine gun and hand grenades and mortar shells.
   Captain Gary Prado Salmón.

   Meeting with Lieutenant Colonel Selich and Major Ayoroa, Prado undertook a detailed inventory of all the items contained in Che's pack, for the purpose of submitting them to the division headquarters at Vallegrande the next day with the help of the Engineer Battalion commander. Notable in this inventory were:

Two notebooks containing Che's diary (one corresponding to November-December 1966 and the other to January-October 1967)
A notebook with addresses and instructions
Two notebooks with copies of messages received and sent
Two small code books
Twenty maps of different areas updated by Che
Two books on socialism
One destroyed M–1 carbine
One 9–mm pistol with one clip
Twelve undeveloped rolls of 35–mm film
A small bag containing money (Bolivian pesos and dollars).

   After checking through all of this documentation and equipment, the company commander took a series of measures to guarantee the security of La Higuera and to be in a position to resist any attempt to rescue the guerrilla chief. According to the intelligence available about the total strength of the guerrilla force, two had died and two had been captured, leaving thirteen men who could attempt any sort of action, given the importance of the capture of their leader.

At 10 P.M. a message from Vallegrande was received, ordering succinctly: "Keep Fernando alive until my arrival by helicopter tomorrow first thing in the morning. Colonel Zenteno."

With this directive in hand and in the interest of security, the captain set up shifts among all available officers (Lieutenants Totti, Pérez, Huerta, and Espinoza) so that one of them would be staying at all times with the prisoners in separate rooms. During the night he visited the guerrillas several times, conversing with them and checking on their condition. He was concerned about the responsibility involved in having Che on his hands, though also relieved at the thought that the guerrilla war was coming to a close with this action.[5]

In the heights east of La Higuera, six men had gathered. With difficulty Pombo, Inti, Darío, Urbano, Benigno, and Ñato—three Bolivians and three Cubans—had managed to elude the siege and separate from the group, but now they were worried about the fate of Che and their other companions, of whom they had no news. Once again no rallying point had been set, although in recent days they had spoken of "clearing out of the area and finding more favorable areas from which to reestablish contacts with the urban support system."[6] The Piraimirí River had been mentioned, but it was so far away from their current positions that they could arrive there without learning anything about the rest of the men. In any case, they decided to walk only at night from that time on in order to avoid being betrayed by the campesinos. Pombo assumed command of the group by mutual accord, and they advanced somewhat farther toward the heights, hiding in nearby canyons.

During the night the Ranger–2 Battalion commander, Major Ayoroa, took the necessary steps to continue operations at dawn. He ordered the transfer of the rest of A Company from Pucará to San Antonio Canyon in order to begin a thorough search from below toward El Churo, controlling the heights on the north side, while B Company would search from above, controlling the heights on the south side.

This action began on the morning of the 9th. The canyons were carefully combed step by step. A Company found the caves where Chino and Pacho had taken refuge. When surrender was demanded, the guerrillas shot and killed a soldier, bringing a quick reaction from the Rangers, who silenced them with hand grenades and machine-gun fire. B Company found the body of Aniceto, who had fallen the day before but had not been located in the confusion of the moment. Transporting these three guerrillas' bodies plus the dead soldier, the troops completed the search without encountering any more resistance and marched to La Higuera, where they learned that by order of the President of the Republic, Che and Willy had been executed.

How had this happened?

The instructions transmitted by the commander of the 8th Division had been followed strictly. Che remained under arrest at the La Higuera school all through the night of the 8th. On the 9th, before leaving with his troops at daybreak to continue the operation, Captain Prado held his last conversation with the guerrilla leader just as the helicopter carrying Colonel Zenteno and a CIA agent known as Felix Ramos was arriving.[7]

The division commander explained to the officers present that Ramos was there to participate in the positive identification of Che, since he knew him well from earlier times.

Colonel Zenteno listened carefully to the report of the commander of B Company, taking notes. After learning the positions taken for that day by the battalion commander, he went into the room where Che was being held, accompanied by Maj. Niño de Guzmán, the helicopter pilot. He greeted Che and then asked him about his condition, receiving only a shrug of the shoulders in reply. Turning to Captain Prado, he asked him to set the prisoner on his feet. Che stood up with the officer's help, looking straight at Colonel Zenteno. At that point, Ramos came up to observe Che carefully, without exchanging any words with him, nodded slowly in the affirmative, and then left the room. Zenteno remained for a few minutes more, looking closely at Che, and asked him if he needed anything. Che answered, "Nothing," and then sat down again on the floor, leaning against the wall. The CIA agent came back in and after a few words with the division commander, who gave him permission, took photographs of Che with a small camera. Lighting conditions were poor inside the room, but the prisoner could not be taken outside, since a good number of campesinos, attracted by the combat and troop movements, had come into the village.

Shortly afterward, the helicopter piloted by Maj. Niño de Guzmán made a first flight with two wounded soldiers and Lieutenant Colonel Selich; it would continue these flights in order to evacuate the dead and wounded, giving priority to military personnel.

In the mayor's house, where the battalion had set up its command post, Colonel Zenteno leafed through the documentation captured from Che and discussed the diary with officers Ayoroa and Prado. The agent, Ramos, requested authorization to photograph some pages so that graphological tests could be taken later. This was authorized by the division commander, who then decided to accompany Captain Prado and Major Ayoroa to the area where the search operation would be undertaken. Lieutenant Totti remained in La Higuera in charge of the prisoners.

At about 8:30 A.M., the division commander and his group arrived at the heights where El Churo Canyon and the adjacent zone could be observed. Colonel Zenteno again asked for a report on how the operation had been carried out, and at the same time he made a panoramic drawing of the area from the position he was in (see Map 9).

Satisfied with the reports, he returned to La Higuera accompanied by Major Ayoroa and an escort of soldiers. After making radio contact with Captain Torrelio, who was already nearing the heights north of El Churo Canyon, Captain Prado agreed to begin the operation, which would come to an end near noon when it was clear that there were no more guerrillas in the canyons.

At La Higuera, Colonel Zenteno contacted the division headquarters at Vallegrande with the radio equipment that had been set up in the village, and asked twice what orders had been received from the high command. Both times he was told to await instructions that would come later from the Miraflores general headquarters at La Paz.

At about 11 A.M., a radio call brought those instructions. With no further explanation, the order simply called for the summary execution of the prisoners. That order, originating from the office of the President of the Republic in accord with the commander-in-chief and the chief of the general staff, had its logic and its justification, which we will try to summarize from the point of view of those who held the political and military power of the nation:

—It was felt more important for international public opinion to show Che defeated in combat and dead than taken prisoner.

—Debray's trial was becoming an annoyance because of its international repercussions. Those would definitely increase if the guerrilla chief were tried.

—Security problems with Che during his trial and after his certain conviction would be difficult. His image would be kept in the public eye. Attempts to free him would undoubtedly be made, so a special arrangement would have to be made to guarantee that the sentence imposed would be carried out.

—If Che were eliminated, a heavy blow would be struck at Castroism, setting back its doctrinaire policy of expansion in Latin America.

Based on these considerations, coded instructions were sent to Vallegrande to proceed with the execution of the prisoners, but terms and methods of making news of it public were not clearly set. This would create a host of problems over the following days. The matter was left in the hands of Colonel Zenteno, who asked for two volunteers from the noncommissioned officer group. Warrant Officer Mario Terán and Sergeant Bernardino Huanca stepped forward, and after receiving instructions from the division commander, they simultaneously entered the classrooms where Che and Willy were being held separately and, without saying a word, fired a volley at each prisoner.

The division commander ordered Che's body to be the last transported to Vallegrande so that he would have time to take some measures. He then left in his helicopter. Back at his headquarters, he made the official announcement at 1:45 P.M.: "Che Guevara died yesterday in combat." The news spread throughout the world within a few minutes, arousing the curiosity of journalists, who wanted more details. From that moment on, a great variety of fictional versions colored the event as it entered into Bolivian political and military history.

NOTES

1. 2d Lt. Alfredo Lara Paravicini of Cavalry Group 8 had remained in the operations zone since the beginning of the conflict. He was sent with a section of Braun Group to Abapó on March 18 and then went on to Ipitá and Tatarenda together with Capt. Emeterio Pereyra, staying in Yumao, Saladillo, and Ñancahuazú in the first days of April. He and his troops suffered incredible hardships. They were unable to receive supplies for some days, and they were sprayed with machine-gun fire on one occasion when they were mistaken for the guerrillas. Later he carried out missions with his troops integrated into other companies in Ñancahuazú, Tiraboy, and Pirirenda. He returned to Florida on June 25, newly transferred to the Eighth Division. The Tiger Company was formed with his soldiers and those from Second Lieutenant Galindo's Manchego Regiment. They participated in the Parabanó operation and were then transferred to Masicurí.

2. Che's diary, entries for September 7, 9, 11, 12, 13, 16, 18, and 19. Pacho's diary, entries for September 6, 15, and 17.

3. Che's diary, entry for September 7.

4. Che's diary, entry for September 27.

5. The author deems it necessary after all these years to make public a series of details concerning that night and the morning of October 9. Since these are above all personal impressions, they appear in an appendix apart from the account of the operations themselves.

6. Che's diary: Analysis of the month of September.

7. This Captain Ramos was the only foreigner who had access to Che during his confinement. He never participated in the operations, and was assigned to the 8th Division Command for intelligence purposes, having arrived at Vallegrande only when the capture of the guerrilla chief occurred. The same Captain Ramos, now known as Félix Rodriguez, was implicated twenty years later in the Iran-Contra affair and identified as a former CIA agent.

The La Higuera school where Che was shot to death by the military.

Above, Captain Prado and other army officers having breakfast with area residents. *Below,* B Company during a halt in San Antonio Canyon.

Julio, Antonio, and Pombo.

Camba detained by the military.

Above, the troops occupy the main guerrilla camp. *Below*, members of the North American Army Green Beret team who served as advisors to the Bolivian Army counterinsurgency operation.

Chapter 12

THE END

By October 9, La Paz news broadcasts reported that fighting had taken place between the guerrilla group and Assault Regiment 2 (Rangers) near La Higuera on the afternoon of Sunday, October 8, with losses on both sides. They also unofficially mentioned the possibility that one of the dead could be Che Guevara.

When the division commander, Colonel Zenteno, confirmed rumors by announcing Che's death officially at 1:45 P.M. on the 9th, the entire population of Vallegrande got worked up and went to the landing field to await the arrival of the bodies of the combat dead. First to come were the wounded soldiers, then the dead soldiers, and finally the guerrillas. On the last trip, the helicopter touched down at 5 P.M. bringing the remains of the guerrilla chief under tight security.

The curiosity of the population was understandable. So much had been said in the last few days about the guerrilla movement, so many people had arrived in the small city, disturbing its usual calm, that everybody had to see the man who was beyond a doubt the main source of all the commotion.

The High Command of the Armed Forces issued Communiqué 45/67 early on October 9, stating:

1. Eight kilometers northeast of Higueras, during the day on October 8, fierce fighting broke out with a red detachment that put up desperate resistance. The reds suffered five losses, among whom presumably is Ernesto Che Guevara. On our side the following casualties were recorded:
   Dead: Pvts. Mario Characayo, Mario La Fuente, Manuel Morales, and Sabino Cossio.
   Wounded: Pvts. Beno Jiménez, Valentín Choque, Miguel Choque, Miguel Taboada, and Julio Paco, all from Assault Battalion 2.

2. Operations are continuing and their results will be reported to the nation's public in due time.
La Paz, October 9, 1967.

That same day the commander-in-chief, Gen. Alfredo Ovando, had arrived by air in Vallegrande, accompanied by the commanders of the army and the naval force, Gen. David La Fuente and Rear Adm. Horacio Ugarteche. Besieged by journalists, General Ovando said only, "No comment. Here you have what was not to be believed. The guerrillas have been liquidated in Bolivia, although a small group of six commanded by Inti Peredo is still operating and will be destroyed in the next few hours. Once again the Bolivian soldier's bravery and love of country have been demonstrated. He has succeeded in destroying the theorist of Castro-communist guerrilla warfare, which could not have been done in other countries with more modern and better equipped armies."

When the bodies had been transferred to the little room that served as a morgue, doctors from Señor de Malta Hospital proceeded with the autopsy and the report, while intelligence experts ran all identification tests. They took special care with Che's remains, which were set aside so that all who wished to see them could do so, in accord with the commander-in-chief's instructions. It was a moment of glory and triumph for the armed forces, who did not hide their satisfaction at having won an important victory over the subversion that threatened the country's institutional stability.

The chief executive's message to the nation, issued on that date, was framed in that context:

The glorious Armed Forces of the Nation continue to accomplish their self-sacrificing, patriotic mission, clearing out the dens of foreign interventionists who were trying to subjugate the Bolivian people through armed invasion.

From Ñancahuazú to the last skirmishes, which are taking place at this moment, the leaders, officers, noncommissioned officers, and soldiers of the Armed Forces have fought only for the liberation of their people, overcoming deadly crises, the constant threat of traps, hunger, thirst, illness, and privations of all kinds, which the people can only repay with gratitude and affection.

The officer or soldier has risked his life for the freedom of his fatherland and of Bolivians because the Armed Forces are the people in arms.

Well-organized positions in the rugged mountain ranges surrounded by thick jungle still continue firing on Bolivian troops, who will finally show the world that Bolivia is a sovereign nation, able to fight on its own for its development and its liberty. Foreign intruders of all kinds are not authorized by any law, motivation, or pretext to intervene in our decisions and to use sophistry, defamation, or intimidation aimed at twisting the resolve of our actions and distorting our own reality.

I regret that I have only words of condemnation and indignation for adversaries who, invoking their ideals, have tried to smash the ideals of the Bolivian people.

I think that those who came to kill were also prepared to die. It is not only in victory that one can be consistent and a hero. Our men have been heroes in both defeat and victory, first in Ñancahuazú and Iripití, later in Vado del Yeso, Higueras, or El Churo Canyon.

If Señor Guevara has died, he has died after killing many of our men and causing greater poverty and suffering.

The National Congress also held a special session in homage to the armed forces, in which speakers stressed the role of the military in defense of national honor and sovereignty.

The forces of the left, crushed and in disarray after the failure of the guerrilla war, said nothing. A few attempts to honor Che did not get off the ground, so other means were sought to tarnish the image achieved by the armed forces—and, paradoxically, it was the military authorities themselves who opened the way to this campaign through their snap decisions, conflicting statements, and lack of seriousness.

The first criticism appeared when no clear statement was made telling what had been done with the guerrilla chief's body. Although the rest of the bodies were buried in the Vallegrande cemetery, the body of the leader was taken out of the city at dawn on the 11th and given to an officer who was ordered to burn the remains so that nothing was left of the guerrilla. This mission was accomplished in a process lasting two days, but the division commander, responding to questions from the press, stated that Guevara had been buried in a safe place. This gave rise to speculation that ranged from transport of the body to the United States for further identification tests to the story that the body had been removed because the remains displayed had not been those of Che Guevara. The confusion grew when the commander-in-chief admitted that the body "has been incinerated," giving way to more commentaries, since neither in Vallegrande nor anywhere else in the country were there facilities for burning bodies. Both the statement and the procedure were thus called into question.

The second act of this drama regarding Che's death occurred when differing stories began to circulate of how and when he had died, and what he had said, and if he had managed to speak before dying. While these various stories were beginning to take shape, two reports from the front took center stage. Fighting with the last guerrillas had broken out.

EL NARANJAL

After the El Churo combat, the military deployment had undergone some modifications with a view to keeping up the search for the scattered remnants of the guerrilla band. There was evidence of two small groups that had been separated, and efforts were made to prevent them from getting back together. On the other hand, it was considered highly likely that, with the certain knowledge that Che had been captured and killed, the guerrillas would try to disperse rather than to offer resistance, and would try to pass unnoticed in nearby towns, changing their appearance and blending in with the people. Thus they would be able to get out to the cities, where they could look for assistance in either lying low or leaving the country. On the basis of these assumptions, civilian authorities were alerted so that they would be on guard, and the deployment was activated. A Company of Assault Battalion 2 was kept in La Higuera, B Company in Abra del Picacho, C Company (-) in Alto Seco, and a section of C Company in Cajones at the junction of the Grande and Mizque rivers. Florida Company was to cover San Lorenzo, while NCO School Company 2 covered Ckasamonte. All units had the mission of establishing patrol bases and searching for the guerrillas in their areas of responsibility. This task was carried out on the 10th and 11th, but no information was forth-coming. On the morning of the 12th a campesino informed Captain Prado's B Company command post at Abra del Picacho that six guerrillas had been observed proceeding along a path in the direction of the Santa Elena River. Pursuit began immediately. The First Section, under the command of 2d Lt. Germán Venegas, was sent on the path the guerrillas had used, in order to keep up the pressure on their rear guard, while Sergeant Huanca's Third Section with Captain Prado and Major Ayoroa moved along the heights, intending to cut off the reds' route farther ahead and thus capture or destroy them. The maneuver gave a partial result when, upon reaching El Potrero Canyon, 2d Lt. Raúl Espinosa, who was at the head of the line, tried to enter the canyon to determine whether the guerrillas had arrived there and met up face to face with Urbano, who was leaving the canyon as the vanguard of the guerrilla group. Both fired instantly and took cover. No one was wounded, but this action made it possible to seal both sides of the canyon with troops. It was almost a repetition of the scene at El Churo Canyon, with the guerrillas closed into the depths and surrounded by soldiers at both ends. Here, however, the troops did not control the heights on the south side, so after abandoning their packs, the guerrillas entered a passage called El Socavón (the hollow), and this allowed them to get out of the canyon. When the company commander discovered their maneu-ver—the search of the canyon had turned up only the abandoned packs—the pursuit maneuver was repeated. Part of the First Section, under Corp. Daniel Calani, was sent through El Socavón to follow the trail, while the rest tried to gain the heights in order to cut off the insurgents' route.

El Socavón rises out of Naranjal Mountain. An island of trees, it has a radius of some 20 meters, and forms a kind of amphitheater with elevations at a distance of 60–70 meters. The only vegetation is in the island; the rest has only *paja brava* (spiky bunchgrass) 20–30 centimeters high. All of these elevations are about 2,400 meters above sea level. In the last minutes of daylight, an attempt was made to set up an encirclement so as to wait for dawn and clean up the area. Meanwhile, Corporal Calani had arrived at the edge of the island of trees, and fell wounded when he was getting ready to move into it. His men spread out and occupied positions below. Medic Franz Muriel came up to attend the wounded man, unarmed and clearly displaying his Red Cross insignia, but was struck down with a shot to the head. Then Corporal Calani was finished off. Night soon fell, and the full moon bathed the whole sector in its light. The temperature went down close to freezing. The troops, having had nothing to eat all day and having walked without stopping, were exhausted and could hardly stay awake. At about four in the morning, the moon went down and a profound darkness covered the area. At that moment the guerrillas broke the siege, killing two soldiers.[1] A chance occurrence allowed this to happen. In the sector chosen for the escape, two soldiers were in position. Pvt. Facundo Cruz of B Company, an excellent combatant, was dozing, fatigued from the day's activity. At his side Abel Callapa, who had joined the unit that day as a replacement for the losses at El Churo, was keeping watch. He did not have the advanced training of the veteran soldiers nor the aptitude for that type of operation. When he heard a noise ahead of his position, instead of firing first and asking questions later as he should have done, it occurred to him to act like a barracks sentry asking, "Halt, who is it?" This gave away his location, and Inti and his men took advantage, attacking and escaping. Callapa, gravely wounded in the kidneys, died bleeding profusely in the company commander's arms. There was no opportunity to assist him. Cruz, who had managed to react, was killed on the spot.

At dawn, the troops began the search once again, trying to find tracks that would permit the operation to continue, but the result was negative. A helicopter was requisitioned to evacuate the dead, who included a civilian guide, and the troops returned to their base at Abra del Picacho.

CAJONES

Meanwhile, the other surviving guerrilla group had taken the opposite direction. Although there is no exact information, it is assumed that after the El Churo combat, the group made up of Chapaco, Moro, Eustaquio, and Pablito, having no rallying point to head for, chose to find a way out of the operations zone on their own. With this aim they moved slowly— probably at night, because they were not seen—toward the bank of the Grande River. They went upriver until they reached the junction with the Mizque River on the night of October 13. There they set up camp and lit a fire in order to prepare food. This fire was observed at 11 P.M. from the opposite bank by the sentry of the third section of C Company of Assault Battalion 2, who immediately alerted his commander, 2d Lt. Guillermo Aguirre Palma, to the development. The type of fire and other details led the officer to believe that it could be a guerrilla group, so they continued to observe until dawn, when one of them was identified, in a camouflage uniform, crawling over to the edge of the river to get water. Having confirmed the presence of the rebels, Second Lieutenant Aguirre adopted a deployment that would assure him success. One part of his force, with Sergeant Bolívar, occupied positions across from the guerrilla camp, while he maneuvered with the rest, crossing the river about 200 meters farther down so as to position himself behind the camp. At his signal, Sergeant Bolívar began firing, forcing the guerrillas to occupy positions to defend themselves in his direction. This facilitated Aguirre's attack, which ended with the deaths of the four guerrillas. The soldiers picked up the bodies and the weapons, consisting of three M–2 carbines and a Winchester rifle, as well as the packs with personal effects. A helicopter, which had been bringing supplies, informed Vallegrande of the event, since the Aguirre section did not have a radio to communicate with the command post. The helicopter transported the bodies, and the Aguirre section remained in the Cajones region two more weeks as part of the deployment intended to finish off the guerrilla foco. The official communiqué about this encounter and its results confirmed the almost total destruction of the guerrilla force, since it was assumed that the group of six survivors could no longer undertake any significant action and surely intended to break up. It would be difficult to find them, since they would avoid contact even with the campesinos.

REPERCUSSIONS OF CHE'S DEATH

The first repercussion following the news that Ernesto Guevara was dead came from Camiri, where the trial of the captured guerrillas was being held. Changing his attitude and displaying a great deal of histrionics, Régis Debray confessed his participation in guerrilla activities. Just in case, however, he kept an escape valve open in his statement, saying, "Although it is true that I entered the zone as a journalist, it is also true that once I was inside, at one with Che's ideals, I asked to join the guerrilla force as a combatant. Che flatly refused to let me in, arguing that I could be more useful from the outside than from a guerrilla hideout in the jungle. I ask the court to do me the honor of declaring me a co-participant in the guerrillas' acts."

This declaration, which was well received in the communications media, had the edge taken off it when the military prosecutor brought to light the entries in Che's diary showing the Frenchman's insistence on leaving the zone—despite Che's offer for him to stay with the guerrillas, and despite the risks that meant for the overall operation—and also showing the guerrilla chief's opinions of Debray's and Bustos's statements about the goals of the guerrilla movement.[2]

The other repercussion came from Havana. After maintaining a tantalizing silence about Che for several days and simply airing news from international agencies, Prime Minister Castro announced and officially admitted the death of Guevara, to whom he paid special homage, expressing in some parts of his long speech the following ideas:

> It is not possible to believe that this is a tissue of lies. Photos can be altered but in this case they were made by journalists that were in Bolivia. This is not a case of falsification.
>
> The campaign diary presented is undoubtedly Che's: it is his handwriting, which is very difficult to imitate, and even if it were a forgery, Che's style and manner of expression would have been impossible to imitate.
>
> There are indications that Che was killed in cold blood, and proof of this is the contradictions in the statements of General Ovando that Che identified himself and the statement made by Colonel Zenteno that he died without recovering consciousness.
>
> This is the politics of revolution; we must recognize that he is dead. Many things could be made up to conceal the death of Ernesto Guevara, but it is preferable to accept the sadly true report of the glorious death of my best friend.
>
> No one will be surprised that in a guerrilla troop's combat he could have been among the first to fall. Very conscious of the mission he had been assigned and of how important it was, he thought, as he had always thought, that men have a value that is relative.
>
> He was always characterized by his daring and by his scorn for danger on numerous occasions.
>
> Che's death deals a heavy blow to the revolutionary movement, but the movement will go forward.

This initial acceptance of Che's death was important, not only because it confirmed the identity of the guerrilla chief for Bolivian authorities, but also because between the lines Castro also was beginning to accept the responsibility he had for planning and carrying out the guerrilla war in Bolivia. In effect, when he spoke of the mission assigned to Che and the importance that it had for the revolutionary movement, he was implicitly recognizing Cuban participation in all of the events that had taken place in Bolivia. Later, at the time when Che's diary was published, Castro would be more explicit in fully and clearly admitting Cuban involvement in the guerrilla war.

In the military sphere, a communiqué was prepared and issued on October 16 for the purpose of cutting off the speculation and discussion that had been going on. According to military authorities, it was the last word on the guerrilla chief's death. Nevertheless, this communiqué and its attachments, together with the curiosity of journalists, would encourage further exploitation of the discrepancies and inaccuracies until the events at La Higuera were definitively cleared up. The military communique said:

ARMED FORCES COMMUNIQUE TO CLOSE THE RECORD ON CHE'S DEATH

1. In keeping with the report made to national and foreign public opinion through the documents issued by the High Military Command on October 9 and later dates regarding the combat that occurred in La Higuera between units of the Armed Forces and the red contingent commanded by Ernesto Che Guevara as a consequence of which the latter, among others, lost his life, the following is established:

   a) Ernesto Che Guevara fell into the hands of our troops gravely wounded and with full use of his mental powers.

      —After combat had ceased, he was transferred to the village of La Higuera at about 8 P.M. on Sunday, October 8, where he died as a result of his injuries.

      —The transfer of the body to the city of Vallegrande was made at 4 P.M. on the 9th in a helicopter of the FAB [Bolivian Air Force].

   b) Doctors Moisés Abraham Baptista and José Martínez Casso in their capacity as director and intern of the Señor de Malta Hospital certified the death (Attachment 1) and issued the autopsy report ordered by military authorities (Attachment 2).

   c) With regard to the identification of the deceased and the authenticity of the diary that belonged to him, the Supreme Government requested the cooperation of Argentine technical organizations, which provided three specialists, a handwriting expert and two fingerprint experts, who verified the identity of the dead man and certified that the handwriting in the campaign diary captured by our troops coincides with that of Ernesto Guevara (Attachment 3).

   d) The campaign diary and the book of reflections are documents containing the account of activities from the date of his entrance to October 7 and this subversive leader's opinions about the members of the organized groups and the individuals that collaborated with them both within the country and abroad.

2. In this way the High Military Command considers all information relating to the death of Ernesto Guevara to be complete.

La Paz, October 16, 1967.

ATTACHMENT 1—DEATH CERTIFICATE

The undersigned doctors, the director of Señor de Malta Hospital and a medical intern, certify: that on Monday the 9th of the present month, at 5:30 A.M., the body of an individual was brought, which military authorities said belonged to Ernesto Guevara, about 40 years old, it having been noted that his death was due to multiple bullet wounds in the thorax and extremities. Vallegrande, October 10, 1967. Dr. Moisés Abraham Baptista. Doctor José Martínez Casso.

ATTACHMENT 2—AUTOPSY REPORT

On October 10 of the current year, by military order, an autopsy was performed on the body that was identified as that of Ernesto Guevara:

Age: Approximately 40 years.

Race: White.

Height: Approximately 1.73 m.

Hair: Curly brown, moustache and beard grown out, similarly curly; thick eyebrows.

Nose: Straight.

Lips: Thin, mouth open in good condition with nicotine stains, lacking the lower left premolar.

Eyes: Bluish.

Build: Medium.

Extremities: Feet and hands well preserved; scar covering almost all the back of the left hand.

General examination showed the following lesions:

1. Bullet wound in the left clavicular area, exit in the scapular area of the same side.
2. Bullet wound in the right clavicular area, with a fracture of the same bone and no exit.
3. Bullet wound in the right costal area, no exit.
4. Two bullet wounds in the left lateral costal area with exits in the dorsal area.
5. Bullet wound in the the left pectoral area between the ninth and tenth ribs, with exit in the lateral area of the same side.
6. Bullet wound in the middle third of the right leg.
7. Bullet wound in the middle third of the left thigh, superficial.
8. Bullet wound in the lower third of the right forearm, with a fracture of the ulna.

When the thoracic cavity was opened, there was evidence that the first wound had slightly injured the apex of the left lung, and the second injured the subclavian vessels, the bullet being found in the mass of the second dorsal vertebra.

The third passed through the right lung, lodging in the costal-vertebral articulation of the same rib.

The wounds mentioned in point 4 slightly injured the left lung.

The wound mentioned in point 5 passed through the left lung in a tangential trajectory.

The thoracic cavities, especially the right, showed an abundant accumulation of blood.

When the abdomen was opened, no traumatic lesion was found, only distension of the intestines from gas and yellowish liquid.

Death was caused by the wounds to the thorax and the resulting hemorrhage.

Vallegrande, October 10, 1967. Doctor Moisés Abraham Baptista. Doctor José Martínez Casso.

ATTACHMENT 3—COMMUNIQUÉ

The committee of technicians assigned by the Argentine government on the request of the Bolivian government, to verify the identity of the remains of Ernesto Guevara, has proceeded to the comparison of the materials that were provided by the office of the commander-in-chief of the Armed Forces with those that are in the possession of Argentine police authorities.

From the fingerprint identification and handwriting analysis performed by the technicians, in accord with current scientific procedures, it is clear that the compared materials correspond without a doubt to Ernesto Guevara, and this has been stated in the report sent to Bolivian authorities. Signed, Inspector Esteban Belzhauser, Deputy Inspector Nicolás Pellicari, and Deputy Inspector Juan Carlos Delgado.

The Argentine experts sent by their government to cooperate with the Bolivian government in the identification of the guerrilla chief undertook their work after receiving two cylindrical containers with the hands of the guerrilla chief, which had been cut off before the body was incinerated. These hands, preserved in formol, provided fingerprints for comparison with those contained in Argentine police records. Similarly, Che's handwriting was compared in the diary and in documents he had written that were possessed by the Argentine Federal Police.

The publication of these official documents, far from clarifying the matter and silencing commentaries relating to Che's death, prompted a series of technical and journalistic opinions clearly demonstrating that it was unlikely that a man with nine bullet wounds, as detailed in the autopsy report, several of them near vital organs and capable of causing grave hemorrhages, could have lasted as many hours as the military authorities insisted he had, from his capture at dusk on October 8 to his death on the morning of the 9th, even if he had received adequate treatment in a well-equipped medical center, let alone an area deep in the mountains with no available facilities.

Nor was it considered probable that the guerrilla, in that condition, could have uttered a single word attributed to him in several official reports, so this gave rise to the most absurd and fantastic versions that the imagination of journalists and their sponsors could put forth. That is understandable if we consider the level of professionals that arrived to cover this event, which became undoubtedly the most important news story of the year on the Latin American scene, surpassed in the world news only by the Six-Day War in the Middle East. The lack of adequate information, the mystery of Che's final resting place, and the contradictions were fertile ground for press speculation, and they were also the source of the crudest and dirtiest commerce with the image of the guerrilla chief. Within a few days books and accounts began to appear, put out by any number of people who sought to take advantage of his death to make a name for themselves or, even worse, make some money from it.

MATARAL

Far removed from all of this, the six survivors, under Pombo's command, were in great difficulty. They did not have the remotest hope of being able to further the goals of the guerrilla war. To Pombo, the failure was clear. It was even foreseen in his diary when at the preparatory stage he had had some disagreements with Che. Obsessed with the victory obtained in Cuba, where after the landing of the *Granma* a handful of men was able to carry on the Cuban Revolution from their base in the Sierra Maestra, the guerrilla leader was eager to begin operations in Bolivia. The Cuban advance man in La Paz noted sententiously in September 1966, after learning of Che's decision to work with Moisés Guevara, the consequences of offending the PCB: "We should forget right now the notion that the [Cuban revolutionary] struggle began with twelve men. The struggle in the present circumstances has to begin with the greatest possible number of forces. Also remember that the impact of guerrilla warfare on the continent is not the same as on the narrow island."[3]

Thirteen months later, the last guerrillas from the adventure, cornered on the heights, were seeking salvation by getting away from the operations zone and avoiding contact with the campesinos. Starving, their clothes in tatters, nearly barefoot, they hung on to their arms and their scant ammunition resolutely in order to avoid capture. When they arrived at the bed of the Piraimirí River, they followed it upriver with the utmost caution, avoiding villages, convinced that their deliverance lay in reaching the Santa Cruz–Cochabamba highway. On their way, in Chujllas, they bought some food from a campesino family, who immediately reported it to the army. The Eighth Division, newly deployed, tried to surround them. Assault Battalion 2 (Rangers) was assigned to set up control posts and patrol the asphalt highway to prevent their leaving, while Florida and NCO School Company 2 ran searches in the area between Alto Seco and Los Sitanos.

The intense combing activity of NCO School Company 2, commanded by Captain. José Meruvia Lazarte, caused the guerrillas to move north. The capture of the civilian guide used by the guerrillas, Honorato Linares, brought the news that after staying in the canyons near his house, the guerrillas were led by him following the heights north of Vallegrande, along the Ckasamonte-Pucará–Santa Ana–Pampa Grande route to the Casas Viejas settlement, 6 kilometers north of the city on the Mataral road. He left them there at dawn on November 9.

In view of this report, the NCO School Company and Florida Company were brought back to Vallegrande to be used in the north sector while efforts to control the asphalt highway were intensified. In spite of these precautions, Pombo and his group reached Mataral on the 13th. Ñato and Urbano approached a small general store to buy some clothing and sandals in order to disguise everybody. Their presence was reported within a few minutes to the closest military detachment, and a section of NCO School Company 2, commanded by 2d Lt. Jorge Castellón, began pursuit, which ended in the heights north of Mataral with a brief combat, causing the death of Ñato and forcing the five remaining guerrillas to run off in a hurry without achieving their goal of getting supplies in Mataral. The search effected by C Company of Ranger 2, the NCO School Company, and Florida Company did not yield significant results and this Mataral skirmish amounted to the last contact between army forces and Che's guerrillas.

CONCLUSION OF THE TRIAL IN CAMIRI

In an atmosphere of anticlimax, thoroughly outranged in importance by the fighting and its consequences, the trial of Debray, Bustos, and the Bolivians accused of participating in the guerrilla attempt in the southeast came to an end on November 17. The arguments of the military prosecutor and the defenders took place without mishap and the verdict was read in the presence of the participants. The resolution of the lengthy document stated:

The War Council of Military Justice, in the name of the Nation and by virtue of the jurisdiction it exercises in her name, finds the accused Jules Régis Debray and Ciro Roberto Bustos guilty of the crimes of rebellion, murder, theft, and assault and battery, and condemns them to suffer the corporal punishment of 30 years in prison, in conformity with Article 17 of the Political Constitution of the State, in addition to payment of damages and costs incurred by the civilian party and the State. Acquitted from punishment and guilt are the accused Pastor Barrero, Salustio Choque, Vicente Recabado, and Ciro Algarañaz, in conformity with Article 12 and Article 108 of the Military Penal Code and the Code of Military Judicial Procedures. Prison warrants for the former two and an order of release for the latter four are to be issued.

Colonel Luis Nicolao Velasco. Colonel Remberto Tórrez Lazarte. Captain Gerardo Tórrez Antezana, Military Judge Advocate. Second Lieutenant Enrique Pérez Llano, Attorney-Secretary of the Council.

The convicted men were allowed to hold short interviews with the press in the next days; their statements were predictable under the circumstances. While Debray said, "The verdict is symbolic because the guerrilla force is being judged through two foreigners," Bustos complained, "It is unjust. I didn't kill anybody, I only came to a political meeting." With the show over, however, no one was very much interested in this kind of opinion, and little by little Camiri began to recover its small-town peace and quiet as the military units and the journalists went away. The same thing happened in Vallegrande, where the withdrawal of military forces had more impact. The city emptied out, spirits were soothed, and all that remained was the memory of those days of uproar and distress. In public memory the death of Che was linked to that of another invader, Brigadier Francisco Javier Aguilera, the last royalist soldier, who even after independence was proclaimed in Bolivia in 1825, kept on fighting, backed by a small group of men in the Vallegrande region. He had his base in Santa Ana, 10 kilometers south of the city, where he was to resist regular troops until he was captured by Colonel Anselmo Rivas, taken to the main plaza of Vallegrande, and shot on October 30, 1828. Referring to this coincidence, the commander-in-chief stated in one of his pronouncements relating to the capture and death of Che, "Here died the last Spanish leader, Aguilera, and today another invader dies."

No one paid any more attention to the five survivors of the destroyed guerrilla movement.

THE ESCAPE

Marching parallel to the highway, the survivors made a painful advance toward the west. Later, finding a campesino family that would help them for the fee they offered, they obtained clothes for Urbano and Inti, who were able to escape disguised to Cochabamba. There they made contacts that enabled them, after several anxious days, to send a vehicle to pick up Pombo, Benigno, and Darío, eluding the police and military controls that had been set up. The truth of the matter was that since the remaining group posed no threat and also avoided combat, it was very difficult for the military to muster the necessary motivation to continue pursuit, a task that is more suited to the police. In any case, the Armed Forces felt that the guerrilla band had been defeated, and thus decided to withdraw their troops and demobilize assigned units. This took effect in the month of December.

That entire month went by without risk for the guerrillas. Government efforts to get information about them was unsuccessful, although fliers were circulated in the area bordering the highway with photographs and descriptions of the five survivors, offering a reward of 10,000 Bolivian pesos ($833 U.S.) for the capture of each of them or for information leading to their apprehension.

Together in Cochabamba, the fugitives made contact with what remained of the support structure, and this allowed them to recover from their fatigue, improve their health, and calm their spirits after so many months of anguish and despair. Although they kept out of sight, far removed from the operations zone, they carefully prepared each step they took to arrange their escape route out of the country.

Nothing was heard about them in official circles until February 14, when a radiogram from the subprefect of Sabaya, in Atahuallpa Province of the western department of Oruro, informed the prefect, Col. Francisco Barrero, that on the day before, five suspicious persons were circulating in the area. They had been observed at midday, and they withdrew toward the west when some of the population went to investigate. Since an order had been issued to all authorities to be on the alert for the presence of the guerrillas or new focos that might pop up, this report was immediately sent on to Oruro so that an assessment of the situation could be made, taking into account the fact that there were no military forces in the altiplano towns.

The fugitives had been brought from Cochabamba to Oruro so that they could try to reach the border from there. Using Estanislao Vilca Colque, a native of the region, as a guide, they began the march trying to pass by unnoticed, dressed like ordinary citizens but carrying small arms in little traveling bags. The seasonal rains had made the Oruro altiplano roads difficult, but nevertheless, near Barras, on the morning of February 12, Vilca approached a truck stopped by the side of the road to ask if they could take him to Sabaya. The driver, Teodoro Araníbar, a resident of the area, knew Vilca and his parents and so he agreed. At that moment four other men appeared and got into the vehicle, which started up again. The strangers' presence worried the driver, who slowed down with one pretext or another and stopped in Characollo at dusk, saying that he had to rest because he had not slept well for several days. The fugitives' impatience led them to abandon the truck at dawn on the 13th and head for Sabaya on foot. Their arrival at midday was observed by residents, for although only Vilca went into the village and the others stayed on a little hill outside, the campesinos of the altiplano have a special sense for spotting strangers at a great distance. So while the guide surreptitiously tried to size up the situation of the place to gauge the risks, the authorities had already sent two scouts to try to identify the outsiders, who hid themselves from the campesinos. Probably up to then they had been taken for cattle thieves. In any case, to cover themselves, the authorities decided to inform the Oruro prefecture of the event when they realized that something out of the ordinary was occurring. Vilca insisted on finding out if there were troops in the area and also asked for help in reaching the Chilean border. The campesinos did not trust Vilca, because he had left the area five years earlier to travel to Cuba and upon returning had spent most of his time in Oruro and the mining centers.

A few minutes after sending the dispatch to Oruro, in the early hours of the 14th, when it was learned that the outsiders had come into town and were in a resident's house, the communal authorities had them called in. They showed up coolly at the town hall, answering questions by saying that they were traveling salesmen on their way to Chile. This attempt to cover up did not last long, however, and they admitted they were survivors of the guerrilla movement. Threatening the unarmed officials (a police sergeant, the subprefect of the province, and the general secretary) with reprisals if they were denounced, they secured their silence. Without revealing that they had already sent a radiogram to Oruro, the authorities allowed the group to stay in the village for a few hours on the condition that they would harm no one. After obtaining some supplies and without saying anything to the residents, the guerrillas left Sabaya at dawn on the

15th, traveling north toward the village of Julo, trailed by a scout assigned to the task by residents of the town.

When the first information from Oruro reached La Paz at midday on the 14th, the commander-in-chief, General Ovando, contacted the prefect of Oruro, General Barrero, and the commander of the Second Division, Col. Amado Prudencio, with whom he outlined a tentative strategy. The idea of sending troops from Oruro by land was rejected because of the poor state of the roads and the time that this would take. Assured that the Sabaya landing field was in operating condition, the commander-in-chief ordered a detail of Camacho Artillery Regiment 1 to prepare to be transported by air that very afternoon. In addition, the order was sent to Cochabamba for a detail of the CITE to be in readiness to be parachuted into the area closest to the guerrillas' location in order to close off their route to the border.

Only at dawn on the 15th did all of these precautions go into effect, because the weather conditions were totally adverse. A light plane transporting Col. Manuel Cárdenas from Department III of the army general staff landed in Sabaya, followed shortly afterward by a C–47 plane of the FAB in which a detail of Ingavi Cavalry Regiment 4 arrived and immediately undertook pursuit of the guerrillas. The C–47 flew to Oruro and returned with another detail of Artillery Regiment 1, which was also dispatched in another direction. Working together, the department prefect and the army command envoy mobilized the campesinos to try to locate the fugitives. The result was confusion, wasted effort, and delays. At dawn on the 16th, together with the commander of the Second Division, a detail of parachutists arrived with presidential aides Captains Villarroel, Salomón, and Orellana. They still did not have adequate information, however, that would permit troops to be dropped in, and they spent the entire day waiting for news that did not arrive. Then, on the night of the 16th, word came that the fugitives had reached the border and crossed into Chilean territory, so that the opportunity to capture them was lost.

Identification of the fugitives by Chilean authorities clearly established that the three Cubans had succeeded in leaving Bolivia aided by two Bolivian citizens linked to the PCB. They were Estanislao Vilca Colque and Efraín Aguilar Quiñones.

The rest is simply history. The president of the Chilean Senate, Salvador Allende, personally assumed responsibility for the care and protection of the refugees and hastily arranged their departure from Chile to Prague. From there, they returned to Cuba to brief Prime Minister Castro about what had happened in Bolivia.

Of the five survivors, the Bolivians Inti and Darío remained in their country, staying underground to continue their political activity and trying to revive the legend of the ELN.

In an encounter in La Paz on September 9, 1969, with police officers who were searching a house, Inti was killed. Darío met the same fate a few months later, and this tragic episode in the history of Bolivia came to an end. After a few brief public appearances for propaganda purposes, nothing more has been heard of the Cubans Pombo, Urbano, and Benigno.

NOTES

1. Inti Peredo, *Mi campaña con el Che*, Chapter 2.
2. Che's diary, entries for March 27 and 28, April 3, summary for the month of April, and entry for July 10.
3. Pombo's diary, entry for September 19.

Part IV

EVALUATION

Chapter 13

SOME CLARIFICATIONS

Much has been written and there has been much speculation about Che's guerrilla war. Without a doubt the silence of Bolivian authorities and the lack of a complete, authentic official version of these events permitted the creation of a pack of distortions clearly aimed at discrediting the Bolivian military. After all, the defeat of the principal ideologue and interpreter of guerrilla war theory could have and did have serious repercussions throughout the Latin American continent. Accordingly, the author deems it necessary to make some precise observations on the major aspects that have been most exploited and most distorted, so that what happened in those months of 1967 can be clearly understood.

THE MILITARY MOBILIZATION

At no time did a mass mobilization take place in the operations zone. In the first place, the forces on the scene—the organic forces of the Fourth and Eighth divisions—were the appropriate ones to deal with the problem. When the conflict began, the Camiri Division had a total of 1,103 soldiers within its dependent units. It was slowly reinforced by companies from other regiments out of La Paz and Cochabamba, who did not exceed 500 men.[1] By May, part of these forces were replaced with other companies, so the same troop level was maintained. When operations shifted to the Eighth Division, those reinforcement units were also shifted to that command to supplement the organic forces in the conduct of operations.

The first difficulty in deploying troops arose by chance. The date when the guerrilla foco was discovered coincided with the period set for discharge of the soldiers who had entered military service in the first months of 1966 and had fulfilled their required minimum year in uniform. Although at that time the law provided for two years of service as a maximum, custom and practice as well as budgetary restrictions had set the norm of discharge after a year in the barracks. This discharge—of 80 percent of the strength of the army—was therefore under way when the Ñancahuazú ambush occurred, and it had to be suspended in the Fourth and Eighth divisions as well as in some units of other divisions. This was the case of the Bolívar, Jordán, Méndez Arcos, and CITE regiments, which were the first to send reinforcements to the operations zone.

It was difficult to use these soldiers, since they felt they had fulfilled their military service and wished to get back home to continue their studies or to work. Their mobilization put off these plans for the sake of a problem that apparently was not yet major. Only in one case, however, did a discipline problem arise: a battery of Artillery Regiment 2, covering the tin-roof house in Ñancahuazú, attempted to mutiny and abandon their superiors at the end of April after the Iripití ambush. They were quickly controlled by their officers and noncommissioned officers with no unfortunate consequences. Disciplinary methods were quickly adapted so as to avoid this kind of incident, and at the end of May, when the troops recruited in March had received accelerated training, the earlier units could be relieved and honorably discharged.

The other important aspect of the mobilization has to do with military training. The troops from the class of 1966 had been trained for regular warfare. The units stationed in the altiplano and the valleys, accustomed to dealing with routine internal problems in the country, had gone through all their periods of instruction. Those belonging to the Fourth and Eighth divisions, however, had received only basic training and had then been employed in road and agricultural work, so that their quality as combatants was very low for the kind of operations that guerrilla warfare required. Hence the disorganization that reigned at the onset of hostilities when soldiers from different units were thrown together under improvised commands to carry out the first missions. This happened basically because there were no complete units within the Fourth Division. The lack of officers was also notable: second lieutenants were carrying out the duties of company commanders, and sergeants those of section commanders, due to the lack of officers at the rank of lieutenant and captain, a consequence of the interruption within cadres caused by the closing down of the military college in 1952 and 1953. The first classes that had entered beginning in 1954, who held the rank of captain by 1967, were very small, averaging from fifteen to twenty officers each, and this was reflected in the units. Besides, two classes of captains were at that time taking the advanced course at the Weapons Application School, which had to be suspended so that they could be sent to the units engaged in fighting the guerrillas.

As regards fields of specialization in military training—which determine the kinds of units and of combatants with certain skills—in the case of operations in 1967, the army was basically composed of infantry units. Two specializations, however, stood out: parachutists and assault troops (Rangers). The former received their training at the Center for Instruction of Special Troops (CITE) in Cochabamba, had good command cadres, and were considered soldiers with good skills. Nevertheless, their training was oriented more toward the geographic center of the country, which is to say the valleys. At no point was there an opportunity to adapt their parachuting skills to the type of terrain existing in the Southeast.

The two parachute companies, CITE 1 and CITE 2, who participated in the Fourth Division's area of action performed as simple infantry, and only their esprit de corps distinguished them from the rest. They had their baptism of fire in Iripití, losing one of their officers and several soldiers.

The other special unit was Ranger–1 Company of Méndez Arcos 24th Regiment from the Challapata garrison in the Department of Oruro. Trained under the Assault Troops program, its members undoubtedly were better prepared than the regular units, with only one drawback: the geographic environment. They came from the altiplano, and all their preparation was geared toward scrub vegetation and the high peaks. This unit lost an officer and a soldier at El Espino within the Fourth Division sector and carried out important missions displaying their ability and sense of responsibility.

As always, though, the best action, the most significant feats of courage, were accomplished by those units that were most neglected or least prepared. Thus, continuing their glorious record since the Chaco War, troops of Campos 6th Infantry Regiment, Boquerón 11th Infantry Regiment, and Abaroa 1st Cavalry Guard excelled in the first operations.

Only in the last part of the campaign did the army have troops available that were especially trained to face guerrilla warfare. On the one hand there was Manchego 12th Infantry Regiment, which after sixteen weeks of instruction finished off its training period with a tactical exercise demonstrating its skills. Coordinated work shared by the Mobile Training Team (MTT) of the United States Army Special Forces, commanded by Maj. Ralph Shelton, and the Bolivian officers led by Lt. Col. José Gallardo and Maj. Miguel Ayoroa, produced a battalion that was well-trained, tough, and eager to enter into combat.

The training center at La Esperanza continued to function once Manchego began operations, and companies from several units were sent there to undergo a four-week course during the months of September, October, November, and into mid-December, when, judging the guerrilla problem solved, the Bolivian government decided that the North American military personnel could return to their country. These companies made a valuable contribution to the regular forces on control and security missions.

On the other hand, while Ranger–2 was being trained, other companies were being prepared by their own instructors in the Third Division from Villamontes and the Fifth Division from Roboré. They were to be used if the guerrilla problem spread. The end of the guerrilla war meant that those units also returned to their bases, and their forces were reunited with their organic units under the respective division commands.

With these reduced forces, which sometimes were poorly trained and lacked complete command cadres, the army faced the guerrilla problem in its initial, most difficult phase, when it did not have complete intelligence about the insurgents' strength, intentions, and goals. Nor was there initially an adequate evaluation of the support the guerrillas might receive from the civilian population, particularly the campesinos, who theoretically constitute the most important support base for a guerrilla movement.

In the second stage, however, when the guerrilla problem had been completely sized up and its chances for expansion circumscribed, the army command possessed better units and resources for facing it. To speak, therefore, of thousands of soldiers encircling the guerrilla force is to lose perspective and to show ignorance of the environment. Over the extent of the operations zone, the military forces scattered and thinned out, creating problems that were hard to solve for the command, which was trying to maintain surveillance over the area and simultaneously conduct operations.

INTELLIGENCE METHODS

Throughout the campaign the main source of information for the army was the campesinos and residents of small urban centers. The intelligence sections of the division general staffs in Camiri and Santa Cruz had barely enough personnel to carry out their routine duties. The principal support so far as internal security was concerned came from the the Criminal Investigation Board (DIC), which from its political control branch kept military authorities informed of the activities of political and labor leaders. Nevertheless, this information, most often fragmentary, did not permit adequate intelligence work to be carried out.

So it was that the first news of the guerrillas came from outside sources (YPFB personnel), while the Ministry of Government at that point had no information on the presence of the Cuban advance team in La Paz since May 1966, nor on the contacts that they had made with the political structures of the Bolivian left. The freedom of action that the Cubans had is surprising, but there was no serious reason to think that an operation of that type was probable. The executive board, recently organized on a constitutional basis in August 1966 after a sound electoral victory, was not likely to imagine that a guerrilla problem of the sort that emerged in Ñancahuazú was incubating in the country.

While operations were going on, as soon as the presence of insurgents was detected in the Southeast, the task of military intelligence was channeled on the one hand toward the identification of the members of the armed group, and on the other toward their contacts outside of the zone so as to isolate them. Success was quickly achieved with the former task. The capture first of the deserters Daniel and Orlando, then of Salustio, and finally of Danton, Pelao and Loro, made it possible to obtain from the statements of all of these men practically the entire battle order of the adversary. In addition, although this first body of information was not very exact and was corrected little by little, it was already enough to form an idea of the scope of the problem and of who was involved in it. Here it is worth recalling the skillfulness with which information about Che's presence and leadership on the guerrilla front was handled. His involvement was not announced from the start although sufficient information was in hand to do so. Instead, the authorities waited for the news to come from other sources, such as Debray, so as later to confirm it and exploit it politically, trading on Che's status as a foreigner meddling in Bolivian affairs.

The DIC cooperated actively in this phase. Of key importance was the information it provided on Moisés Guevara's trip to Camiri and then on to Ñancahuazú, with full identification of his companions—thanks to the registry of the hotel where they had stayed overnight upon arrival and had needed to show identification. Since Moisés Guevara was known in the political-labor sphere, the DIC had been alerted to observe his movements from a list of those suspected of "trying to organize guerrilla movements." Clearly, something about his activities had leaked out. The arrival of this information at the headquarters of the Fourth Division command alerted the police, who observed and followed him, verifying that he and his companions had gone to Ñancahuazú in two groups, using the same vehicle—Coco's Jeep—and also linking him to Tania and Coco. This information, obtained on March 14, 15, and 16, was communicated to Section II of the Fourth Division and was swiftly confirmed when Daniel, Orlando, and Salustio were captured, at which point the first reports were also obtained about foreign participation in the guerrilla war and the probable presence of Che Guevara in Ñancahuazú.

Combat intelligence was produced in two ways by the units engaged in operations: initially, through the use of guides for familiarization with the terrain and campesinos for getting news of guerrilla movements and activities; later, when experience had shown that campesino reports were not always accurate and were sometimes fanciful, each unit organized its own information teams, consisting basically of sergeants and privates who, dressed in civilian clothes and pretending to be businessmen and travelers, moved around the zone in search of the guerrillas' trail so as to report it to their units. At times police personnel were used in the same circumstances.

The allegations that the CIA had provided Bolivia with sophisticated methods of electronic surveillance capable of detecting the heat of human bodies and their cooking fires to track down the guerrilla groups (for example in the article signed by Andrew St. George in *True* magazine, April 1969), and that all plans were approved and finalized in the United States, in the Pentagon, are also of course untrue. One need simply recall, for example, how the information leading to the two principal actions (Vado del Yeso and El Churo) was obtained. In both cases campesinos were the ones who provided army officials with the news of the guerrilla presence. No sophisticated method of tracking or detection was used in these cases.

As an example of what was going on in the country, we shall quote President Barrientos's official statement regarding the *True* article and other similar publications, which tried to put things in true perspective. The president said:

Thousands of phantasmagoric stories have circulated—and will continue to circulate—about the so-called Castroite guerrilla wars. Some speculate with them; others earn money for glorifying through publicity not so much Che Guevara as Castro, an individual who feeds his popularity on his friends who have died in the macabre task of killing and in the adventure of making our peoples poorer and more dependent.

The people of Bolivia and their government fought for their freedom and their sovereignty without receiving any aid from President Johnson, as is alleged in the publication referred to by the journalists who asked for my opinion.

The other story about supposed CIA participation is another way of lessening the glories of our Armed Forces and justifying the defeat dealt to the adventurist "revolution" of Castroism by the realistic and heroic Bolivian revolution. The CIA exists only in the imagination of those who defame Bolivia and the Bolivians.

Che Guevara died because he came to kill. And he came to kill invading the nation's territory with mercenaries and traitors who sowed mourning and blood in campesino villages and where paths crossed. This invasion was met by our Armed Forces, whose triumph can be blemished by nothing and by no one but those who act out of spite, mediocrity, and cowardice.

We who have the responsibility of guaranteeing the self-determination of our people and of maintaining respect for the most noble attributes of the fatherland have led the fight. The Captain General of the Republic was in all combat sectors. I could have fallen into one of those macabre, cowardly ambushes. No one speaks for the more than sixty anonymous sons of workers and campesinos, military men and ordinary citizens, who died defending the sacred cause of the sovereign nation.

No one can blame General Ovando, General Zenteno, Colonel Reque Terán nor Captain Gary Prado for the death of Che Guevara. The blame is his for having obeyed Señor Castro, who continues to celebrate in holiday fashion the revolution of the firing squad, guerrilla warfare, Vietnamization. It would be more in keeping with his cause if he first did himself what he demands so insistently of others.

In my capacity as Captain General of the Armed Forces of the Nation, as constitutional president of the Republic, I assume all responsibility for the events that occurred as a consequence of the Castroite invasion and the Bolivians' defense.

Nearly two years after the brutal aggression, I renew the determination of the revolutionary people of Bolivia and their government: we will again crush any intent to subjugate our fatherland.

As regards strategic intelligence—set up as a result of the agreements reached in the Conferences of Commanders of American Armies from 1962 on, with special emphasis on those aspects relating to subversion—it remained on a normal level of exchange of information that allowed other countries even more than Bolivia to investigate on their own some links with the guerrilla apparatus—for example the Uruguayan, Ecuadorean, and Panamanian passports used by the Cubans to gain access to Bolivia. Thanks to the information provided by Bolivia, those countries were able to discover shortcomings in their systems of identification and issuance of documents, which were being exploited by international subversion to facilitate its members' movements.

The report presented later by Bolivia at the Eighth Conference of American Armies, held in Rio de Janeiro in 1968, helped to identify some of the tactics and techniques used by Castroism in its activities in the hemisphere and to assess its future perspectives in light of them.

ARMAMENTS USED

Since 1959, Bolivia, like nearly all countries in the hemisphere, had been receiving war matériel from the United States as part of the Military Assistance Program (MAP), consisting of infantry arms used in World War II. The North American army's adoption of newer arms, with the M–14 rifle as the basic weapon, made obsolete the M–1 rifle and carbine and other collective weapons, such as the Browning automatic rifle (BAR), the light machine gun, and all 30–caliber weapons.

In the case of Bolivia, these deliveries were made in small lots, first to equip a battalion—material that was distributed in 1959 to three companies, one in the Maj. Waldo Ballivián Presidential Escort Regiment, another in the 4th Cavalry Regiment, and a third in the Noncommissioned Officer Military School at Cochabamba, these being the units most often used for problems of internal security. The terms of the military aid agreement clearly established that these resources were intended for that use.

In the years following, as other lots arrived, the 24th Infantry Regiment (Rangers, in Challapata), the motorized Toledo 23rd Infantry Regiment, and the CITE were organized at the same time that the equipping of the first units was completed.

The modernization plan was therefore in full swing when the guerrilla war broke out, but the Fourth and Eighth division units had not received any of the equipment up to that time. Priority had been set for the western part of the country, so that in the East, the soldier's basic weapon consisted of the Mauser 7.6–caliber rifle used in the Chaco War.

In the first battles of 1967 those were the weapons used, as can be verified in details noted in Che's diary and other documents.[2] They were notably inferior to the arms used by the guerrillas, nearly all of whom possessed automatic weapons with greater firepower.

After the setbacks of Ñancahuazú and Iripití other weapons were sent to the units to improve their offensive capability. Among the material received was the FAL 7.62–caliber rifle made in Argentina, with which some units were equipped. For its part, Manchego Regiment received for its training the matériel covered in the program, the basic weapons for which were the M–1 Garand rifle and M–1 and M–2 carbines. So at no time was any modern or special weaponry used, nor was additional support received from other countries, except for the shipment of Argentine rifles and ammunition that arrived by rail. With these precarious means, the Bolivian Army faced the guerrilla force.

SUPPLIES

If on the guerrilla side hunger was a constant factor due to the difficulties in obtaining food that were present from the beginning, on the side of the regular forces the situation was not very positive either. The basic ration of the Bolivian soldier consists of *lagua* (a thick soup of corn flour in which pieces of meat, potato, or yucca are cooked, according to the region, with the addition of rice or noodles and some vegetables and beans). This diet, served in generous portions, has always sustained the army, but with troops in operations, the logistic systems that worked more or less regularly in normal times had great difficulty in fulfilling their mission.

As for the supply of food, the main problem was that the degree of mobility imposed on the units, with patrols and constant movement, made traditional meals impractical. It meant carrying heavy loads, pots (normally fuel barrels cut in half), condiments, and the like, limiting the troops' effectiveness in their movements. Nevertheless, this system was used during nearly all the operations, with brief attempts to use combat rations from other armies—such as North American C rations, which were not widely accepted by the Bolivian soldier after the initial novelty had worn off. The food tasted different and there was little variety. The same thing happened with the Brazilian Army combat ration. The use of these rations, however, did allow a certain degree of autonomy to be given to some units. Toward the end of the campaign, through the initiative of some military engineers, there was an experiment in Santa Cruz in manufacturing a dry ration based on Bolivian eating habits. This ration, packed in a plastic strip divided into compartments, contained dehydrated, powdered lagua as the principal food. The disadvantage lay in the need to cook this ration, but its taste and quality were acceptable. It was complemented with beans and toasted corn, *pito* (ground toasted cereal dissolved in water with spices), dehydrated bananas, and some sweet. The end of the campaign precluded thorough experimentation with the ration's quality, but the attempt to prepare a dry ration based on the food habits and customs of the Bolivian soldier was praiseworthy.

The other basic supply problem was ammunition. The use of units coming from different garrisons and different kinds of organization, and above all supplied with different weapons, created total confusion in ordering. At one time four calibers of individual weapons could be counted: 9–mm, 7.65–mm, the Argentine 7.62–mm, and the American 30–mm, for both rifles and carbines. Forty-five-caliber for pistols, and in support arms 7.65– and 30–caliber, were needed, the latter linked for light machine guns. It was common to receive ammunition that did not match the order. This would require additional transport staff and would restrict the units' firepower for long periods.

TRANSPORT

When operations began, the Fourth Division units had only one truck per regiment, of the type called "caimán" (alligator), provided by North American aid and intended for Civic Action. The division command was reinforced with some vehicles that proved insufficient to serve the needs of troop movements, supply, and evacuations. So it was necessary on a number of occasions for both the Fourth and the Eighth divisions to resort to the requisitioning of civilian vehicles for military use, with appropriate payment. The few available roads and their poor condition limited the use of vehicles to certain areas. Elsewhere, it was necessary to use helicopters for supply and evacuations of the more remote units. In several instances horses were also rented to carry supplies, thus relieving the soldier of the task of transporting all these articles by hand. The Cochabamba-Sucre-Camiri road was used preferably in Fourth Division operations as the principal supply route, due to the security it provided, entering the operations zone as it did at one of its extremities and guaranteeing permanent unrestricted use. Th Eighth Division used the Cochbamba–Santa Cruz highway as its main supply route throughout the entire operations period.

MEDICAL SERVICE

This service was perhaps the hardest to organize efficiently so as to provide the care that was so necessary to the fighting troops. Before the outbreak of hostilities, the military medical service amounted to one or two doctors per division who, with the support of a noncom or sergeant medic (nurse), fulfilled the mission of attending to minor illnesses and healing. They turned to the easy expedient of evacuating the seriously ill to Cochabamba and Santa Cruz hospitals when possible, or going to other health centers. When the first ambush occurred with its aftermath of dead and wounded, it became necessary to thoroughly organize a military medical service that could effectively support the units. There was a notable lack of necessary professional personnel, since the doctors, normally working half-time in the army and having other obligations, could not easily be mobilized. These limitations notwithstanding, the system would be organized, as in the Fourth Division with a hospital in Camiri and another on the way to completion in Lagunillas. In addition, medics were assigned to companies operating independently.

The lack of resources for attending the wounded and sick was nevertheless depressing. Considering that some units came from the western part of the country with its great heights and cold climate, their first weeks in the operations zone constituted a very difficult period owing to mosquito and other insect bites that became quickly infected. Dehydration also claimed victims, and on top of everything else there was hardly enough tincture of iodine and other ointments. Those wounded in combat suffered the most, because they had to be transported on improvised stretchers to first-aid posts. Occasionally helicopters could be used, but communication difficulties prevented an efficient use of that kind of transport. Typical examples were Piraí and Morocos in the Eighth Division, where they had to wait much too long after the fighting for evacuation, and the wounded died for lack of medical attention.

These conditions undoubtedly affected the troops' morale. A combatant who knows he will be attended to promptly and efficiently if wounded is more at ease than one who sees his comrades bleeding to death with no dressing to stop the blood.

The medics, both professional and amateur, accompanied the troops despite all the limitations, and became valuable assets during the campaign. A characteristic example is Pvt. Franz Muriel of Ranger–2, who, having been trained as a nurse, died trying to rescue a wounded man at Naranjal, carrying out his duty in the finest tradition.

COMMUNICATIONS

From the first, communication lines were the great problem for the regular forces committed to fighting the guerrilla band. The existing system of military radio comprised an unreliable network linking the army command in La Paz with the division commands in Camiri and Santa Cruz, subject to interference and listening in because of the frequencies used. There was no radio equipment in the regiment commands in Charagua, Carandaití, much less tactical radios for short-range use. When operations began, additional equipment was installed in Lagunillas, where the advance command post of the Fourth Division was set up. The Santa Cruz command had radio communication with Vallegrande, La Esperanza, and San Ignacio de Velasco, the headquarters of its dependent units. It, too, lacked tactical radios.

The first solution adopted for providing liaison equipment to units committed to operations was to send all existing equipment from the Military Geographical Institute in La Paz, used by its brigades in field work for the national map survey. This equipment was sent to the division commands affected by the guerrilla war. It was made up of AN/GRC–9 units from the United States Army that had seen better days and worked only with great difficulty. Bulky and heavy, they required two men for transport and operation. Their receivers worked by battery, but the transmitters required the use of a noisy and ineffective manual generator. Besides, in order for them to be used, a proper antenna installation was needed, pointed perpendicular to the station to be contacted. This required a compass and sufficient knowledge of the location of the receiving and transmitting stations, often difficult to achieve due to the lack of up-to-date plans and maps of the area. This equipment, used throughout the campaign, represented the only possibility of communication between companies assigned to the operations zone and the division commands. As a matter of course operating failures prevented good communication, and there were cases when units remained isolated until they had regained contact or solved the problem by sending messengers or liaison officers, or by other means, such as messages carried by the air force.

Some units, such as the CITE, Ranger–2, and Ranger–1 companies, equipped through military aid in earlier years, had PRC–10 and short-range PRC–6 tactical radios (6 and 2 km respectively) which facilitated communication to a degree, though conditions of terrain (mountains and woods) greatly reduced their effectiveness, and the supply of replacement batteries was severely limited. Messengers traveling on foot, on horseback, or by motor vehicle became the principal medium of communication, with delays resulting from their use. Whenever possible, the communication facilities of some public enterprises such as YPFB, ENFE (National Railways Company), and State Telegraph were used. The disadvantage lay in the difficulty of maintaining confidentiality and the fact that these were fixed installations, not always appropriate for operational needs.

FOREIGN INTERVENTION

Contrary to all the speculation and wishful thinking, foreign intervention, particularly the North American, did not have an important effect on the development of antiguerrilla operations in 1967. Although the aim and purpose of the guerrilla war consisted in securing armed intervention by North American soldiers to organize "two, three, or ten Vietnams" and convert the Andes chain into the "Sierra Maestra of South America," this did not happen, because from the beginning it was possible to isolate the foco and reduce the problem to national scale in spite of its foreign links.

When the guerrilla force and its leader were identified by the intelligence service of the Bolivian Armed Forces, it is evident that aid was sought abroad but under some specific guidelines:

—Resources assigned to the program of military aid for 1967, when it was planned to organize a new unit of the motorized infantry battalion type for the western area of the country (Coro Coro), were transferred to Manchego 12th Infantry Regiment of the Eighth Division in order to convert this production unit into an operative unit.

—The United States Army was to send a training team from its special forces (Green Berets) to Bolivia to assist in preparing this unit, which besides receiving normal basic training was to receive additional training for assault troops (Rangers).

—The North American instructors were to remain barracked in La Esperanza, 80 km north of Santa Cruz, where this battalion would be trained. They eventually would be able to go to Santa Cruz, the eastern capital city on some weekends, in coordination with the Eighth Division command.

—It was expressly prohibited for North American instructors to enter the zone of guerrilla operations under any circumstances.

—Besides equipping Ranger–2, the United States Army was to provide the Bolivian Army with enough ammunition for their training, as well as additional ammunition for operations. Similarly, it would immediately supply a lot of C combat rations for the troops to use in operations. In fulfillment of these accords, Maj. Ralph W. Shelton arrived in the country at the end of April with Capts. Edmond Fricke, William Trimble, and Margarito Cruz, and twelve sergeants of varying specializations to make up the training team that set up in La Esperanza, where together with Bolivian officers they readied the contingent from Manchego Regiment for the operations in the Southeast. Equipment for the unit arrived within a few weeks, as did the ammunition and rations, which were distributed to the division commands in the operations zones. The only time that North American military men were in the vicinity of the combat zone was a few days after the Ñancahauzú ambush, at the beginning of April, when the adjunct military attaché, Major Kirsch, was authorized to travel to Camiri to obtain some information from the division command. The result of that report and of his assessment of the situation was the signing of the accord that paved the way for North American military aid to the Bolivian military.

Although the members of the training team at La Esperanza followed with interest the development of operations during the months when Ranger–2 was being trained (May through August), they always considered this a Bolivian problem, and they tried to carry out their assignment to the best of their abilities. Their presence was useful and necessary at a time when the Bolivian Army needed that assistance. No argument can be made against it. Their arrival in the country and their work were covered by the military-aid agreements signed by the MNR governments in the years 1954–58, and this was not the first time that foreign military missions had assisted the country (we have the cases of the German, Belgian, and Italian missions in the first decades of this century), nor is it a special case in Latin America, where military missions have always existed, even between area countries—such as the Brazilian military mission in Paraguay, or the Chilean mission in Ecuador, and the Argentine mission in Bolivia. Military cooperation is therefore a permanent fact of life.

Another topic refers to the CIA agents who appeared at a certain point in the conflict. From mid-September on, after Vado del Yeso, when it had become certain that the end of the guerrilla war was near, particularly because of the lack of support from the campesino and worker sectors, the North American government offered to provide the armed forces with two CIA agents who might cooperate in the identification of the Cuban guerrilla leaders and in other areas that might be considered necessary. For this purpose the agents known as Félix Ramos and Eduardo Gonzales arrived in Santa Cruz, both of them Cuban and supposedly familiar with Che and his collaborators. In the Eighth Division command they were assigned to Section II-Intelligence, and with that status they were transferred to Vallegrande on September 26 when the command post was moved up, joining Col. Zenteno Anaya and his general staff. They did not go in with the troops who were combing the area, and on October 9 Félix Ramos arrived by helicopter in La Higuera together with the division commander, to make positive identification of the prisoner who said he was Che Guevara. This mission accomplished, he returned to Vallegrande, and a few hours later he and Gonzales left that city for Santa Cruz and from there surely continued on to Washington.

That was the participation of the United States in the 1967 operations.

Two other countries interested in the guerrilla problem who could have been affected if it developed and spread were Brazil and Argentina. Their lengthy borders with Bolivia were difficult to safeguard, and their domestic situations were not stable, so from the first they established intelligence liaisons that allowed them to follow everything that was happening in Ñancahuazú without intervening. Requests for logistical support from Bolivia were given priority attention, with the result that Brazil sent combat rations in great quantity and Argentina sent FAL rifles of its own manufacture and supply to equip two battalions, replacing the Mauser from the Chaco War.

Foreign participation in the fight against the guerrillas was limited to that. There was no direct action, nor special teams, nor was a massive logistical effort undertaken. The hardships undergone by the Bolivian troops are proof enough of this fact.

THE CAMPESINOS

A basic factor in guerrilla warfare is the rural population. Their participation and support of one of the sides of the conflict tips the balance decisively, as a general rule. It is not for nothing that tribute is paid to it in guerrilla manuals. In the case of Bolivia in 1967, the performance of the campesino class was so important that a good share of the success achieved by the armed forces must be attributed to it.

From the beginning of hostilities, campesino organizations, comprising syndicates and federations, spoke out against subversion. Although one can say that these clusters of leaders were obeying government orders or were involved with the government, it is no less true that they were in touch with the grass-roots level at the time. One proof of this is that they were ready to mobilize several thousand men into the operations zones to fight at the side of the army. The military authorities did not accept this offer, since with little military background civilian combatants would be easy prey for the guerrillas and could hinder operations of the regular forces, but the will of the campesinos, particularly those from the Cochabamba valley, who were strong fans of General Barrientos, held firm at all times.

In the operations zone itself, the campesino population was not so concentrated as in the western part of the country. In the East, communities are more spread out and less numerous, so there is neither a very strong nor a very active campesino syndical organization. Nevertheless, after the first battles the campesinos began to organize, particularly in the vicinity of Ñancahuazú, to protect themselves and to deny support to the guerrillas. So it was that the decision was made, as a rule of thumb, for men to disappear when the insurgents came on the scene, for fear of being recruited or taken hostage. That attitude was observed during the entire campaign and in virtually every community. The elderly, women, and children were the only ones who received the guerrillas. On the other hand, when a military unit arrived, the entire population received it and participated in discussions and exchange of news without fear. The fact was that the army's presence in those areas had never been associated in the past with repression or political persecution, so the campesinos trusted men in uniform.

Except in the case of Honorato Rojas, the army did not offer special inducements nor did it buy information from the campesinos. Their backing and cooperation was obtained by simply appealing to nationalist sentiments. In no case did the military pressure the campesinos in order to obtain news of the guerrilla force. On the insurgent side, however, attitudes were taken on several occasions that had a negative effect on the communities: the taking of hostages, requisitioning of their cattle, and threats to their security.[3] It is therefore no surprise that campesino support was denied to the rebels.

THE GENERAL POPULATION

For a country like Bolivia, where political convulsions have unfortunately been a permanent fact of life, the rise and development of the Ñancahuazú guerrilla war did not constitute a problem of the first magnitude. In its first phase, its peculiarity and novelty helped the guerrilla war to grow, especially owing to the setbacks suffered by the army at Ñancahuazú and Iripití, but getting into the phase of isolation and attrition, the guerrilla force became less newsworthy, recapturing public interest only on occasions like Samaipata, Vado del Yeso, and the like. Throughout this period, the vast majority of the Bolivian population neither felt anything for nor was affected by the guerrilla problem.

In the first place, the military action was taking place in a remote, sparsely populated area. It did not have any immediate repercussion on the lives and activities of the rest of the Bolivians. On the other hand, the government did not adopt strict measures of control and allowed a climate of normality to reign in the rest of the country. Only on the occasion of the military incursion into the mines on St. John's Eve was there a confrontation outside of the operations zone.[4] Nor did the politicians play a significant role at that time. Their fear of getting involved with the foreigners in the guerrilla band kept them cautiously silent most of the time.

NOTES

1. See the Unit Mobilization Chart, Table 3.
2. Che's diary, entry for March 23. Rolando's diary, entry for April 10.
3. Che's diary, entries for April 19; June 19; July 3, 4, and 8; September 18 and 24.
4. The La Paz morning daily, *Presencia*, in June 1986 carried an interview with two clergymen who had been working in the mining town of Siglo XX in 1967. They told how the military reaction was provoked by a truck driver and his son who, in an attempt to create a confrontation, fired on the troops and caused the first casualties.

Chapter 14

ASSESSMENT

The failure of the Ñancahuazú guerrilla war can be explained in many different ways. For some, military reasons are primary, for others political reasons; causes of a social and even economic nature can be cited, and there will be some truth in each explanation. The present essay could not be considered complete if we did not try to systematize these aspects in an effort to understand the overall problem and the repercussions that it has had over the two succeeding decades, not only in Bolivia but throughout Latin America.

THEORY

For that purpose one first needs to analyze the theoretical framework, and that is provided in the writings of the guerrilla chief himself, Commandant Ernesto Guevara, who as a result of his experience in the Sierra Maestra and his participation in the process of consolidation of the Cuban Revolution, is considered by friends and foes to be an authority on this type of war against imperialist domination. In his book *La guerra de guerrillas*, Che said:

1. Essence of Guerrilla Warfare

The contributions made by the Cuban Revolution to the mechanics of revolutionary movements in America are:

1. Popular forces can win a war against the army.
2. It is not always necessary to wait until all conditions for the revolution are in place; the insurrectional foco can create them.
3. In underdeveloped Latin America the fundamental setting for armed struggle is the countryside.[1]

The first point has been effectively demonstrated only twice in the period since 1960. In Cuba and Nicaragua, strongly motivated popular forces were able to destroy the armies of the Batista and Somoza governments; but those two military structures reflected in their organization and methods all the corruption and despotism of the tyrannies that they represented. They did not amount to anything more than Pretorian guards intended to keep their leaders in power and protect their interests. They did not bear within them the seed of nationalism that sustained and continue to sustain the armed forces elsewhere, nor any degree of popular and social partic- ipation on the part of their cadres. They felt no identification with the people and their aspirations. The other armies that have had to confront the guerrilla problem in Bolivia, Argentina, Colombia, Venezuela, El Sal- vador, Guatemala, etc., have managed to find sufficient internal support to render the fighting in the mountains ineffective and to reduce it to a problem localized generally in a remote area, which does not affect the life of the country on a large scale.

Nor has the second statement been proven. The insurrectional focos created in Latin America have not been able to provoke the promised popular revolutions or changes. It is true that they have spilled blood over the land, but without provoking the confrontation with the colonial power by involving it directly in the fighting that was its first goal. They have caused the destruction or weakening of communal systems of production, transport, and energy production, affecting not so much the oligarchies as the campesinos and workers, who feel threatened from both sides and flee their lands and homes for the poverty belts of the cities. The current examples of El Salvador and Peru are clear and pathetic.

Che's guerrilla war in Bolivia did not create revolutionary conditions, but instead contributed to a long process of political and social disorien- tation that has convulsed the country for many years, in which the real crux of the problem has been lost from view due to the discrepancies between men and theories.

As for the third statement, in Latin America in general an accelerated process is under way of abandonment of the countryside for the cities as a consequence of the economic crisis that plagues the region, so definitions of the social order are being transferred to the urban context, where living conditions and subsistence are more difficult every day. Almost all gov- ernments in the area, good and bad, are trying to keep their populations in the agricultural sector, giving incentives for production and improving living conditions in order to circumvent migration. Under these conditions it is more and more utopian to imagine a theater of fighting in areas that are gradually losing importance in the nations' economies.

Where a government has risen to power through some form of popular vote, fraudulent or not, and at least an appearance of constitutional legality is kept up, the outbreak of guerrilla war cannot be forced since the possibilities of peaceful struggle have not yet been exhausted.

If this was Che's point of view, we can only ask, why then did he come to Bolivia?

René Barrientos's government was constitutional, the result of an election with wide popular participation, in which the candidate's image won the sympathies of the campesinos above all. The Congress and all constitutional mechanisms were in full force, there was freedom of the press, there were no political prisoners or exiles (though political leaders were detained after the guerrilla war broke out). Although we cannot call the Barrientos government excellent or totally honest, we cannot fail to recognize that it was a legitimate, popular government, against which the guerrilla band could not hope to prevail.

Other examples have shown up in Latin America. Colombia, with its long democratic tradition, has constantly blocked the guerrilla struggle, backed by the legitimacy of its governments. The Sendero Luminoso guerrillas have achieved nothing against the constitutional governments of Fernando Belaúnde and Alan García in Peru, and not even in El Salvador, with all its limitations and problems, has the guerrilla movement succeeded in breaking down the mechanism of government.

So it seems obvious that intuitively or consciously we Latin Americans are learning to live in democracy, we wish to respect our institutions, and it is through legal channels that change can be achieved. What happened in Bolivia in 1982 is a clear example. Through joint political and civic pressure the armed forces were obliged to hand the government over peacefully, depositing power in the hands of the Congress so that it would elect the president of the republic. In this way the process interrupted on July 17, 1980, went on. This degree of civic and political maturity demonstrates the democratic vocation of the Bolivian people, which they share with other countries.

Guerrilla warfare is a mass struggle, a war of the people. The guerrilla band as an armed nucleus is the fighting vanguard of the people. Its great force resides in the mass of the population. The guerrilla fighter thus depends on total support from the local population. This is a sine qua non.

If the guerrilla band is the fighting vanguard of the people, in the case of Bolivia in 1967, its people did not want to fight. The support of the general population—Mao Zedong's comparison of the guerrilla band to "the fish in the water"—was not present in the country. In fact, we can say that the common citizen did not understand, much less feel in any way affected by, the guerrilla war; thence the isolation and complete lack of support for Che's forces. Perhaps the isolation of the guerrillas achieved by the army once the foco had been prematurely discovered had something to do with it, but what is clear is that neither in the political and labor institutions of the period nor on the level of the ordinary citizen was there any enthusiasm for the guerrilla war. That meant that no combatants could be recruited, one of the causes of the failure.

The guerrilla fighter will carry out his action in wild, sparsely populated areas, in which the people's struggle for redress focuses preferably and indeed almost exclusively on changing the social make-up of landholding. This means that the guerrilla fighter is first and foremost an agrarian revolutionary. He interprets the aspirations of the great campesino mass to own the land, their means of production, and their animals.

The Agrarian Reform of 1953 brought about radical changes in Bolivia, not only in terms of land ownership, but more basically in terms of the social conditions of the campesinos. This was felt more strongly in the western sectors of the country, the altiplano and the valleys. In the eastern region, the Agrarian Reform meant little, due to the fundamental fact that lands were readily available and the population density was low. In the East large latifundios have never existed. For centuries campesino families were always landowners, so that the guerrilla aim relating to the land made practically no sense to those who for centuries have neither had landowners over them nor been exploited. It can be argued that the means of production are and were primitive, and that commercialization of their products leaves the campesinos impoverished. That is true, but nothing was said of this, nothing was explained to them, seemingly because the guerrillas did not trust them.

2. Guerrilla Strategy

At the beginning, the guerrilla fighter's basic job will be to avoid being destroyed.

The precarious condition of the guerrilla band was evident from its first moments. The small number of men was not the main problem. The limitations arose because after the first ambushes they could not depend on a secure base, having no supply chain or route to guarantee their survival. From the beginning the guerrilla operation—because of Marcos's or Loro's lack of discipline, because of Che's lack of precision in his dealings with Joaquín—carried the seeds of its own destruction.

The hammering should be constant. The enemy soldier in an operations zone must not be allowed to sleep. His outposts should be attacked and liquidated systematically.

At no time did the guerrilla band mount an offensive against military installations. The ambushes and armed encounters sustained were undertaken mainly to slow down the advance of the regular troops. Undoubtedly if attacks had been made on military posts in the operations zone, a situation of fear and insecurity could have been created that might have influenced the final outcome. Considering how easy it is to send a small patrol of two or three men to harass barracks or security posts, it is surprising that this was not done. Even by acting from a distance, responses from the troops would have been provoked that would have meant wasted hours of ineffective searching, with concomitant physical and nervous exhaustion, while the guerrillas who had originated the operation, after firing one or two bursts, could calmly withdraw to a safe, restful place. If during one night this were done two or three times, most certainly on the next day those troops would be so tired out and alarmed that they would be rendered ineffective. When the army, in the first phase of operations, sent troops to villages in the area such as Lagunillas, Gutiérrez, Ipitá, etc., they were never attacked nor harassed, and were able to develop a sense of security.

There are two conditions that must obtain during every minute of the guerrilla fighter's life: absolute cooperation of the people and a perfect knowledge of the terrain.

We have already observed that cooperation of the people, practically speaking, did not exist. In the nomad phase of the guerrilla war it was harder to establish any kind of relationship with area residents, and it was necessary instead to detain the campesinos in order to prevent them from denouncing the presence of the insurgents to the army.

As for knowledge of the terrain, this was uncertain in the best of cases. Other than the route followed by Che on his February reconnaissance trip, the rest of the terrain was unknown to the guerrilla band. Time after time, as can be seen by reading the campaign diaries, they got lost searching for a way out of very difficult places. They would tire themselves out and lose time trying to find some reference point or some hamlet where they could get supplies.

The guerrillas' wandering led them on several occasions into dead ends or encounters with the army at times when they were not prepared to fight. When they entered the jurisdiction of the Eighth Division to operate in the sector of Florida and Samaipata and then in the Alto Seco-La Higuera sector, their ignorance of the terrain and of the social characteristics of the population were such that they committed one error after another until they ended up in El Churo.

A strong base of operations must be maintained and fortified throughout the course of the war.

The Ñancahuazú base did not become completely established, nor was consideration given to the need for an alternative base in case the first had to be abandoned. Excessive confidence after the first ambush led them to believe that the army would not be capable of penetrating so far as this base. When the military reacted, however, and began to encircle the area and conduct raids in the direction of the base, the guerrillas were forced to abandon it, both in order to get Danton and Pelao out of the operations zone and to escape the military pressure themselves. This ensured the loss of the base, to which they were able to return once in May, only to have to abandon it definitively later in the face of the military occupation, which closed off any chance of access to their supplies.

Having no alternative base, no safe refuge, the guerrilla band went nomadic and grew weaker. Yet it is well known that after periods of intense activity, an insurgent force needs a period of rest in safe zones where they can recover their strength, cure their wounds, and receive new fighters. The Ñancahuazú base did not fulfill these conditions, nor were other bases provided for that would fulfill them.

3. Guerrilla Tactics

One of the enemy's weakest points is highway and railroad transport. It is practically impossible to guard a transport line, a road, or a rail line. Surprise attack on the enemy's communication lines yields notable dividends.

Obviously a good share of the vulnerability of regular forces lies in their need to carry out a double mission: guaranteeing the security of localities and communication lines, and pursuing and fighting so elusive and mobile an enemy as the guerrilla band. To try to accomplish both tasks simultaneously exhausts and weakens an army.

In the operations zone selected by Che, within the sector of the Fourth Division, clear objectives were at hand: the railroad and the highway from Santa Cruz to Yacuiba on the Argentine border; the road from Lagunillas to Sucre; and the YPFB facilities in Tatarenda, Camiri, and the Camiri-Sucre oil pipeline. Nevertheless, except for the brief raid on Carahuatarenda, undertaken to get supplies and not to cut off the Santa Cruz–Camiri highway, there was never any attempt to attack or threaten communication lines. Their approach to the El Espino station did not have this aim, as was shown by their immediate withdrawal to the Grande River. In the Eighth Division's northern sector, the Samaipata raid was a notable event and a brave surprise action, but it was not followed up with others that would pose a threat to the vital Cochabamba–Santa Cruz highway. The guerrillas' withdrawal south, rapidly confirmed by the army, gave the army peace of mind and freedom of action.

Communication lines with the outside should include a series of intermediate points with completely trustworthy people, where products can be stored and where contacts can go to hide out at critical times.

Premature discovery of the guerrilla foco prevented the implementation of the "Instructions for Urban Cadres" drawn up by Che and taken out of the encampment by Loyola. The rectangle drawn by the guerrilla chief—with Cochabamba, Sucre, Santa Cruz, and Camiri as support bases from which communication lines to the interior of the operations zone would originate—was adequate, but "intermediate points" were not set up nor were there completely trustworthy people to maintain contacts with the outside. The isolation of the guerrilla band was total after Debray and Bustos left.

Stable communication lines must be maintained so that a minimum of food is always available in caches in the event of any unfortunate occurrence.

Since the urban support network could not be used as expected, the supply problem became critical. The guerrilla band could count only on food products from the area, which being sparsely populated had limited farming, although cattle-raising was more abundant. The whole southeast region depended on the West for products such as potatoes, quinoa, and vegetables, and on the area north of Santa Cruz for rice, beans, sugar, coffee, etc. Availability was severely limited in the area. When this situation was combined with rigid military control, the insurgents' possibilities were stifled.

On the other hand, other kinds of supplies, such as medicine, clothing, some kinds of equipment, etc., practically did not exist in the region. This prompted risky incursions such as the one at Samaipata, yielding virtually negative results, although they had propaganda value. Once again the cordoning off of the guerrilla band achieved in the first stage by the regular forces prevented them from setting up an adequate logistical network, leaving the fighters to their own fate in an area that was poor in resources and sparsely populated.

4. "The Guerrilla As Combatant"

The social composition of the guerrilla band ought to conform to that of the zone chosen as the center of operations, which is to say that the fighting core of the guerrilla army ought to be campesinos.

The guerrilla band at Ñancahuazú was made up of people of all types save campesinos, and—worse yet—save natives of the area. Leaving aside the foreigners, who were in the struggle for other reasons, the only one of the Bolivians who admitted to being a campesino was León, a native of Beni, who in any case had not done farmwork in the last few years. All the rest were students or miners and artisans used to the cold climate of the altiplano and the mountains, who had to go through a period of suffering and desperation in order to adapt to the tropics and their inconveniences. The desertions in that period therefore are not surprising. Recruits neither found the men they were expecting to find (Che was on his reconnaissance trip) nor received adequate orientation. This was particularly the case with Moisés Guevara's group, which in addition to being poor material for a guerrilla war was not received under the best conditions. Indisputably, a guerrilla band has to be in touch with the region where it is operating, and its people have to be local. This factor was decisive for the future action of Che's group, in addition to the fact that he and the other leaders were foreigners.

The guerrilla fighter needs an iron constitution that will allow him to resist every adversity without getting sick and to make his life as a hunted animal one more strengthening factor.

In order to keep a guerrilla force in good health, there is a need for a constant supply of medicine, in addition to balanced nutrition. None of this could be had at Ñancahuazú; supply defects and an associated weakening were present even before the foco was discovered. The reconnaissance trip to the north was full of those episodes of weakness, hunger, and exhaustion that became common after the Ñancahuazú and Iripití ambushes.

Too, the guerrilla chief himself was not in the best of health, and at times he had to be carried by his men when he lost consciousness. He did not lose his authority, however, since he commanded such respect among the members of the guerrilla band.

5. On the "Organization of the Guerrilla Band"

What must never be done is to break up the unity of a guerrilla band.

Failure to observe this rule was a fundamental flaw that deeply influenced the guerrillas' performance. When the foco was discovered and the guerrillas were obliged to abandon the encampment, Che decided "to get everybody out and operate for a while in the Muyupampa zone,"[2] thus entering a region that had not been previously explored and was unknown to all. When the commandant decided three days later to proceed directly to Muyupampa to arrange for the departure of Danton and Pelao, he ordered Joaquín, the leader of the rear guard, "to stay in the area and wait for them until their return,"[3] without clearly setting one or more alternative rallying points.

This splitting of the guerrilla force into two groups weakened it and made it possible for it to be destroyed piecemeal. Although for four months the two groups were constantly searching for each other, they were never to meet up again, so Che lost one of his most faithful men, Joaquín, who had served under him since joining up in the Sierra Maestra in 1958, first as a simple soldier, then as lieutenant and captain, until he reached the level of commandant.

6. On the "Organization of the Guerrilla Front"

Good supply is fundamental to the guerrilla band. Supply in the first stages is always internal. As guerrilla conditions develop, there must also be a source of supply outside combat lines or territory.

The supply problem became critical when the operations zone was cut off, making it impossible to set up lines to the outside. Since the guerrillas were obliged to carry their supplies along with them in the absence of a secure base, their capability of transport was limited. This required constant raids or contacts with the campesino communities for resupply purposes, enabling the army to obtain information on their location and movement, keeping them on the defensive, cutting off their freedom of action, and limiting their initiative.

The organization of the insurrectional movement is important on both the external and the internal fronts. Functions are different on the external front. For example, propaganda should be of a national type. It should point the way, explaining the victories obtained by the guerrilla band, calling the worker and peasant masses to fight, and giving news, if there is any, of victories obtained on that front.

Circulation of the revolutionary idea through the necessary channels should be accomplished in the greatest depth possible. This involves full equipment and a responsive organization.

The civil organization on the external front rapidly crumbled as soon as the guerrilla band was discovered and the government's repressive apparatus went into action. The arrest and imprisonment of suspicious political and labor leaders, the restriction of their movement, and lack of instructions from the leader of the movement on how to stand up to these circumstances made it impossible even to make effective propaganda. The "Instructions for Cadres" and the communiqués drafted in the operations zone could not be circulated, so the aims and objectives of the movement were not known. Only the press spoke of their victories and their actions, but this was not enough because the reporting did not particularly favor them.

In later years, as a result of that experience, other guerrilla attempts have paid more attention to this aspect, trying to set up radio stations and newspapers that would serve to provide wide sectors of the population with the guerrilla version of each feat of arms.

The most effective propaganda is produced within the guerrilla zone. Priority will be given to spreading ideas among natives of the zone, explaining in theory the insurrection which they already know in fact.

The scant contacts with area residents did not yield favorable results. Fear of the guerrilla force was a constant, a fear that was widespread because the campesinos are naturally wary of people from outside the community. There was no fear of army reprisals, because in no village or community did the troops act under orders of that kind. On the contrary, from the beginning of operations, the military took special care in its relations with campesinos and community members, whereas the guerrilla band, obliged to supply themselves from the meager resources of the area residents and to try to recruit fighting people among them, could not establish good relations. When denunciations became constant, each contact became more difficult. On the few occasions when they spoke about the objectives of the guerrilla war, in the vicinity of Muyupampa, in Alto Seco, and in Abra del Picacho, the response was more fearful silence than enthusiasm, a situation which discouraged the guerrilla fighters and made them more violent and secretive in their dealings with the campesinos.

7. From "Guerrilla Warfare: A Method" (1963)

Guerrilla warfare is a people's war, it is mass struggle. To attempt to carry on this type of war without the support of the population is the prelude to inevitable disaster.

The minimal preparation of the support system, the secrecy necessary for the first stage of organization, and the concealment of the true aims of the guerrilla foco, which is to say the international character of the struggle, drained effectiveness from the movement. When the guerrilla band went public, its foreign character acquired a connotation that prevented open support from leftist political organizations, which would have compromised them and lost popular support for them. Thus the insurgents in the Southeast were cut off and abandoned to their fate.

The guerrilla band is supported by the campesino and worker masses from the region and from the whole territory in question. Without this basis guerrilla warfare is not possible.

There is no doubt that this support was never achieved at any time, and this was one of the principal factors in their destruction.

Armies organized and equipped for conventional warfare are the force sustaining the power of the exploiting classes. When they must confront the irregular warfare of campesinos fighting on their home ground, they turn out to be absolutely powerless. They lose ten men for every revolutionary fighter who falls. Demoralization spreads rapidly among them when they have to face an invisible and invincible army that denies them the opportunity to show off their academic tactics and their military fanfare, which they are so quick to display in order to repress the city workers and students. (Second Declaration of Havana).

This concept underwent radical transformation after the first losses at Ñancahuazú and Iripití. In fact, the Bolivian Army was not prepared to stand up to guerrilla warfare, but with its cadres' great decisiveness and force of will this situation was overcome in a few months. The proportion of guerrilla losses to those of the regular forces averaged two to one at the end of the campaign. This has not been accomplished in any other country that has confronted guerrilla warfare, thus showing the degree of effectiveness and adaptation to this type of fighting achieved by the Bolivian regular forces.

If the military situation will be difficult from the first moments, the political situation will be no less delicate; if a single military error can liquidate the guerrilla, a political error can slow down its development for long periods.

The political error that affected the development of the guerrilla band and notably reduced its possibilities originated in two interrelated events. First there was the attempt to conceal the true aims and objectives of the guerrilla war from the upper levels of the PCB. In the first contacts with Monje, Kolle, and Reyes, the coming of Che and his companions was presented as a support action for the struggle undertaken by the Bolivians against the Barrientos government, aimed at creating conditions favorable for a general insurrection. They were never informed—not at Ñancahuazú nor on the occasion of Monje's interview with Commander Guevara, nor even on Kolle and Reyes's visit to Fidel Castro—of the international nature of the struggle, the intention of creating the multiregional training center from which, after taking control of the base country, columns of guerrilla fighters would be sent into other countries. There was a deliberate attempt to hide the character of a politico-military school that they wanted to give to the Ñancahuazú base.

Secondly, the social characteristics of Bolivians and their ardent nationalism were ignored, intentionally or not. Che Guevara did not receive complete, well-rounded information about the true political situation in the country, nor about the progress achieved in the years following the revolution of 1952. The Cubans were led to believe that Bolivian was ripe for violent change, that the political and labor organizations would plunge into the struggle in support of the insurgents, and that the armed forces simply amounted to small units that were not prepared for a war like the one they were planning. Doubt was cast not only on their operative capabilities but also on their identification with the Barrientos regime.

It should therefore be no surprise that the secretary of the PCB, Monje, stated so vehemently his disagreement with the Cubans' approach and argued the necessity of giving the rebel forces a "national command." The incomprehension of the Bolivian character and the somewhat prideful and messianic attitude adopted by Che, stating that "All of America was his fatherland" and that the magic of his name would be enough to attract fighters, constituted the prelude to failure.

THE ARMED FORCES SIDE

1. Organization

The structure of the Bolivian Armed Forces in 1967 revealed a high command unified in the office of commander-in-chief, where the undeniable authority of Gen. Alfredo Ovando Candia stood out. He had exercised the supreme military function since 1962. The chief of the general staff, Gen. Juan José Tórrez, and the armed forces general staff—the highest officers of the three branches (army, air force and naval force)—did not, however, take an active role in the course of operations. These had been entrusted to the land forces, to which were added a squadron of T–6 planes and two helicopters for air support and a company (120 men) of marines in the Abapó sector, from the Naval Force.

The army command and general staff, under the direction of Gen. David La Fuente Soto, were thus charged with planning and executing antiguerrilla operations. Their work was initially full of difficulty because of the lack of adequate information on the enemy and the terrain, and because they lacked resources for the type of problem that had arisen.

The Fourth Division in Camiri—in whose jurisdiction the base encampment at Ñancahuazú was located—had to be reinforced, first with troops from other units and then with officer personnel to fill out its general staff and its command cadres.

All these initial organization problems demonstrated very visibly that the armed forces were not adequately set up to face a subversive plan of rural guerrilla warfare, although they had been receiving advice and information on the inter-American level about the possibilities of expansion of the Castroite model. It became clear that only in the western part of the country and in the major cities (La Paz, Cochabamba, Oruro) did organized units exist that were equipped to meet internal security problems, but in conditions of climate and terrain different from those existing in the Southeast.

Realization of this fact ultimately led to a complete reorganization of the military and demonstrated the need for the commands of the branches of the armed forces and their major units in the respective jurisdictions to pay more attention to training the troops, to liaison and support functions with the civilian population, and to an adequate knowledge of the terrain through reconnaissance, tactical excursions, monographs, etc.

2. Strategy

The guerrilla problem was not thought out in strategic terms, having been limited from the time it was discovered to a tactical framework of operations. Nevertheless, when Debray's statements confirmed the international character of the movement and the strategic plan it was following, its implications began to be analyzed in the office of the commander-in-chief. The result of this study was a series of directives to the branch commands, pointing out:

—The importance of the guerrilla war in the Southeast, as an effort directed from Cuba to provoke the intervention of North American troops in Bolivia and then in other countries.

—The necessity of preventing guerrilla expansion in the territory, through the effective control of areas of probable internal conflicts (mining centers, important cities, oil fields, etc.) in cooperation with state security organisms so as to deny the adversary the possibility of attaining his goal: provoking a situation of the type that would facilitate or favor foreign military intervention (from the United States or neighboring countries).

—The urgency of denying the subversives the support of the people, both in the cities and the rural area, by reactivating all means of control and of approach to popular organizations, through Civic Action, the Campesino-Military Pact and other areas of activity, with special attention to campesino sectors close to the existing guerrilla base and others that might emerge in the future (in Alto Beni, Chapare, etc.).

—The decision to keep the guerrilla problem on a limited plane of both information and operations, thus to deprive the subversives of access to propaganda channels. (This decision proved difficult to carry out, partly because of the attitude of President Barrientos, who was eager to make the greatest possible political capital as a result of the antiguerrilla struggle, the outcome of which he never doubted. Also it was impossible to adequately regulate the role of the press, which from the beginning of operations featured the events in the Southeast in the forefront of the international news, especially when Debray and Bustos were captured and when Che Guevara's presence at the head of the guerrilla movement in Bolivia was reported.)

These directives from the office of the commander-in-chief were complemented with precise instructions to:

—Work out in cadres and troops an accelerated, adequate antiguerrilla training within a short time so as to be able to have prepared personnel on hand throughout the national territory.

—In parallel fashion, undertake the work of indoctrination and reaffirmation of national values in the cadres of officers, noncommissioned officers, and soldiers, to make them immune to the appeals of subversion.

Simultaneously with these actions the commander-in-chief's office undertook two other tasks:

—On the international level, it perfected the mechanisms for exchanging intelligence reports and for monitoring known extremists so as to detect possible installations of new guerrilla focos.

—On the domestic level, it organized and carried out a psychological campaign among the general population, providing for demonstrations of support for the armed forces, the formation of committees of support for the soldiers, and a general reaffirmation of the civic spirit of the citizenry.

All these actions bore fruit throughout the campaign, facilitating the elimination of the guerrilla group.

3. Tactics

The operations entrusted to the army general command, after the losses at Ñancahuazú and Iripití, and once the Fourth Division command had been properly organized and assigned means of air support, had these primary goals:

—The isolation of the area near the guerrillas' base, for the purpose of denying them supplies, support from the population, and recruits.

—The gradual reduction of the operations area, followed by the destruction of the guerrilla force.

The first goal could not be accomplished efficiently. The guerrillas evaded the first encirclement set up by the Fourth Division in mid-April, and headed for Muyupampa, upsetting the whole military plan. Subsequently they again eluded the encirclement when they pursued their maneuver toward the east (El Espino–Muchirí) and finally when they crossed the Grande River and entered into the jurisdiction of the Eighth Division.

Only at the end of July, more because of the guerrillas' movement than because of the action of the troops, can one speak of a real isolation of the guerrilla band. After their raid on Samaipata, they headed south toward the Grande River, thereby facilitating coordinated action of the Eighth and Fourth divisions and effectively reducing the operations area. It was newly widened by Che and his men, however, when they headed west (Los Sitanos, Alto Seco) leaving the military forces frustrated once again.

The use of units, their size, coordination, and control were other problems that had to be solved on a tactical level. In the first phase, the use of company-type units yielded some positive results. It gave the commanders freedom to act with initiative and aggressiveness. Nevertheless, this also produced setbacks and in some cases negligence, when they chose to stay put rather than search out the guerrilla band.

The decision of the Fourth Division command to issue orders to "organize defensively and undertake short-range patrols," taken after Ñancahuazú and Iripití, although justified by the need to readjust deployment and recover morale and fighting spirit, brought along as a consequence a passivity that could be dangerous. In any case the guerrillas did not take advantage of that passivity to attack military installations (a move that would have helped them maintain the initiative and constantly threaten the security of the troops), and it was later overcome when new units were used.

Although the subsequent decision to organize battalions so as better to conduct operations improved coordination and control in the Fourth Division, it reduced mobility, reaction time, and the initiative of company commanders, for each operation necessarily had to be planned, organized, and led by the battalion command, which did not always have resources available to do it. This needlessly lengthened the duration of the guerrilla war, which could have been liquidated sooner.

Finally it was realized that the best solution for problems of this type, caused by a group of guerrillas without a stable base and with a great facility of movement in a sparsely populated area of difficult access, boiled down to using independent companies with administrative autonomy and freedom of action, with areas of responsibility assigned by the upper echelon. They could operate by setting up a base from which they could send out patrols of section strength (thirty to forty men) to try to locate the guerrilla group and force it to fight. These bases, normally established in a small village, had the advantage of simultaneously exercising control over the area residents and receiving permanent and continuous information. Bases such as the ones at La Laja, Pucará, La Higuera, and Abra del Picacho got briefings and were able to act quickly to make contact with the guerrillas and fight them.

On the other hand, given the nature of the operations, the division commanders always had to have available in reserve one or two motorized companies so as to be ready to deploy them in the most appropriate directions according to the reports received from campesinos and other sources.

The need to protect some communication lines, plants, and villages required a wide dispersion of forces and a loss of effectiveness. These little garrisons quickly fell into routine and neglect, encouraging situations such as the one at Samaipata, with its great publicity impact. Nevertheless this type of arrangement inevitably had to be maintained, particularly when there was no clear understanding of the guerrillas' intentions and their real chances of success.

4. Logistics

It was in this branch of military art that the most serious problems arose for the regular forces in their combat against subversion. The lack of adequate logistical organization was obvious from the first, when in order to move only a hundred or so men from Camiri to Lagunillas civilian trucks had to be used; when the troops had to march with their pots and supplies on their backs; when units assigned to distant positions had to go for several days without supplies because there was no way of getting them there. The units' mobility and radius of action were thus affected by logistical limitations, which were a permanent restraint.

The lack of comprehension by some leaders of just what a counterinsurgency operation was, due to their adherence to classical norms, also affected tactical operations.

Throughout the campaign supply hardships were common to all units. Difficulty in obtaining and shipping adequate ammunition, because of the variety of calibers used and the lack of transport and communication facilities, caused the regular forces to lose significant blocks of time in movements on foot, for which the guerrilla band was better prepared. The troops also had to halt in mid-pursuit to allow logistical support to reach them or to carry out evacuations of dead, wounded, and prisoners.

Given problems of this type, it is better to organize small logistical units that can utilize vehicles, radios, horses—whatever is needed—to service a fixed number of companies operating in the area, so that supply can be almost automatic and incumbent on these logistical units.

The fundamental task of feeding the soldiers should be well organized through the use of dry rations, which facilitate movement since otherwise so much has to be carried along. The dry rations must always be the type of food that satisfies the troops.

5. Intelligence

Strategic intelligence provided by neighboring countries, the United States, and domestic sources amounted in the first stage simply to a string of unconnected reports of little value. Since 1964 the continental armies had been receiving a continuous series of data on subversive intentions and procedures—data that were more general than particular in nature.

On the domestic level, the intelligence services of both the armed forces and the Ministry of Justice did not manage to detect the presence of the advance members of the Cuban team, who from mid–1966 had undertaken their reconnaissance and made contacts. Nor did they manage to link the Bolivian Communist party to these activities. In January 1967, some data were obtained about the recruiting of combatants initiated by Moisés Guevara. This information was converted into instructions in February for all divisions of the Bureau of Criminal Investigation to exercise surveillance over a list of ten names, among whom were Moisés Guevara and Simón Cuba (Willy). They were suspected of trying to organize a guerrilla movement, although this attempt had not yet been linked to Cuba.

This directive had its effect in Camiri when the presence of Moisés Guevara and his companions was detected upon their arrival in that city and later when they traveled to Ñancahuazú.

On the tactical level, combat intelligence was obtained by the units from two sources: area residents and personnel in civilian dress who investigated the area of each unit to try to determine the presence or the activity of the guerrilla group. The results of this work were permanently favorable; there was no need to resort to pressure or remuneration. Examples are clear over the entire course of the campaign, and this was one of the decisive factors leading to the destruction of the guerrilla force.

6. Political Handling of the Guerrilla Problem

Many difficulties arose on this level. From the Ñancahuazú ambush on, discrepancies showed up between the military leadership and the political leadership. On the one side, President Barrientos regarded the guerrilla war almost as a personal affront and deeply involved himself in a political campaign aimed at depriving it of support and provoking the campesinos to reject it—in which task he succeeded. Meanwhile, on the other side, the military command, more cautious, tried to reduce the impact of the guerrilla war and make it more manageable, simultaneously seeking a degree of confidentiality regarding the operations and their outcome. This clashed with General Barrientos's habit of making statements on a daily basis, often without sufficient information, and with the work of the press, which cannot be circumvented.

Barrientos constantly imposed his will, and his attitude neutralized the political parties, disconcerted friends and foes, but achieved its aim: the guerrilla force was rejected on the whole, and that allowed him easily to dominate the political scene. His image was also projected on the international level, and he secured the support of neighboring countries and the United States for the fight against subversion, while maintaining control of the situation.

More laconic and more reserved, General Ovando on occasion got caught up with the president's enthusiasm, and when it became clear that the guerrilla band had been isolated, he did not hesitate to announce that they had been destroyed. At all times the commander-in-chief showed himself conscious of what the guerrilla war meant and its implications for the armed forces, and he tried to guide the work of the military with calm.

Only upon Che's death did all of this effort come apart. The lack of a previous decision about what to do with the guerrilla chief in case he was captured, and the lack of coordination among all the authorities so as to give a coherent report of his end, gave rise to all the discrepancies that persist even today. Doubtless contributing to this were a certain tendency to show off that was visible in some leaders, the euphoria of victory, and a lack of experience.

There remain, however, the lesson of all that took place and a legitimate feeling of pride throughout the Bolivian military. Like it or not, what had been called "the worst army in South America" scored an important victory over the guerrilla movement and its ideologues. After the Chaco War, the Ñancahuazú campaign constitutes the most important armed action accomplished by the Bolivian Armed Forces. The errors in leadership and the shortcomings observed, all the negatives, are overshadowed by the reality of victory—a victory obtained by us ourselves, the Bolivians, the military, conscious that it was and will continue to be our obligation to stand up to any attempt to use our territory and our poverty and backwardness as a theater of experimentation that is alien to our national character.

Those of us who were privileged to participate in those operations, sharing with our officers and soldiers hard days, hunger, fear, fighting, defeat, and victory, have learned to love our campesino more, to respect his traditions and customs, to love our country more, and to have faith in its future. We will have to build that future ourselves, not with weapons in hand but shoulder to shoulder through creative effort, work, and patriotism.

The changes that our society requires can be achieved without recourse to violence, which as in Ñancahuazú and El Churo only brought pain and suffering. The blood shed by all in the Southeast has not been in vain, since we all learned a lesson there: service to country is a permanent task in peace and war.

NOTES

1. Quotations in this chapter come from Ernesto Guevara, *La guerra de guerrillas*, first published in 1950 and often reprinted, and (in section 7 of the chapter) from Guevara's article "Guerra de guerrillas: un método," first published in the journal *Cuba Socialista*, September 1963, pp. 1–17. Both texts are available in

English in Che Guevara, *Guerrilla Warfare* (Lincoln: University of Nebraska Press, 1985). The Guevara quotations in this chapter were translated by John Deredita.

2. Che's Diary, entry for April 14.

3. Che's Diary, entry for April 17.

APPENDIX: IMPRESSIONS AND CONVERSATIONS

I was on duty with Braun 8th Cavalry Group in the city of Santa Cruz when the Ñancahuazú ambush occurred. It broke the usual calm of barracks life and alerted us to coming risks. My first concern arose when I saw how irresponsibly soldiers from my unit without adequate training were sent to Camiri on March 26 to reinforce the Fourth Division. They were taken off farming and grazing properties where they were involved in production work. For months these soldiers, about ready for discharge, had not held a weapon. My observations to the commander of the Eighth Division were dismissed with the argument that higher orders issued by the army general command had to be obeyed. We were forced to select thirty men, along with 2d Lt. Alfredo Lara, to be transported by air to the south.

Looking ahead in view of the evidence that emerged in the following days that there really was a guerrilla problem in the country, I took special care when recruits were brought in at the end of that month to choose the effective force for my squadron—120 men—so that I would have a homogeneous group able to face the combat that doubtless awaited us later. I started training that contingent with plenty of enthusiasm and after three weeks began to see favorable results, as well as an evident commitment on the party of my men.

After the Iripití setback, which made a deep impression on everyone, an order came from a higher level for me to send fifty of my men to the recently activated Manchego Regiment, which was about to begin its training at La Esperanza. It had been noted that all of the troops assigned to the 12th Infantry Regiment came from valley and altiplano communities, and it was deemed necessary to add some Easterners to them to facilitate their adaptation. Since the closest unit was Braun 8th Cavalry Regiment, this change was ordered. I made some effort to resist it, because I was becoming fond of my soldiers and was getting to know them, but there was nothing to be done, so I sent fifty "Cambas" (Easterners) to La Esperanza in exchange for fifty "Collas" (Westerners). To my surprise, however, a couple of days later, I myself received the order to join Manchego Regiment as a company commander.

From the first day on the premises of the former sugar refinery, all of us officers understood the responsibility and the seriousness of the task that lay ahead of us.

With no opportunity to choose them in advance, we were going to convert 650 young men from all over the country, first into soldiers and then into Ranger specialists so as to go in with them as a battalion exclusively trained to meet the guerrilla problem in the Southeast. At that point—the first days of May—that problem threatened to become a long, bloody process. The Ñancahuazú and Iripití ambushes had been followed by serious reverses for the army, so that the need for well-trained troops was obvious.

The arrival of the team of North American instructors allowed us to establish training programs and teaching strategies quickly so that the best results could be obtained in the shortest time. We set up a sixteen-week timetable, at the end of which we were to be in combat readiness. Difficulties of communication with the Green Beret team, whose members did not speak Spanish except for two Puerto Ricans, were overcome thanks to my knowledge of English.

It was a period of intense work, broad experience, and great benefit. We substantially modified the usual methods of recruit training, deemphasizing the formal, showy aspects of military instruction such as close order, marching, and presentations, and stressing combat instruction—marksmanship, ambushes and counterambushes, patrols and reconnaissance—at the same time that we developed the physical aptitude of our men.

Using much more ammunition than we were accustomed to, we produced soldiers that were very skilled in the use of their weapons, aggressive, and brave. After a short time of difficulties due to the change of climate, men from the altiplano and the valleys adapted to the heat and the jungle very well and began to operate confidently and ably in the jungle, surprising all of us with the high quality of their performance. My unit, B Company, was made up of 165 soldiers, forming three platoons (reinforced sections) of riflemen and a support arms platoon (60–caliber mortar and 3.5–inch rocket launcher). I had under my command three second lieutenants, Germán Venegas P., Tomás Totti A., and Raúl Espinoza L.; a cadet in his last year at the Military College, Johnny MacKay; a company NCO, Carlos Marín; and Sgt. Bernardino Huanca, all of whom took very well to the rigors of instruction. There was one factor that favored our work and made it more serious and responsible: we were all aware that when our instruction was over we would go into combat and not, as usually was the case, simply receive another contingent and begin over again with the routine barracks task of the annual training of reserves. This time the task was real, and we knew that each one of our men must be ready to meet the demands of irregular combat and that our mission was defined in advance. This premise, which I did not tire of pointing out every day, developed esprit de corps in my troops and made them work seriously.

I constantly endeavored to apply—and encouraged my officers to apply—leadership principles expressed in mottoes such as "Know your men" and "Know your task." Well applied, they assure a high degree of efficiency and performance due to the bond that is established. In this way I got to know each one of my soldiers, with all of their capabilities and defects, their characters and personalities, earning the respect and good will of all of them, attitudes that persist today when we get together.

The other battalion companies, A under Capt. Celso Torrelio Villa, C under Capt. Haroldo Pinto, and D under Capt. Ángel Mariscal, undertook similar efforts, so by the end of the training period we were able to count on a homogeneous battalion, well-trained and eager to meet the problem posed by the guerrilla war, which until then, the end of August, had remained latent, limited to small encounters and exchanges of fire.

When we learned at La Esperanza the outcome of the Vado del Yeso ambush, we were at once pleased with what that meant for the army and concerned that the subversive foco might be exterminated before we had time to take to the field with our battalion. It was thus with some fear and also some satisfaction that we received the order to enter the operations zone via Vallegrande on September 25, 1967.

When we arrived at about noon on the 26th in the provincial capital, where I had spent my childhood, we learned that 2d Lt. Eduardo Galindo had ambushed the vanguard of the guerrilla group at La Higuera, inflicting three losses on them and causing them to disperse.

With full confidence, I offered my company as replacement for A Company under Captain Torrelio—who had stated that he had personnel problems—to undertake the pursuit. Thus I arrived at Pucará close to midnight of that same day and proceeded on foot toward the Grande River, so as to cut off any possibility the guerrillas might have of crossing in the direction of Chuquisaca Department.

At dawn on September 27, while searching San Antonio Canyon on a campesino's tip, we captured Camba after a brief resistance, and thereby acquired our first prisoner and made our first contact with the insurgents. I gave every one of my men the opportunity to see the guerrilla close up so that they would realize how vulnerable and weak the rebels were, in contrast to the invincible image they were trying to project. Worn out, weak, and in rags, Camba inspired pity rather than fear, and his capture gave a lift to my troops, since in just a few hours we had already achieved something positive, unlike other units which, after spending months in the operations zone, had never seen a guerrilla.

Energized by his capture, we questioned Camba in the presence of the S–2 of the battalion, Capt. Raúl López Leyton and in the presence of the battalion commander, Maj. Ayoroa Montaño. We did not obtain much information, however, because Camba made it clear that he did not know the whereabouts of the rest of the guerrilla band and, in addition, rallying points had not been set in the event that they were separated. We continued our search mission for the next few days without finding the guerrillas' trail, and then established a patrol base at Abra del Picacho, from which we continued operating in the first week of October.

When 2d Lt. Carlos Pérez of A Company, stationed at La Higuera, requested my support at dawn on the 8th to verify campesinos' reports that seventeen men were present in nearby canyons, I agreed and traveled there with a reinforced squad of fifty men to help them.

Once combat had begun and reconnaissance of El Churo and La Tusca Canyons was being effected, I took pride in the calm and bravery that my men were displaying. A high degree of efficiency was apparent in all of their movements. The procedures we had gone over so often—security, communications, deployment, and the like—were accomplished automatically. My officers and NCOs acted calmly; in short, I was reassured by the fact that everything seemed to be turning out well. Although the picture was not clear in the first moments of combat, I had full confidence in my men and their ability.

When we realized that, due to the blockade set up by Second Lieutenant Pérez at the upper end of El Churo Canyon, the guerrillas would try to leave by way of our position at the confluence of the two canyons, I ordered the 60–caliber mortar to be positioned and set up to shoot grenades 100 yards into the canyon, and the light machine gun to be aimed at the same area, a clearing in the canyon, full of rocks, and having some vegetation. They would need to pass through there if they wanted to get out of the encirclement we had mounted.

In fact, within a few minutes we observed some figures, shadows in the vegetation that were approaching the clearing, observing it, and preparing to cross it. Maintaining absolute silence, we waited; then all of a sudden, a burst of automatic fire from the heights scattered its bullets near our position, and other weapons firing at the same time forced us to take cover. The fire was intended to permit movement, so I gave the order to open fire with the mortar and machine gun. Supporting that action with our individual arms (carbines and rifles), we succeeded in repulsing the first attempt to get out.

Since I had only eight men with me up to that time (the four members of the mortar crew, two from the machine-gun crew, my radio operator, and my runner), I radioed Second Lieutenant Pérez, immobilized by guerrilla fire from the upper part of the canyon, to send me two squads (eighteen men) to reinforce the command post, since at that time Sergeant Huanca's platoon—he had assumed command upon entering into operations as the replacement for Cadet MacKay, who by order of the army commander had retuned to the Military College to complete his studies—was combing La Tusca Canyon. With that reinforcement, which took barely fifteen minutes to cover the 300 meters separating Pérez's position from mine, and which I positioned at the mouth of El Churo, we succeeded a short time later in repulsing a second and more violent attempt to break the siege, forcing the guerrillas to retreat toward the interior of the canyon.

When Sergeant Huanca concluded his search of La Tusca without finding anything, I ordered him to come into El Churo down below, pushing the guerrillas up against Pérez's forces. The fighting was violent, but the decisiveness and courage of Huanca and his men made it possible to overcome the guerrilla resistance and to gain some fifty meters inside the canyon.

It was then that I received news from one of my soldiers, stationed for security purposes some meters above the command post, who called to me, "Captain, Captain, there are two here, we have caught them." I went up there together with my runner and found two members of the guerrilla band, disheveled, covered with dust, gaunt, and showing signs of great fatigue, still holding their weapons and covered by my two soldiers, who were aiming at them.

The first was undoubtedly a foreigner. He had an impressive gaze, clear eyes, long, nearly red hair, and a rather thick beard. He wore a black beret with the CITE emblem, a completely filthy private's uniform, and a jacket with a hood. His chest was nearly bare, because his shirt had no buttons. He was holding a carbine in his right hand. The other man was short, dark, with long hair and a little goatee. He was also holding his weapon.

As soon as I saw them, I ordered them to get rid of their weapons. They dropped them to the ground.

"Who are you?" I asked the taller one, although I was almost certain of his identity.

"I am Che Guevara," he answered in a low voice.

I pretended not to pay much attention and addressed the other one: "How about you?"

"I'm Willy," he replied.

"Are you a Bolivian?"

"Yes," he stated.

"What is your real name?"

"Simón Cuba."

Then I drew close to Guevara to observe him at some length. He had protuberances on his forehead. I asked him to show me his left hand and I saw the scar on the back of it.[1] Satisfied, I ordered that their equipment be taken and that they be searched. My runner, Alejandro Ortiz, took charge of everything that Che was carrying: a pack, two knapsacks, and a pistol at his waist. Another soldier picked up Willy's pack.

"They destroyed my weapon," Guevara said suddenly.

I saw then that his carbine had its barrel perforated from a hit. "When was that?" I asked.

"Down here, when your machine gun began to fire. I'm also wounded. I suppose you're not going to kill me now. I mean more to you alive than dead. We have always healed wounded prisoners."

"We'll heal you. Where is your wound?" I asked. He showed me his right leg, rolling up his pants. He had a bullet entry mark on his calf, with no exit mark. It was bleeding very little, and the bone did not appear to have been touched.

"Take them farther back to the command post," I ordered my soldiers.

"Can you walk?" I asked Che.

"I have to," he replied, leaning a bit on Willy.

In those few meters, while we were going to the command post, a single thought entered my mind: "What a relief. This is over. Now we can go back home."

It really was a relief to see how easily the legendary guerrilla chief had fallen. I was absolutely certain at that moment that the guerrilla war was over, that Che's capture eliminated any possibility of its continuing. The insurgency had continued solely because of the authority and the personality of the man who was now my prisoner.

Once at the command post, I took some measures. We were under the shade of a small tree at the bank of the canyon but some ten meters above it, protected by a small depression. I ordered the prisoners to be tied up, hands and feet, with their own belts and leaned with their backs against the tree, with two soldiers continuously aiming their rifles at them.

When these orders were being carried out, Che said to me, "Don't bother, Captain, this thing is all over."

"It is for you, but there are still some good fighters out there and I don't want to run any risks," I replied.

"It's no use, we have failed. . . . "

I looked at him while he was talking that way. It didn't square with the image that we had formed of Che, arrogant and successful, but then I understood, when I saw him drop his chin on his chest and lose himself in thought. All of us have had this experience at a time when fatigue, demoralization, anxiety made us feel there was nothing left to be done. It was, I imagine, a time of great depression for the guerrilla chief, seeing his hopes and illusions destroyed, remembering how many deaths this had cost, and thinking how uncertain his future was.

I felt a little pity. Willy, quiet and stoical, was in a better state. Perhaps his life as a miner had led him, in his native Huanuni, not to expect much from life.

I shook off these thoughts, because there was still much to do. I ordered my radio operator to contact our base. The PRC–10 radio that we had with us finally managed—with great difficulty and with the help of Second Lieutenant Venegas's section at El Quiñal—to get in touch with Second Lieutenant Totti, whom I ordered to transmit the following message to the Eighth Division command at Vallegrande: "I have Papa and Willy. Papa slightly wounded. Combat goes on. Captain Prado."

When they confirmed that the message had been transmitted and received in Vallegrande on the GRC–9 equipment at the base, I put my efforts toward controlling the progress of the fighting. Everything recounted here had taken only a few minutes.

The state of affairs in the canyon remained uncertain. It was, however, the first time that we were forcing the guerrillas to sustain a combat in which they were at a disadvantage because of the lay of the land and the tactical situation. They were not used to this type of action.

Within a few minutes I was called to the radio again. Second Lieutenant Totti relayed a message to me from the Eighth Division command post in Vallegrande urgently requesting that I confirm Che's capture. Apparently the news had been received with skepticism. I lost patience and replied that it most certainly was Che and that I had neither time nor any reason to make up stories.

Meanwhile, the advance of Sergeant Huanca's squad was beginning to produce results. He notified me that he had managed to break a first line of defense and eliminate two guerrillas (Antonio and Arturo), but that he had one seriously wounded man. Leaving instructions at the command post to care for the prisoners, I went down into the canyon accompanied by the medic Tito Sánchez. When I reached Huanca's position, I was able to see the terrain and the situation close up. Directly in front of us we had rugged, well-protected ground from which my men's movement was being observed. After Huanca made some attempts to break the resistance and to continue the advance, I went to see the wounded man, Sabino Cossío, who was having difficulty breathing. Sánchez, the medic, had no bandages to cure him with, no dressing—nothing. I left him there trying to do something and returned to the command post.

A few minutes later, Huaca reported Cossío's death to me by radio. I felt overcome with sadness. He was the first soldier in my company who had given up his life. Tito Sánchez came up out of the canyon, his face contorted and his eyes full of tears.

"Cossío died, Captain, there was nothing I could do."

I tried to calm him down by reminding him that thus far in spite of everything, we had been successful and that he shouldn't lose hope. He seemed calmer when he answered, "This is going to be over, Captain, that bum who was the head has fallen."

Che, who had been listening to everything, answered immediately, "The revolution has no head, comrade."

I replied, "Maybe the revolution you advocate has no head, but our problems end with you."

Just then a soldier came out of the canyon bleeding. It was Valentín Choque. He had two wounds, one in the upper part of his neck and the other in his back. Neither was serious. Sánchez tore up a shirt that was in Che's pack to make some bandages.

"Do you want me to heal him, Captain?" Che asked quickly.

"Are you by any chance a doctor?"

"No. First and foremost I'm a revolutionary, but I know medicine. Also in the Sierra Maestra I even learned to pull teeth. Shall I take care of the soldier?"

"No, let it go," I said. I devoted my attention to the fighting. Huanca's squad was continuing its advance farther into the canyon.

"Captain," the guerrilla prisoner asked, "doesn't it seem cruel to you to have a wounded man tied up?"

The question touched me and I ordered the men in charge of security to untie the prisoners' hands.

"Can I drink a little water from my canteen?"

At that point it occurred to me that Che might try to poison himself, seeing that all was lost, so I offered him my canteen. He drank eagerly, and then I passed it to Willy, who did the same. Then he asked permission to smoke. I offered him my cigarettes, but he refused them because they were Pacifics, a mild brand. He said that he preferred strong tobacco. One of my soldiers, who had Astoria cigarettes, offered him one, which he smoked with enjoyment.

The afternoon grew late and the fighting was nearing its end. We had nearly finished combing the canyon, and it was getting hard to see inside it. To avoid clashes among my own troops, I decided to suspend the operation. After all, the main goal had been achieved. Che's capture was worth more than the rest of the guerrillas, and I considered it important to guarantee his safekeeping so as to turn him over to my superiors. So I cut off combat, left a small blocking force, and headed for La Higuera.

In the heights surrounding the canyons, several dozen campesinos had gathered from nearby towns to watch the fighting. When I came up there with my men, I also found my battalion commander, Major Ayoroa. He had come from Pucará when he found out about the combat we were engaged in. Lt. Col. Andrés Selich, commander of the 3rd Engineer Battalion, had also come from Vallegrande in the helicopter to act as guide for the pilot, Maj. Jaime Niño de Guzmán. After I gave my battalion commander a quick report of everything that had happened, we all proceeded to La Higuera, some two kilometers from there, arriving nearly at nightfall. All the residents of the town were in the main street, and we decided to occupy the school as the most appropriate place to deposit the prisoners. Che was in one room, Willy in another, where we deposited the bodies of Antonio and Arturo. Our dead and wounded were taken to the home of a campesino, where we proceeded to hold a wake for the former and attend to the latter with the resources we had at hand.

I organized the guard detail so that we would be ready to meet any attempt to rescue Che, and I ordered that an officer remain with him at all times. After taking these precautions and seeing to it that food was prepared for the troops, I was able to meet with Lieutenant Colonel Selich and Major Ayoroa to draft the report of the operation, discuss tomorrow's continuation of it, and go through the contents of the guerrillas' packs and knapsacks.

After eating something I felt uneasy on account of all that had happened and went over to the school to see the prisoners. They had been given food and water. After seeing Willy, I went into the room where Che was being held. I found him seated, leaning against the wall, his eyes closed against the light of one candle. Second Lieutenant Totti, on duty there, had bound up the prisoner's calf with a bandage; it was spotted with blood.

I had a pack of Astoria cigarettes, which I offered to the prisoner with a box of matches. He thanked me and immediately unrolled two cigarettes, placed the tobacco in the bowl of an old pipe, and began to smoke. I struck up a conversation with him. I was very interested in getting to know him better.[2]

"How do you feel?"

"Fine. The lieutenant has bandaged me, and though I feel some pain, that's inevitable, right?"

"I'm sorry we don't have a doctor with us, but in any case the helicopter will come first thing in the morning and you will be taken to Vallegrande where they will take better care of you."

"Thanks. I imagine they must be anxious to see me there."

"That's for sure. Is there anything else I can do for you? I'll send you some blankets."

"Yes, there is one thing, Captain, although I hardly know how to say it."

"Go ahead, tell me."

"It's like this. I had two watches with me. One is mine and the other belongs to one of my comrades. They were taken from me by the soldiers when we were on our way here."

I reacted quickly. I hadn't authorized anything like that. I knew which soldiers had accompanied him on the trip from El Churo, so I went out and had them called immediately. In fact they had the watches, two identical stainless steel Rolex Oyster Perpetuals. I took them back and returned to the school after severely reprimanding the soldiers.

"Here are your watches. Hang on to them. Nobody will take them away from you."

"I think they are too noticeable for me to hold on to. I would prefer that you keep them for me until I can take them back or so that you could send them to my people when it's possible. Would you do me that favor?"

I hesitated a moment, but then decided to accept, because they would certainly take them away from him again in Vallegrande.

"Which one is yours?" I asked.

"I'll mark it," he said, and taking a pebble from the dirt floor, he traced an "x" on the inner side of the watch. "This one is mine, the other is Tuma's," he explained, handing over both watches. I put them in one of my pockets.

"Is there anything else?"

"No, nothing. Thanks, Captain."

"I have a request. I'd like to know first hand the reason for this exploit of yours, which is so foolish, so senseless. . . . "

"Maybe, from your point of view. . . . "

I sat down on a small bench, lit a cigarette, offered one to Second Lieutenant Totti, who was seated beside me, and we continued the conversation.

"No, I think that's the way it is from any point of view. I have the impression that you made a mistake from the start by choosing Bolivia for your adventure."

"The revolution is not an adventure. Didn't the war of South American independence start in Bolivia? Aren't you Bolivians proud to have been the first?"

"Yes, but we were the last to achieve it. Your performance here, so far as we have seen up to now, goes against all the principles of guerrilla warfare advocated by Mao, yourself, all the 'masters.' "

"Maybe it was a mistake to choose Bolivia, I don't know. Ultimately, the decision was not wholly mine; other comrades also participated."

"Fidel, I imagine?"

"Other comrades at other levels. The most enthusiastic ones were the Bolivians."

"What happened later? Not very many Bolivians came along. But do you think that we are going to solve problems this way, with gunfire? As a result of this encounter I have four dead and four wounded, whom I had learned to love and respect in this time we were together. I ask you: what am I going to say to their parents, when I talk about them and why they died."

"For the fatherland . . . fulfilling their duty . . . "

"That sounds poetic, and you know it. That's why you're saying it in that tone. Give me a realistic answer."

"Your background wouldn't allow you to understand it."

"I think you're wrong there. I don't know if you really understand what has happened in this country. Don't you know that we Bolivians had our revolution already in 1952?"

"Of course, I was in Bolivia shortly afterward."

"But what you don't know, for example, is that I was educated at the Military College after the revolution, with another mentality, with more sense of the people and the fatherland. Our army is part of the people."

"But it oppresses the people."

"Do these campesinos that looked at you so indifferently today, yet show affection for my soldiers, seem oppressed to you? Right now they are cooking for them."

"Their ignorance, the backwardness they are kept in, doesn't allow them to understand what is happening on this continent. Their liberation is on the way."

"Look, Commandant, my family is from here, from this area, Vallegrande. I was brought up in these valleys, these mountains. I had to walk two leagues from Guadalupe to Vallegrande to go to school together with the children of the campesinos. I have come across schoolmates here, friends of mine from childhood, and they are all willing to help us, to help the army. Those bonds are stronger than the ideas you may bring in from outside."

"They have to realize that all of us Latin Americans are in a struggle that is continental, in which there are and there will be many deaths, a lot of bloodshed, but the war against imperialism can no longer be stopped. It has its centers here in Bolivia, in Colombia, in Venezuela and in Central America, and you military men also have to decide whether you are on the side of your people or in the service of imperialism."

"And isn't there any other attitude, neither accommodation nor submission, but our own attitude—I mean the attitude of each country? If we don't like the Cuban model, that doesn't mean that we are serving the Yankees."

"But look at your own case. You've been trained by the Americans, you're carrying American weapons, American equipment. What more proof do you want?"

"Would it be different if I were carrying Russian arms and equipment? I don't think that's where the difference lies."

At that point, a runner called me out to say that Major Ayoroa needed me.

"I'll be back later to continue our talk."

"I'll be here, Captain, I'll be here."

Major Ayoroa, Lieutenant Colonel Selich, and I began to look over the documentation Che had been carrying. We were particularly interested in his diary and a note pad with codes. We leafed through the diary, deciphering the guerrilla's tiny handwriting with some difficulty. We checked his entries for several dates that had been important in the brief span of the guerrilla campaign. We read over his comments after Ñancahuazú, Iripití, Morocos, and other clashes. We analyzed the codes, letters, and all the material. Later the three of us went over to the school. We went into Che's room. He was lying down, covered with a blanket. Second Lieutenant Espinoza was on guard.

"How are you feeling?" Major Ayoroa asked.

"Fine," Che replied.

"Tomorrow we will take you to Vallegrande. The division commander will be here first thing in the morning."

"You'll have to look your best. There are a lot of people who will want to take your picture," Lieutenant Colonel Selich observed sarcastically. "How about if we shave you first?" he said, leaning down to pull the prisoner by the beard.

Guevara looked straight at the officer. He calmly raised his right hand and pushed Selich's hand away. Selich moved back with a laugh, saying, "Your parade is over, buddy. Now we're playing the tune, don't forget it." And with that he left the room.

Ayoroa and I stayed with the prisoner for a while. "How many men are still available for combat?" the battalion commander asked.

"I don't know," Che replied.

"Where were you going to meet? Where was the rallying point?"

"We didn't have one. We were lost, there were soldiers everywhere. We had no place to go."

"So why did you come here to La Higuera in the daylight?"

"It doesn't matter anymore. . . . Who cares why? One question: Have any more of my men fallen?"

"There are probably some inside the canyon that we haven't been able to find. We'll look for them tomorrow. Why?"

"Just wanted to know. They were good people. I'm concerned about them, that's all."

"We'll keep you posted. You should rest now. See you tomorrow."

We left the room. Major Ayoroa and I talked things over as we walked through the narrow streets of La Higuera. The town was quiet. In one area a group of soldiers were singing around a campfire. In spite of the losses sustained, there was a general feeling of euphoria and triumph because Che had been captured. We went over to spend a moment with them. Battle cries and rival cheers between the two companies that were there—A and B—could be heard every so often.[3] I left

Major Ayoroa to tour the security perimeter with Second Lieutenant Huerta. The night was cold with clear skies. We checked all posts and found everything quiet. The soldiers were alert and aware of their responsibility. Satisfied, I went back to the command post to get a couple of hours' sleep. It was past midnight by then.

At about three in the morning, I got up and checked the security deployment once again. Everything was quiet. I went into the school and found the prisoners resting. Second Lieutenant Pérez was on duty.

Che opened his eyes when he heard me come in. "Can't you sleep, Captain?"

"It's not easy after all that has happened. What about you? You're not sleeping either?"

"No, by now I've forgotten what it's like to sleep soundly."

"Now you have one advantage. You don't have to think about your safety or the danger of being overtaken by the troops."

"I don't know which is worse. There's also the uncertainty.... What do you think they'll do with me? They said over the radio that if the Eighth Division captured me they would try me in Santa Cruz, and if it were the Fourth, in Camiri."

"I don't know, I guess it will be in Santa Cruz."

"Your division commander, Zenteno, what's he like?"

"Very good. He's correct, a gentleman. Don't worry."

"You're quite unique, Captain. Your officers mentioned some things to me ... don't take it wrong, we had some time to talk. They appreciate you, that's obvious."

"Thanks. Can I do anything else for you, Commander?"

"Maybe a little coffee. That would be a big help."

"I'll see that some is sent to you. Try to rest. Tomorrow begins another phase."

I left the room. I didn't feel at all tired despite having rested very little. I ordered coffee and bread to be sent to the prisoners and went to the command post. Everything was very calm. A few roosters were crowing, although dawn had not arrived yet. Leaving orders to be awakened at six, I lay down to rest.

At dawn, after checking everything in keeping with the orders I had received from my battalion commander, I formed two platoons with Second Lieutenants Totti and Espinoza to continue combing the canyons in search of the remaining guerrillas. Before seven, I ordered them to leave while I waited for the division commander to arrive. The helicopter landed, bringing Col. Zenteno Anaya and the CIA agent, known to us as Félix Ramos. It returned to Vallegrande, transporting Lieutenant Colonel Selich and two wounded soldiers, and continued ferrying the other soldiers and then the guerrillas for the rest of the day.

Colonel Zenteno listened very calmly to the entire report and the description of the operation of the day before and what had happened since. He told us that up to the time he left Vallegrande no instructions about the prisoners had arrived. The high command had simply told them to await orders. After the discussion, we headed for the school. Colonel Zenteno's visit with the prisoner, already recounted, went forward without incident, and we then went over to the command post to look at the documentation, which was photographed by Ramos with Colonel Zenteno's authorization.

When Major Ayoroa explained the operation we were effecting that day, Colonel Zenteno announced his intention to go to El Churo to observe the troops' work, so we headed for the canyon with a small escort. We arrived there a little after eight in the morning. Captain Torrelio was already in position with the rest of A

Company, so we immediately began searching the area while Colonel Zenteno made a panoramic sketch from the heights. When I was about to enter the canyon, in response to a call from my officers who had informed me of the presence of a guerrilla, the division commander informed me that he was returning to La Higuera to get in touch with Vallegrande, so I provided him with an escort and took leave of him.

The joint operation of the two companies produced its result. Pacho, Aniceto, and Chino fell into our hands and, with evidence that the rest had left the canyons, we met up with Torrelio on the path to La Higuera and began the march to the hamlet together, satisfied with the task we had accomplished. When we were approaching the town, Major Ayoroa came out to meet us. He informed us briefly that a few minutes earlier (it was now noon) the prisoners had been executed on higher orders.

We looked at each other in silence. That wasn't what we had been expecting. We moved faster and arrived at the school. The bodies of the seven guerrillas fallen in those two days of combat were being prepared for helicopter transport. Che's body was the last remaining. I went up to look at him. His face was becoming distorted. I don't know why, but every time I saw dead guerrillas in photos or in person, their faces showed an angry expression, with their mouths open and their glance wandering. On the other hand our soldiers always seemed to be sleeping, with peaceful faces. To prevent further deformation of the guerrilla chief's face, I took my handkerchief and placed it around his lower jaw, tying it at the top of his head. Someone observed that he looked as if he had a toothache. Nobody laughed at the joke, and we secured the stretcher to the outside rail of the helicopter, which within a few minutes disappeared into the mountains, leaving us with an empty feeling.

The next day we had visitors. Barrientos and Ovando arrived separately to congratulate our troops for the success achieved. Then we continued operations in search of the rest of the guerrilla band. Meanwhile, unknown to us who remained in the operations zone, contradictions were showing up in the statements made by the military authorities, who, in an attempt to cover up what had happened at La Higuera, were laying themselves open to all kinds of news commentary.

Later on some of this reportage troubled and angered me. The first instance occurred when I left for Vallegrande with my troops, at the end of October. Some Bolivian and international journalists still remained in the city, eager to uncover the most minute details of what had happened to Che. When one of them, Franco Pierini, a correspondent for an Italian magazine, asked me if I had executed Che, I angrily replied that I was "a soldier and not an executioner." On the basis of this and other unpleasant moments, I made a request to my superiors that my role be duly clarified, to protect my honor and my good name.

Some efforts were made in this direction in the months that followed, but there were some unscrupulous publications that took advantage of the subject to exploit Che's image commercially and put out falsehoods and distortions. One example is Ricardo Rojo's book, *Mi amigo el Che* (My friend Che), where I am shown coldly machine-gunning the prisoner. In any case, with the passing of time, the facts have been cleared up. The truth, which cannot be hidden, has been coming to light with no need for me to be concerned with promoting it. The best proof is my own calm. I can say in all frankness that I was never worried because those erroneous reports were circulating. In more than two decades since then, I have never been threatened, nor have I been forced to adopt special security measures.

On only one occasion did anything happen to cause any doubt. I was enrolled at the Brazilian Army's Command and General Staff School in 1968 in Rio de Janeiro with a scholarship from the Bolivian Army, when a classmate of mine, Major Edward Von Westerhagen of the German Federal Republic, was assassinated by unknown assailants. In their preliminary investigations the Brazilian federal police and military intelligence service considered the possibility that Edward had been assassinated in my place. This hypothesis was picked up by the press, which naturally gave it plenty of coverage. Unfortunately, the perpetrators were never found, and no organization took responsibility for the crime, which is unsolved to this day.

Years later, some publications portrayed this assassination as an action of Israeli terrorist groups, although Major Westerhagen had participated in only the last weeks of World War II, as a simple soldier and at a very young age. Rumor had it that some relatives of his could have been involved in some anti-Jewish activities and thence the reprisal, but none of this was substantiated and the mystery was never unveiled.

Since then, although the Brazilian army obliged me to take some safety precautions for a while, nothing has ever happened that made me fear for my life. For that reason I was greatly surprised by the assassination of Gen. Joaquín Zenteno Anaya in Paris in 1976, where he was serving as Bolivian ambassador, by a supposed "Che Guevara Command" that never surfaced again. The stories linking that event to Bolivian political problems were not confirmed either, so that his death is still a question mark, not necessarily attributable to the guerrilla war in Bolivia.

The fact is that those of us who acted as officers in the operations against the guerrilla war led by Che did so with the full conviction of our institutional role, obeying the laws of war and devoting ourselves wholly to the defeat of that force, who were regarded as invaders of our national heritage and opponents of the democratic principles we have always upheld.

Our subsequent performance, with some exceptions of course, has been guided by those norms. I believe that the fact that our names have become known on the national and international level because of our participation in those military actions has led us to act as a general rule responsibly, honestly, and with deep faith in everything we have done. These pages, which constitute an eyewitness account as well as an analysis, will have confirmed the truth of the matter for the inquiring reader.

NOTES

1. From the author's campaign diary.

2. That same night and over the next few days, I reconstructed the dialogue in my campaign diary so as not to forget it. I transcribe it now with practically the same words that were used. This is neither a fictionalized version of reality nor a pure invention.

3. The stories about widespread drunkenness among officers and soldiers that night are false. Considering the size and the poverty of a town like La Higuera, with scarcely 200 inhabitants, one can see that there could hardly have been enough alcoholic beverages on hand for the troops.

Table 1
Battle Order of the Guerrillas

Alias, Full Name, and Background   Fate

<u>Bolivians</u>

ANICETO - Aniceto Reinaga Gordillo   Died at El Churo October 9.
    Teacher from La Paz. Came from Cuba to join
    the guerrillas. Arrived in Nancahuazú Jan-
    uary 21.

BENJAMIN - Benjamín Coronado Córdova   Drowned in Grande River
    Background unknown.   February 29.

CAMBA - Orlando Jiménez Bazán   Captured at San Antonio
    From Beni. PCB militant. Trained in Cuba   September 27.
    1962. Recruited by Coco.

CARLOS - Lorgio Vaca Marchetti   Drowned in Grande River
    Came from Cuba, where he was trained. Ar-   March 17.
    rived in Nancahuazú December 11, 1966.

COCO - Roberto Peredo Leigue   Died in La Higuera Septem-
    From Beni. PCB militant. Responsible for   ber 26.
    acquiring the Nancahuazú property.

CHAPACO - Jaime Arana Campero   Died at Cajones October 14.
    From Tarija. PCB member.

CHINGOLO - Hugo Choque Silva   Deserter. Captured in
    From La Paz. Newsboy.   Monteagudo July 20.

DANIEL - Pastor Barrera Quintana   Deserter. Captured in Mu-
    From La Paz. Carpenter.   yupampa March 14.

DARIO - David Adriazola Velzaga   Survivor.
    From Cochabamba. PCB member.

ERNESTO - Ernesto Malmura Hurtado   Died at Vado del Yeso Aug-
    From Beni. Medical student on scholarship   ust 31.
    in Cuba. Sent from there to join the guer-
    rillas, arriving in Nancahuazú November 27,
    1966.

EUSEBIO - Eusebio Tapia Aruni   Deserter. Captured in
    Background unknown.   Monteagudo July 20.

INTI - Guido Peredo Leigue   Survivor.
    PCB militant. Named Political Commissar of
    the guerrilla force.

JULIO - Mario Gutiérrez Ardaya   Died in La Higuera Septem-
    From Beni. Medical student on scholarship   ber 26.
    in Cuba.

LEON - Antonio Domínguez Flores   Deserter. Captured in Pu-
    From Beni. Campesino.   cará September 27.

LORO - Jorge Vázquez Viaña   Captured April 22. Escaped
    Urban liaison in the first phase, in charge   May 31.
    of supplies.

MOISES - Moisés Guevara Rodríguez   Died at Vado del Yeso Aug-
    From Oruro. Mining union leader. Militant   ust 31.
    of Communist Party (Marxist-Leninist).

Table 1 (continued)

NATO – José Luis Méndez Conné
From Beni. Supply chief.

Died in Mataral November 15.

ORLANDO – Vicente Rocabado Terrazas
From La Paz. Mechanic.

Deserter. Captured in Mu-
yupampa March 15.

PABLO – Francisco Huanca Flores
From La Paz. Student.

Died at Cajones October 14.

PACO – José Castillo Chávez
From Oruro. Upholsterer.

Captured at Vado del Yeso
August 31.

PEDRO – Antonio Jiménez Tardío
Background unknown.

Died at Iñao August 9.

PEPE – Julio Velasco Montaño
Miner.

Deserter. Captured and
Died in Itf May 24.

POLO – Apolinar Aquino Quispe
Joined as of December 1, 1966.

Died at Vado del Yeso August 31.

RAUL – Raúl Quispaya Quispe
From Oruro. Student

Died at Morocos July 30.

SALUSTIO – Salustio Choque Choque
Campesino.

Captured at Nancahuazú
March 17.

SERAPIO – Víctor Gonzales
Background unknown.

Died in Iquira July 9.

VICTOR – Casildo Condori Vargas
From Potosí. Cab driver.

Died in Ticucha June 2.

WALTER – Walter Arancibia Ayala
Miner.

Died at Vado del Yeso August 31.

WILLY – Simón Cuba Saravia
From Oruro. Mining union leader.

Died in La Higuera October 9.

LOYO – Loyola Guzmán
UMSA student. National treasurer for the
guerrillas, member of Communist Youth. Visited Nancahuazú encampment January 26, 1967
bringing Moisés Guevara for interview with Che.
Returned to La Paz with instructions for urban cadres.

Captured by Ministry of
Government September 17.

Cubans

ALEJANDRO – Comm. Gustavo Machín Hoed de Beche
Chief of Operations of the guerrilla force.
Founder of the Revolutionary Student Direc-
torate. Fought in the Escambray during the
Cuban Revolution. Vice-Minister of the
Treasury. Military Chief of Matanzas. Entered Bolivia with Ecuadorean passport #49836
under name of Alejandro Estrada Puig, December 9, 1966.

Died at Vado del Yeso August 31.

258

Table 1 (continued)

ANTONIO - Capt. Orlando Pantoja   Died at El Churo October 8.
Head of Coast and Harbor Surveillance in Cu-
ba. Che's lieutenant in the Sierra Maestra.
Connected with Interior Ministry. Entered
Bolivia with Ecuadorean passport #49040 under
name of Antonio León Velasco, December 12,
1966.

ARTURO - Capt. René Martínez Tamayo   Died at El Churo October 8.
From Cuban Army Department of Investigation.
Graduate of the Matanzas officers' course.

BENIGNO - Capt. Daniel Alarcón Ramírez   Survivor.
Head of canecutters at the Central España
sugar plantation.

BRAULIO - Lt. Israel Reyes Zayas   Died at Vado del Yeso Aug-
From Comm. Raúl Castro's escort. Veteran of   ust 31.
the Sierra Maestra and the Escambray Second
Front. Entered Bolivia with Panamanian
passport #72538 November 25, 1966.

JOAQUIN - Comm. Juan Vitalio Acuña Núñez   Died at Vado del Yeso Aug-
Sierra Maestra veteran. Member of Central   ust 31.
Committee of Cuban PC. Second in command of
guerrilla war in Bolivia and head of rear
guard. Entered Bolivia with Panamanian passport #65736 under name of Joaquín Rivera
Núñez November 19, 1966.

MARCOS - Comm. Antonio Sánchez Díaz   Died at Peña Colorada-
Head 1st Infantry Regiment, Ciudad Libertad,   Ticucha June 2.
Cuba. Second Chief of Operations in the Es-
cambray. Head of Camagüey Army Corps. Member of Central Committee of Cuban PC. Entered Bolivia with Panamanian passport #65986
under name of Marco Quintero Díaz November
18, 1966. Initially named head of guerrilla
vanguard; removed from post March 25 for lack
of discipline.

MIGUEL - Capt. Manuel Hernández   Died in La Higuera Septem-
Sierra Maestra veteran. Entered Bolivia with   ber 26.
Spanish #40137 under name of Miguel Angel
Martos Laporta. Named head of vanguard to
replace Marcos.

MORO (MUGAMBA) - Med. Lt. Octavio de la Concep-   Died at Cajones October 14.
              ción y la Pedraja
Sierra Maestra veteran. Head of surgery,
Calixto García Hospital. Entered Bolivia
with Ecuadorean passport #49833 under name of
Calixto García December 7, 1966.

PACHO - Capt. Alberto Fernández Montes de Oca   Died at El Churo October 8.
Member of 26 July Movement. Administrator
Central Washington sugar plantation. Director of Mines for Ministry of Industry. Entered Bolivia with Uruguayan passport #12394
under name of Antonio Garrido.

259

Table 1 (continued)

POMBO - Capt. Harry Villegas Tamayo   Survivor.
Sierra Maestra veteran. Aide and confidant
of Che. Entered with Ecuadorean passport
#027094 under name of Arturo González López
July 25, 1966. His alias, like those of
Moro, Mbili, and Mongo was a souvenir of his
campaign with Che in the Congo.

RAMON (MONGO, FERNANDO) - Comm. Ernesto "Che"   Died in La Higuera October 9.
                    Guevara de la Serna
Sierra Maestra veteran. Commandant of Column
4 in La Mesa Valley. Commandant of Column 8
in Las Villas. President of Central Bank of
Cuba. Minister of Industry. Was in Congo in
1965 trying to organize liberation movements
in several African countries. Entered Bolivia using Uruguayan passport #130748 under
name of Adolfo Mena González November 4,
1966.

RICARDO (PAPI, MBILI, CHINCHU) - Comm. José María   Died at Morocos July 30.
                    Martínez Tamayo
Sierra Maestra veteran. In charge of preparing guerrilla foco in Bolivia. Entered
the country in May, 1966 to coordinate activities with PCB and other groups, with Ecuadorean passport under name of Ricardo Ma-
turana Flores. Brother of Arturo.

ROLANDO (SAN LUIS) - Capt. Eliseo Reyes Rodrí-   Died at El Mesón April 25.
                guez
Member of 26 July Movement. Battalion Chief
at La Cabaña Fortress. Head of Intelligence
and Security, Pinar del Río Province. Entered Bolivia with Panamanian passport #66019
under name of Rolando Rodríguez Suárez November 18, 1966.

RUBIO - Capt. Jesús Suárez Gayol   Died at Iripití April 10.
Veteran of Sierra Maestra Second Front. Di-
rector of Mineral Resources. Vice-Minister
of Sugar Industry. Entered Bolivia with
Ecuadorean passport #490389 under name of
Jesús Cuevas Ulloa Deember 12, 1966.

TUMA - Lt. Carlos Cuello Cuello   Died in Florida, Bolivia
Confidant of Che. Entered Bolivia during   June 26.
preparatory phase together with Pombo July
25, 1966 with Ecuadorean passport #83749
under name of Tomás Suances.

URBANO - Capt. Leonardo Tamayo Núñez   Survivor.
Secretary of Cuban delegation to Punta del
Este Conference August 1961. Entered Bolivia with Mexican passport #910637 under name
of Julio Cabrera Benítez November 18, 1966.

Peruvians

CHINO - Juan Pablo Chang Navarro   Died at El Churo October 8.

Table 1 (continued)

<table>
<tr><td>Alias, Full Name, and Background</td><td>Fate</td></tr>
</table>

Peruvian Communist leader. Entered Bolivia
with false Peruvian passport #177971. Visited Nancahuazú encampment December 1, 1966 to
talk with Che and coordinate action. Left to
recruit people and returned with two compa-
triots March 17.

EUSTAQUIO - Lucio Edilberto Galván Hidalgo   Died at Cajones October 14.
Joined up with Chino as radio operator and
technician. Arrived Nancahuazú March 17.

NEGRO (MEDICO) - Restituto José Cabrera Flores   Died at Vado del Yeso Aug-
Used Bolivian passport #607397 under name of   ust 31.
Nemesio Negrón Alonso. Joined March 17.

Argentines

PELAO - Ciro Roberto Bustos (Carlos Alberto   Captured in Muyupampa
                       Fructuoso)   April 20, tried, and sen-
Argentine leftist. Participated in failed   tenced to thirty years in
guerrilla attempt 1964. Entered Bolivia end   prison. Amnestied Decem-
of February. After joining Tania and   ber 24, 1970 by government
Debray in La Paz, traveled to Camiri with   of Gen. J. J. Tórrez.
them, arriving in Nancahuazú March 6.   Left Bolivia on that date.

TANIA - Laura Martínez Bauer (Tamara Bunke)   Died at Vado del Yeso Aug-
Responsible for setting up liaison in cities   ust 31.
and for purchases. Made first entry into
Nancahuazú December 31, 1966 with Mario Monje
and returned later with Debray and Bustos.
Army action after March 23 identified her,
forcing her to stay with guerrilla force to
avoid apprehension.

Frenchman

DANTON - Régis Jules Debray   Captured in Muyupampa April
                                         20, tried, and sentenced to
                                         thirty years in prison.
                                         Amnestied December 24, 1970
                                         by government of Gen. J. J.
                                         Tórrez.

Table 2
Casualty List: Regular Forces

Combat and Date	Unit	Dead	Wounded
Nancahuazú 3/17	4th Div.		Pvt. Sebastián Rojas N.
Nancahuazú 3/23	4th Div.	2nd Lt. Rubén Amézaga F.	Cpl. Guido Terceros S.
Iripití 4/10	CITE	Lt. Luis Saavedra A. Lt. Jorge Ayala C. Pvt. Raúl Cornejo C. Pvt. Angel Flores C. Pvt. Jaime Sanabria S. Pvt. Marcelo Maldonado M Pvt. José Migabriel S. Pvt. Zenón Parada M.	Pvt. Justo Cervantes B. Pvt. Humberto Carvajal M. Pvt. Freddy Alave C. Pvt. Ignacio Hirasini B. Pvt. Bernabé Mandeporá T. Pvt. Gerardo Gallardo R. Pvt. Armando Martínez S.
	4th Div. Comp.	Pvt. Víctor Miranda V.	
	4th Div. Comp. Inf. Reg. 11	Pvt. Marcelo Avalos P.	
El Mesón 4/25	National Guard for Public Security	Guard Villanueva Sánchez C. Señor Luis Beltrán R. (Also: the dog "Storm")	
Taperillas 4/26	Infantry Reg. 2	Sgt. Guillermo Tórrez M. Pvt. Miguel Espada Ch.	
Nancahuazú 5/9	NCO School Comp.	2nd Lt. Henry Laredo A. Stud. Cpl. Alfredo Arroyo Stud. Cpl. Luis Peláez A.	Pvt. José Villaroel V. Pvt. Rodolfo Pinto C.
El Espino 5/30	Inf. Reg. 24	2nd Lt. Eduardo Velarde R. Pvt. Wilfredo Banegas D.	Cpl. Carlos Peredo G. Pvt. Florencio Valdés B. Pvt. Armando Salas C. Pvt. Simón Escobar L.
Muchirí 6/1	Inf. Reg. 11	Señor Alejandro Saldías	2nd Lt. Max Siles V. Pvt. Felipe Arancibia Pvt. Anastasio Mamani Señor Leonor Villagómez (driver)
El Cafetal 6/10	Trinidad Comp.	Pvt. Antonio Melgar A.	Pvt. Eladio Arias G.

Table 2 (continued)

Combat and Date	Unit	Dead	Wounded
Florida 6/26	8th Div. Mixed Comp.	Cpl. Gerónimo Martínez R. Pvt. Mario Bautista Arnez Pvt. Augusto Córdova A.	Pvt. Pablo Chirinos S. Pvt. Jorge Viruez S.
Samaipata 7/6	Inf. Reg. 13	Pvt. José Verazaín Llanos	
Corralones 7/27	Trinidad Comp.	Señor Armando Cortés E.	Pvt. Jesús Gutiérrez M.
Morocos 7/30	Trinidad Comp.	Pvt. Zenón Zabala V. Pvt Manuel Vejarano V. Pvt. Antonio Zabala R. Pvt. Rodolfo Mendía S.	2nd Lt. José Rivera S. Pvt. Domingo Avila A. Pvt. Julián Nava Z. Felipe Leigue Ichú
Grande River 8/26	3rd Div. C. Comp.		Pvt. Vicente Choque M.
Vado del Yeso 8/31	Inf. Reg. 12 (1966)	Pvt. Antonio Vaca C.	
Yajo Pampa 9/3	Inf. Reg. 13	Pvt. Benito Velasco G.	
El Churo 10/8	Ranger 2	Pvt. Mario Characayo M. Pvt. Mario Lafuente P. Pvt. Manuel Morales L. Pvt. Sabino Cossío M	Pvt. Beno Jiménez C. Pvt. Valentín Choque F. Pvt. Miguel Taboada M. Pvt. Julio Paco Huacani
Naranjal 10/12	Ranger 2	Cpl. Daniel Calani Q. Pvt. Franz Muriel C. Pvt. Facundo Cruz G. Pvt. Abel Callapa C. Señor Ciro Robles M.	

Table 3
Unit Mobilization Chart

Unit And Strength	Of The	Of The	Assigned To	Time Period	Observations
Division Comp. (62)	----	4th Div.	4th Div.	3/17-11/3	
Campos Comp. (64)	Inf. Reg. 6	4th Div.	4th Div.	3/17-11/3	
Boquerón Comp. (46)	Inf. Reg. 11	4th Div.	4th Div.	4/15-11/3	
Avaroa Sqdrn. (81)	Cav. Guard 1	4th Div.	4th Div.	6/22-11/6	
Bullaín Batry. (17)	Art. Guard 1	4th Div.	4th Div.	4/15-11/6	
Bolívar Batry. (174)	Art. Reg. 2	1st Div.	4th Div.	3/24-5/26	
Manchego Comp. (63)	Inf. Reg. 12	8th Div.	4th Div.	3/25-10/30	To 8th Div. 6/24
Braun Sqdrn. (37)	Cav. Guard 8	8th Div.	4th Div.	3/18-10/30	To 8th Div. 6/24
NCO School Comp. 1 (85)	NCO School	7th Div.	4th Div.	4/12-10/20	
CIOS Comp. (71)	Inf. Reg. 9	6th Div.	4th Div.	4/14-10/20	
Sucre Sec. (24)	Inf. Reg. 2	7th Div.	4th Div.	4/15-8/13	
CITE Comp. 1 (67)	CITE	7th Div.	4th Div.	3/26-10/30	To 8th Div. 6/26
CITE Comp. 2 (81)	CITE	7th Div.	4th Div.	5/26-12/1	
Ranger Comp. 1 (82)	Inf. Reg. 24	2nd Div.	4th Div.	5/18-11/21	
Colorados Comp. (81)	Inf. Reg. 1	1st Div.	4th Div.	5/18-11/21	
Toledo Comp. (81)	Inf. Reg. 23	1st Div.	4th Div.	5/18-11/21	

Table 3 (continued)

Unit And Strength	Of The	Of The	Assigned To	Time Period	Observations
Ingavi Sqdrn. (81)	Cav. Reg. 4	1st Div.	4th Div.	5/23-10/30	To 8th Div. 6/30
Trinidad Comp. (158)	Cav. Reg. 2	6th Div.	4th Div.	5/12-8/4	To 8th Div. 6/24
A Comp. (87)	----	3rd Div.	4th Div.	8/2-11/30	
B Comp. (86)	----	3rd Div.	4th Div.	8/2-11/30	
C Comp. (87)	----	3rd Div.	4th Div.	8/2-12/1	
Sec. Eng. Reg. 8 (50)	----	8th Div.	8th Div.	6/15-12/2	
Ustarez Comp. (72)	Inf. Reg. 13	7th Div.	8th Div.	6/15-11/30	
Marine Comp. (56)	Alianza Batt.	Naval Force	8th Div.	5/25-11/30	
Florida Comp. (145)	----	6th Div.	8th Div.	8/8-12/2	
Ranger 2 Batt. (650)	Inf. Reg. 12	8th Div.	8th Div.	9/25-12/30	
NCO Comp. 2	NCO School	7th Div.	8th Div.	9/12-12/1	

Map 1a. The Operations Zone

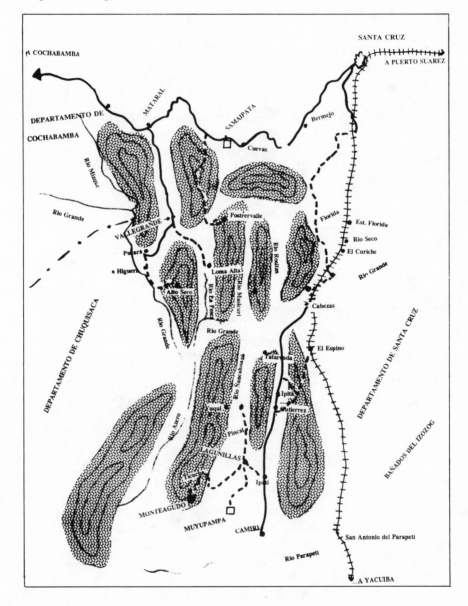

Map 1b. Area of Operations

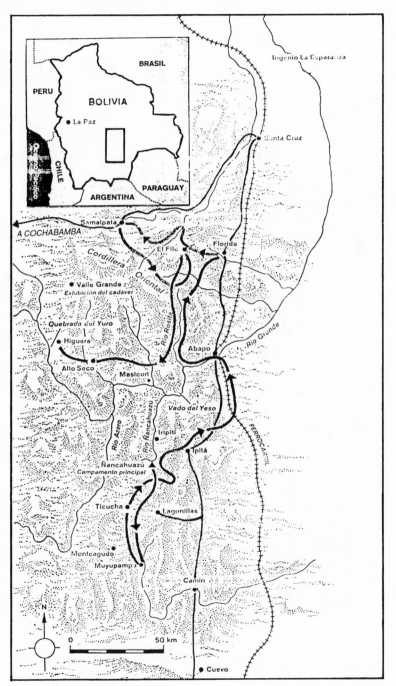

Map 1c. Geopolitical Position of the Area of Operations

Map 2. The Reconnaissance Trip

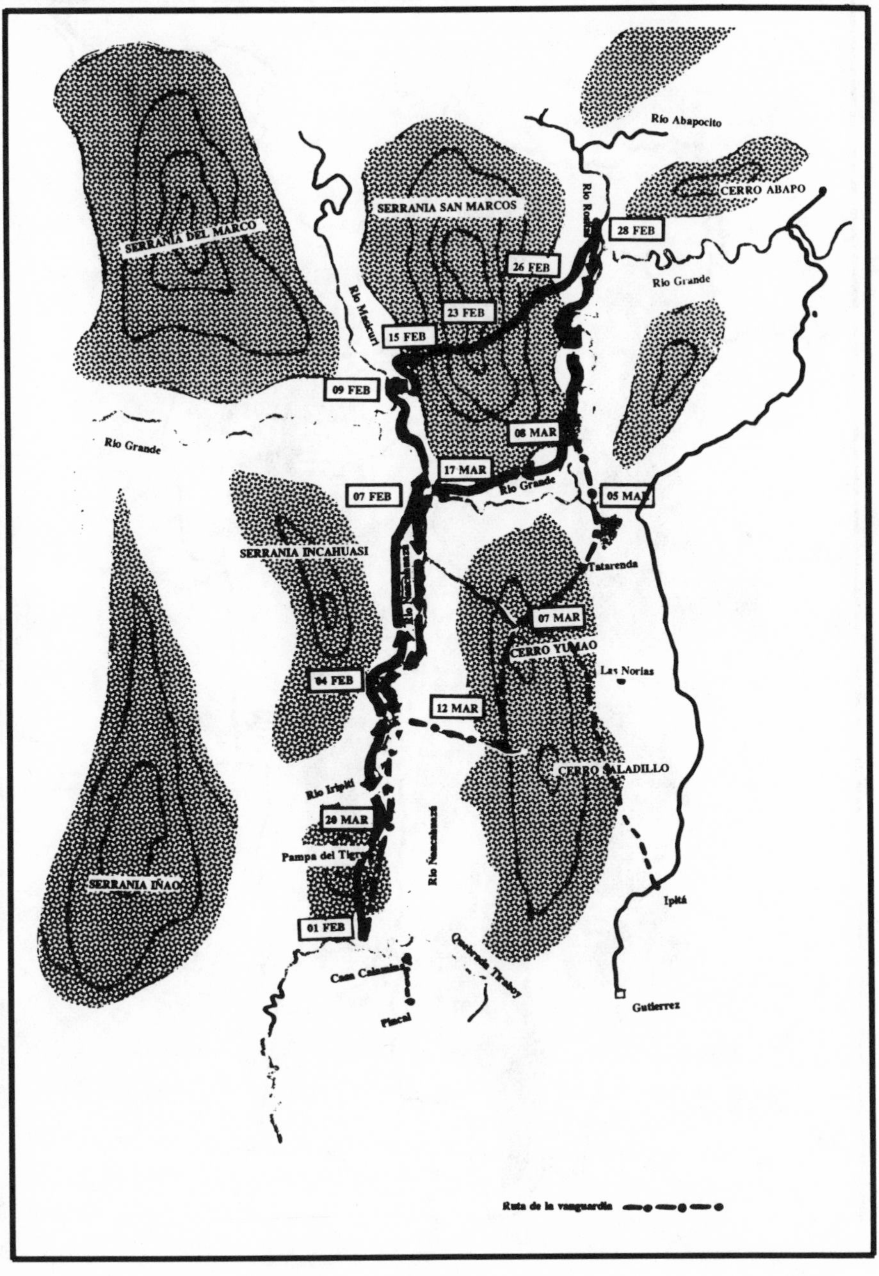

Map 3. The Tactical Encirclement

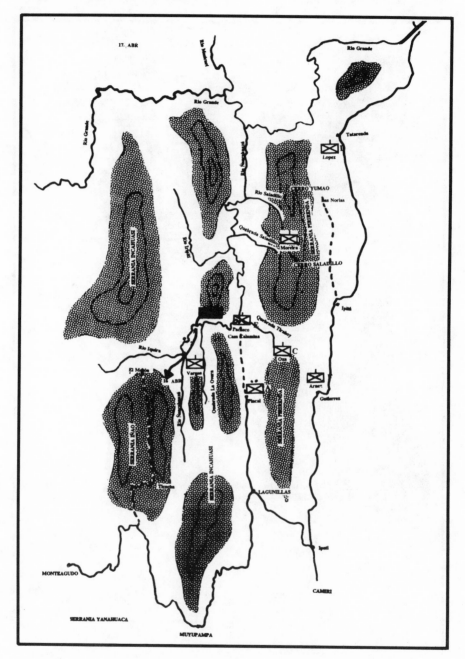

Map 4. Joaquín's Route

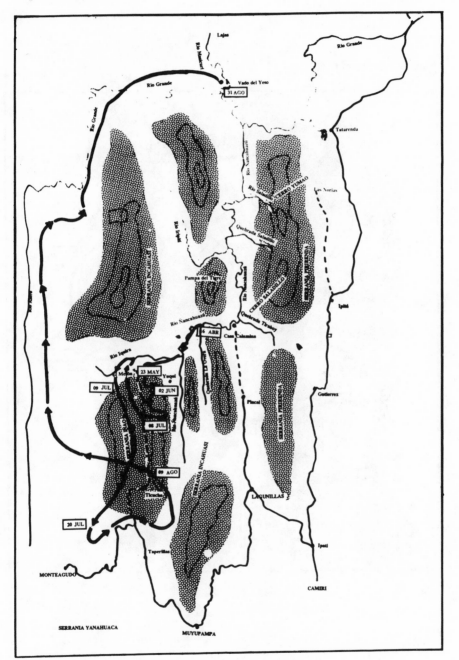

Map 5. Che's Route (I)

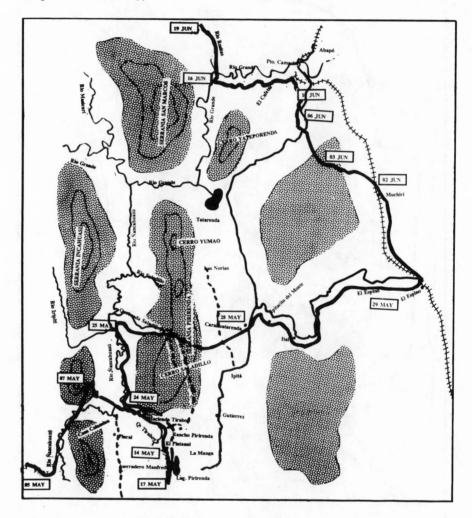

Map 6. Che's Route (II)

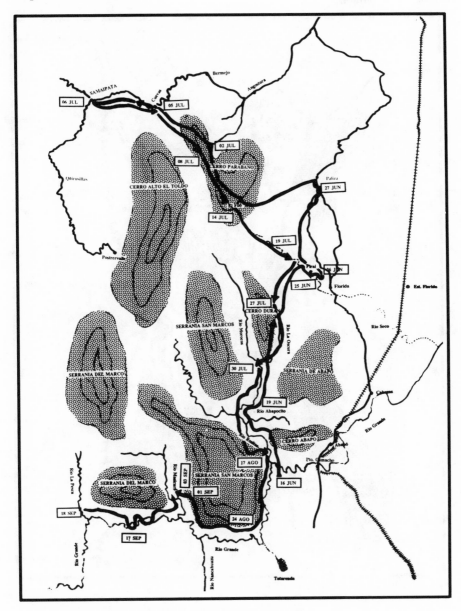

Map 7. The Military Plan

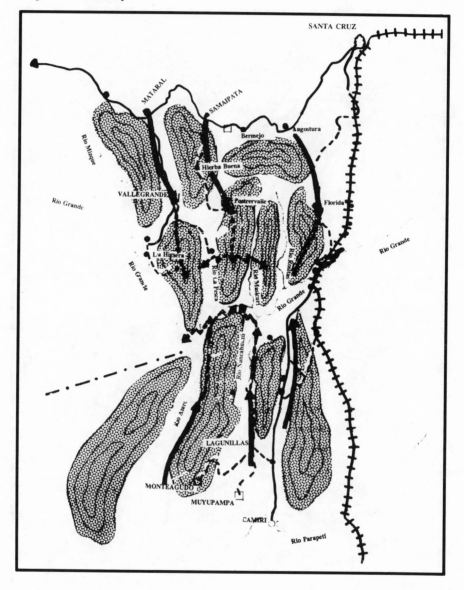

Map 8. The Road to La Higuera

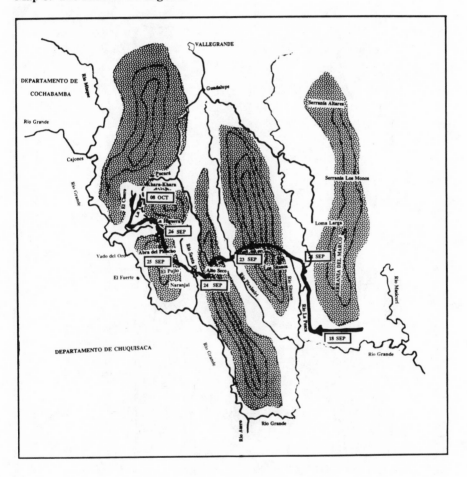

Map 9. El Churo

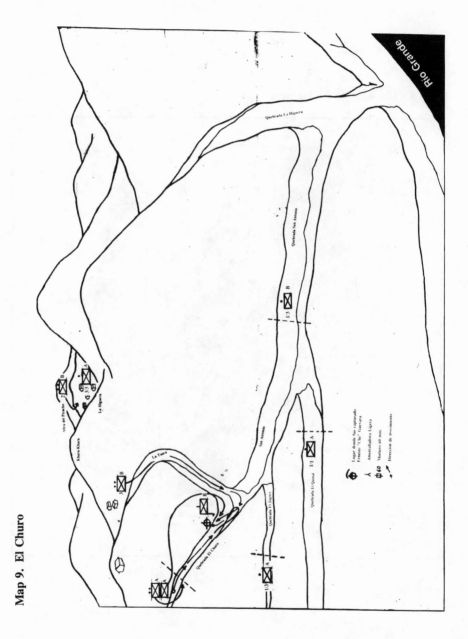

SELECTED ENGLISH READINGS

Corbett, Charles D. *The Latin American Military as a Socio-political Force: Case Studies of Bolivia and Argentina*. Coral Gables, Fla.: Center for Advanced International Studies, University of Miami, 1972.

Dunkerley, James. *Rebellion in the Veins: Political Struggle in Bolivia 1952–82*. London: Verso Editions, 1984.

Guevara, Che. *Guerrilla Warfare*. Edited with an introduction and case studies by Brian Loveman and Thomas M. Davies, Jr. Lincoln: University of Nebraska Press, 1985.

James, Daniel, ed. *The Complete Bolivian Diaries of Che Guevara and Other Captured Documents*. New York: Stein and Day, 1968.

Klein, Herbert S. *Bolivia: The Evolution of a Multi-ethnic Society*. New York: Oxford University Press, 1982.

Malloy, James M. *Revolution and Reaction: Bolivia, 1964–1985*. New Brunswick, N.J.: Transaction Books, 1988.

Mitchell, Christopher. *The Legacy of Populism in Bolivia: From the MNR to Military Rule*. New York: Praeger, 1977.

INDEX

About the Author

GARY PRADO SALMÓN is a recently retired general in the Bolivian
Army. He has spent two decades accumulating materials and preparing
charts in his efforts to reconstruct accurately the events of 1967—an important part of contemporary Bolivian history.

About the Translator

JOHN DEREDITA is a critic and translator. He has taught Latin American literature at Bryn Mawr College, Columbia University, and other
institutions.